Date Due

JUL 1 0 1975		
OCT 2 0 1975		
NOV 1 4 1975		
DEC 3 1976		
NOV 1 6 1977		
DEC 1 5 1989		
MAR 30 1995		
OCT 2 4 1998		
3·12·99		
OCT 0 9 2009		

DEMCO NO. 38-298

The School upon a Hill

The School
upon a Hill

EDUCATION AND SOCIETY IN COLONIAL NEW ENGLAND

James Axtell

NEW HAVEN AND LONDON, YALE UNIVERSITY PRESS, 1974

Designed by Sally Sullivan
and set in Baskerville type.
Printed in the United States of America by
Vail-Ballou Press, Inc., Binghamton, N.Y.

Published in Great Britain, Europe, and Africa by
Yale University Press, Ltd., London.
Distributed in Latin America by Kaiman & Polon,
Inc., New York City; in Australasia and Southeast
Asia by John Wiley & Sons Australasia Pty. Ltd.,
Sydney; in India by UBS Publishers' Distributors Pvt.,
Ltd., Delhi; in Japan by John Weatherhill, Inc., Tokyo.

For Jamie, Than, and Susan

Children, leprechauns, women beutifulle and yonge,
these be forrainers alle.

Contents

Foreword

Both Ends of the Log

The entire man is, so to speak, to be seen in the cradle of the child. . . . We must see the first images which the external world casts upon the dark mirror of his mind, and the first occurrences that he witnesses, we must hear the first words which awake the sleeping powers of thought and stand by his earliest efforts if we would understand the prejudices, the habits, and the passions which rule his life.

Alexis De Tocqueville

The rebirth of the history of education can be dated from 1960, when Bernard Bailyn issued a challenge to American historians to secure some "historical leverage on the problems of American education" by bringing educational history "into relation with a general understanding of the course of American development." It was Bailyn who redefined the scope and nature of education, pointed to the broadly cultural dimensions of the educational process, and offered a provocative hypothesis about the role of *Education in the Forming of American Society.* Perhaps his main achievement was to urge the necessity of asking the right questions about education— and in asking some good ones himself. But the fulcrum of his whole effort—and of the most promising efforts made since he wrote—was the redefinition of education.[1]

1. Bernard Bailyn, *Education in the Forming of American Society* (Chapel Hill, 1960). In 1954 a distinguished group of American historians and teachers met in New York under the auspices of the Ford Foundation's Fund for the Advancement of Education to discuss the need for studying the role of education in American history. Their report, first

Thanks to Professor Bailyn, and more recently to Lawrence
Cremin, we are now familiar with the limited, Whiggish, in-
stitutional view of education held by most historians who
inhabited *The Wonderful World of Ellwood Patterson Cubberley* at the turn of the century. The title page alone of Cubberley's popular interpretation was a dead giveaway. When it
was first published in 1919, it was called *Public Education in
the United States*—as if the history of American education
began with the district school in 1789.[2]

How different was Bailyn's definition in 1960. Taking a cue
from Edward Eggleston, the gentleman-scholar of *The Transit
of Civilization* and former Hoosier schoolmaster, he proposed
that education be considered as "the entire process by which a
culture transmits itself across the generations." In this sense it
was synonymous with the anthropologists' "enculturation,"
the pervasive process in which informal, as well as formal,
agencies help to transform children into full members of a
specific human society, sharing with other members a specific
human culture. This was what Eggleston had in mind when
he attempted to analyze "the original investment from which
has developed Anglo-Saxon culture in America" by probing
"the complex states of knowing and thinking, of feeling and
passion of the seventeenth-century colonists." In chapters on
"The Mental Outfit of the Early Colonists," medical notions,
language and literature, norms of conduct and behavior, and
domestic economy, as well as formal education, he presented
what was in 1900 the broadest, most viable history of education to have appeared in American historiography. Unfortunately, its distinctive conception was not recognized by
contemporaries—as Eggleston told his daughter, "I know we

---

published in 1957 and revised and reissued in 1965, stated that "the
group was unanimous in its conviction that, relative to its importance in
the development of American society, the history of educational forces
in this country both in and out of the schoolroom had been shamefully
neglected by American historians" (*Education and American History*
[New York, 1965], p. 4).

2. Lawrence Cremin, *The Wonderful World of Ellwood Patterson
Cubberley* (New York, 1965).

have no public sufficiently intellectual to justify the spending my resources on such a work"—and six decades passed before Professor Bailyn rescued and refurbished it.[3]

But to some, the idea of education as enculturation was *too* broad, too diffuse to be of any help in focusing upon the complex relations between a society and the education it provides. Lawrence Cremin was one of them. In 1965 he suggested that "culture" in an anthropological sense was a mere *descriptive* category, which could be applied to any society of the world, even the most primitive. As an alternative, one which focused on and humanized the meaning of education and gave it *value,* Cremin substituted Werner Jaeger's *paideia*—"the conscious ideal of human perfection." In this light, true education implies "the deliberate, self-conscious pursuit of certain intellectual, ethical, and aesthetic ideals" or, as he expressed it in 1970,"the deliberate, systematic, and sustained effort to transmit and evoke knowledge, attitudes, values, skills, and sensibilities." He is perfectly ready to grant that "nondeliberate influences are often, if not always, more powerful and pervasive and that the educational historian must be concerned with both," but, as a practical matter, the emphasis must be on the deliberate. Otherwise we will spend our time and energy floundering around in total history and tilting at metaphysical windmills.[4]

This is the general direction my own thinking on education has taken. Trying to unite the best of the anthropologists' universal and Jaeger's classical understanding of the nature of education, I have approached the past with an idea of education as *the self-conscious pursuit of certain intellectual, social, and moral ideals* (which makes it normative) *by any society* (from the family to the nation) *that wishes to preserve and*

3. Bailyn, *Education in the Forming of American Society,* p. 14; Edward Eggleston, *The Transit of Civilization from England to America in the Seventeenth Century* (Boston, 1959), pp. xiii, 1, and preface.

4. Cremin, *Ellwood Patterson Cubberley,* p. 75; Lawrence Cremin, *American Education: The Colonial Experience, 1607–1783* (New York, 1970), p. xiii; Werner Jaeger, *Paideia: The Ideals of Greek Culture,* 2nd ed., 3 vols. (New York, 1945).

transmit its distinctive character to future generations (which makes it conservative). Perhaps the most homely expression of this essentially classical ideal came appropriately from colonial America, from the pen of Hector de Crèvecoeur. While he was visiting the fishing villages and lonely beaches of Nantucket, he observed that "the easiest way of becoming acquainted with the modes of thinking, the rules of conduct, and the prevailing manners of any people, is to examine what sort of education they give their children; how they treat them at home, and what they are taught in their places of public worship." If our predecessors had taken this simple advice, we would not have had to wait until 1970 for Lawrence Cremin's history of colonial *American Education* to receive the first major assessment of "the impact of American education on the American mind and character." [5]

In approaching the history of colonial New England I have made several assumptions and emphases which ought to be articulated. First and most generally, I have assumed that fixity, not change, is the requisite starting point for the study of not only social order but social change. For like many students of society, especially anthropologists, I have been impressed with the *conservative* bent of human behavior and norms, the "manifest desire to preserve, hold, fix, and keep stable," and with the patterns of "fixity punctuated now and then by modification and change" that mark societies, past and present.[6]

I have also chosen to designate the general body of English inhabitants of New England as the *New English* rather than *Puritans,* for two reasons. First, on a commonsense level, not all New England inhabitants, either in the seventeenth century or the eighteenth, were in a religious sense Puritans, although most of them shared in varying degrees a common adherence to the English brand of Calvinistic Protestantism

---

5. J. Hector St. John de Crèvecoeur, *Letters from an American Farmer* (London: Everyman, n.d.), p. 113; Cremin, *American Education,* p. xi–xii.
6. Robert Nisbet, *Social Change and History* (New York, 1969), pp. 242, 271 (emphasis omitted).

and a social ethic that can be appropriately deemed Puritan.[7] And second, I wish by the term to emphasize, at least initially, the essential continuity between old England and New, between the social ideals and educational agencies of English culture and their earliest American counterparts. The point is perhaps obvious, but even today most American historians give only lip service to the English origins of American culture.

To forestall as many misunderstandings as possible, it is also well to state clearly at the outset what I think I have done in this book, what I have not tried to do, and how what I have done complements the work of other historians. First, what I have not done. I have not attempted to write a comprehensive history of education in colonial New England, much less in colonial America as a whole, as Lawrence Cremin has done. My general focus has been the education of only the English in New England. I have not tried to tell the equally important story of the English efforts to educate Negroes and Indians, although, as chapter 7 shows, I have been interested in the Indian education of the English.

The second thing I have not tried to do is present all the facets of the educational process in New England, which, at least at this point in the historiography of education, seems an impossible task. For ideally the historian of education should balance his account between the *substance* (what is taught), the *dynamics* (the means by which teaching occurs), and the *process* of education (the interaction between what is

7. Darrett Rutman, *American Puritanism* (Philadelphia, 1970). Stephen Foster has defined the Puritan social ethic as "the imperatives, aspirations, and inhibitions which collectively comprised the way a seventeenth-century New Englander thought he ought to act toward other seventeenth-century New Englanders when they came together in an organized civil society" (*Their Solitary Way: The Puritan Social Ethic in the First Century of Settlement in New England* [New Haven, 1971], p. xi). Michael Zuckerman has extended Foster's argument to the second half of the eighteenth century in emphasizing the "Principles of Peace" that were the instruments of New England's persistent normative concern for consensus and conformity (*Peaceable Kingdoms: New England Towns in the Eighteenth Century* [New York, 1970], chap. 2). One theme of my own study may be seen as a detailed exploration of the *inculcation* of the social values described by these two books.

taught and the means by which teaching occurs with the child).
The two previous historians of colonial education, Samuel
Eliot Morison and Lawrence Cremin, have understandably
dwelt upon the substance and the dynamics, what Professor
Cremin described as "the knowledge the colonists developed
for coping with the New World and the agencies they established for transmitting that knowledge." [8] What they have
neglected, and what I have tried to recapture, is some sense of
what the educational process was like at the level at which it
actually occurred. In part I have attempted to portray a waist-
high view of education, one that enables us to see the educational process, if not actually through children's eyes, at least
from their position in a lilliputian universe. Unfortunately,
such an attempt can only be partial because of the necessity of
dealing largely with adult sources, and the equally necessary
task of trying to strike a balance between attention to the adult
society that is educating and to the child that is receiving,
adapting, and reacting to that education. For such biased
materials, the only antidote is a large dose of imagination and
empathy and a long memory for what it was like to be a child
—and even that, I fear, will not cure a virulent case of maturity.

Finally, in obedience to my conception of education, I have
not taken as my subject everything that New English children
learned from their educational experiences, deliberate and
random, everything that made them become the individuals they became. What I have chosen for scrutiny are the
ways in which they were educated for life in society, whether
it was the family, the church, or the larger community,
what they as a whole were taught that transformed them from
cultureless newborns into functioning, obedient, and coopera-

8. Cremin, *American Education*, p. 24. Samuel Eliot Morison's *The
Puritan Pronaos* (New York, 1936) is not strictly a history of education
but rather a collection of static *Studies in the Intellectual Life of New
England in the Seventeenth Century*. And in attempting to treat all the
American colonies, Professor Cremin's encyclopedic survey necessarily
relies upon the existing literature that he has criticized so well, a literature that does not move beyond the content and agencies of education.

tive members of a distinctive society and culture. In short, I am primarily interested in the socialization of New English children, in the cultural ties that bound them to their society, and not in the many forces in their culture—ideas, social change, alternative life-styles—that may have been individually liberating.[9]

I am therefore interested in the kinds of habits New English society tried to teach its children and, because the medium is so often the loudest part of the message, the ways in which it taught them. For it is by its habits—its regularities of behavior and feeling and thought—that a culture is known. Those habits *are* the culture.[10] Thus, for example, in treating formal institutions of education such as schools and colleges, I have dwelt not on the potentially liberating lessons to be gained by the individual from the actual content of the books read—and there were obviously many such lessons—but rather on the implicit lessons in social conformity and obedience to authority offered by the very physical, pedagogical, and social conditions in which those books were read. In the end what I am concerned to show is how the processes of education contributed to the preservation and transmission of New England's cultural identity in the face of mounting social change, Puritanism's inherent paradoxes, and the seductiveness of alien cultures on its very borders.

9. Socialization is "the process by which someone learns the ways of a given society or social group so that he can function within it." It includes both "the learning and internalizing of appropriate patterns, values, and feelings" (Frederick Elkin, *The Child and Society: The Process of Socialization* [New York, 1960], p. 4).

10. Culture, wrote Philip Bagby, summarizing a long line of anthropologists, is "the regularities in the behaviour, internal and external, of the members of a society, excluding those regularities which are clearly hereditary in origin" (*Culture and History* [London, 1958], p. 84).

Acknowledgments

Domestic life and literary pursuits were my first and my latest inclinations.

Thomas Jefferson

William Blake once said that "To Generalize is to be an Idiot, To Particularize is the Alone Distinction of Merit." He must have been thinking of the pleasant time at the completion of a book when an author can finally acknowledge—if never fully pay—his intellectual and personal debts.

Librarians must often have the nightmare that prompted Thomas Fuller, only two hundred years after Gutenberg, to lament "the numerosity of needless books." But a book is needless only until someone needs it, and in the course of writing this book I have been grateful on countless occasions to the staffs of several libraries for harboring books whose only crime was gathering proverbial dust—and for many personal kindnesses. I hope it will not appear as an untoward irony to the librarians of Yale University, Harvard University, the Massachusetts Historical Society, the Connecticut Historical Society, and the Connecticut State Library that I am discharging my debt in "country pay."

I am also grateful to Enid Williams and Charlotte Moss for transmuting my unkempt drafts into clean copy with unerring accuracy and cheerful aplomb.

Future historians of colonial America will carry a large debt to Lawrence Cremin for his history of *American Education,* but I owe him more. To his encouragement, his infectious enthusiasm for education, and especially his generosity of

xvii

knowledge and interest, I owe my vision of the community of scholars.

Two other historians have confirmed that vision. At various stages of writing Timothy Breen lent his knowledge and a critical pencil to my efforts, but probably not sufficiently for the result to satisfy his own high standards. And to the puckish warmth, the generous perfectionism, and the consummate craftsmanship of Edmund Morgan, I wish to remain indebted in perpetuity. Although he has read every chapter with care and improved more sentences than I like to remember, I am more grateful for his personal example.

An author's wife suffers a terrible lot. Not only does she have to live with his "genius-at-work" irascibility and watch his pet theories stampeded by herds of brute facts, but once it is born she also has to live with the brain-child, of whose warts she is no mother. And yet in spite of all this, my wife Susan has read and listened to every page of every draft and taken it—and me —with incredibly good humor. For such sufferance—and for much more— this book is dedicated to her and to our ineffable two.

Abbreviations

Learning hath gained most by those books by which the printer has lost.

Thomas Fuller

Since the new history of education presumes, like Bacon, to take all knowledge for its province, a bibliography would be superfluous, as well as impossible. Readers wishing to pursue the history of colonial education may best consult the comprehensive ninety-one-page bibliographical essay in Lawrence Cremin's *American Education: The Colonial Experience, 1607–1783* (New York, 1970).

I have reproduced all original sources as they were written, with the small exception of occasionally expanding contractions and of substituting the modern *th* for the Anglo-Saxon thorn (*y*). To save the reader from undue interruption by footnote superscriptions in the text, sources are cited at the end of each paragraph in the order in which the references or quotations appear in the paragraph. Abbreviations of sources frequently cited in the footnotes follow:

Conn. Archives	Connecticut Archives, State Library, Hartford.
Conn. His. Soc.	Connecticut Historical Society, Hartford.
Conn. Records	*The Public Records of the Colony of Connecticut.* Edited by J. H. Trumbull and C. J. Hoadly. 15 vols, Hartford, 1852–90.

Colls. MHS	*Collections of the Massachusetts Historical Society.*
Dexter's Yale Graduates	*Biographical Sketches of the Graduates of Yale College.* Edited by Franklin B. Dexter. 4 vols. New York, 1885–1907.
Essex Co. Court Records	*Records and Files of the Quarterly Courts of Essex County, Massachusetts.* Edited by George F. Dow. 8 vols. Salem, 1911–21.
EIHC	*Historical Collections of the Essex Institute.*
Maine Records	*Province and Court Records of Maine.* Edited by Charles T. Libbey *et al.* 5 vols. Portland, 1928–60.
Mass. Archives	Massachusetts Archives, State House, Boston.
Mass. His. Soc.	Massachusetts Historical Society, Boston.
Mass. Records	*Records of the Governor and Company of the Massachusetts Bay in New England.* Edited by Nathaniel B. Shurtleff. 6 vols. Boston, 1853–54.
NEHGR	*New England Historical and Genealogical Register.*
New Haven Col. Records	*Records of the Colony or Jurisdiction of New Haven, from May, 1653, to the Union.* Edited by Charles J. Hoadly. Hartford, 1858.
New Haven Town Records	New Haven Town Records. Edited by Franklin B. Dexter and Zara J. Powers. 3 vols. New Haven, 1917–62.

PAAS	*Proceedings of the American Antiquarian Society.*
PCSM	*Publications of the Colonial Society of Massachusetts.*
Plymouth Records	*Records of the Colony of New Plymouth in New England.* Edited by Nathaniel B. Shurtleff *et al.* 12 vols. Boston, 1855–61.
PMHS	*Proceedings of the Massachusetts Historical Society.*
Sibley's Harvard Graduates	Sibley, John L. and Shipton, Clifford K. *Biographical Sketches of Those Who Attended Harvard College.* 16 vols. to date. Cambridge, Mass., 1873– .
Suffolk Co. Court Records	*Records of the Suffolk County Court, 1671–80.* Edited by Zechariah Chafee, Jr. and Samuel Eliot Morison. *Publications of the Colonial Society of Massachusetts,* vols. 29–30 (1933).
Winthrop's Journal	*Winthrop's Journal, "History of New England" 1630–1649.* Edited by James K. Hosmer. 2 vols. New York, 1908.
Winthrop Papers	*Winthrop Papers.* 5 vols. Boston, 1929–47.
WMQ	*William and Mary Quarterly.*

Prologue

The Way to New England

*The Atlantick Ocean, like a river of Lethe, may easily cause us to
forget many of the things that happened on the other side.*

Cotton Mather

When Roger Clap was old enough to be apprenticed, he left
his family in Devonshire and went to Exeter to live with "as famous a Family for Religion as ever I knew." There, with
several maid servants and seven or eight men of the household, he attended church in the city, where he heard many
famous preachers, especially John Warham. "I never so much
as heard of New England," he reminisced, "until I heard of
many godly Puritans that were going there, and that Mr.
Warham was to go also. My Master asked me whether
I would go? I told him were I not engaged unto him I would
willingly go: He answered me that should be no hindrance, I
might go for him or my self which[ever] I would." When the
apprentice wrote to his father for permission, he failed to
receive it, so he walked the twelve miles home to "Intreat his
leave." Fortunately "God sent the Reverend [John] Maverick,
who lived Forty Miles off, a Man I never saw before: He
having heard of me, came to my Father's House, and my
Father agreed that I should be with him and come under his
Care." So at the age of twenty-one Roger Clap came to New
England in May 1630. "Mind by what I have already expressed," he told posterity, "That it was God that did draw

1

me by his Providence out of my Father's Family, and weaned me from it by degrees. . . ." [1]

The first generation of New Englishmen were weaned, not only from a "fruitfull Land, stately Buildings, goodly Gardens, Orchards, yea, deare Friends and neere relations," but from the smothering embrace of an English Church presided over by a wilful patriarch, William Laud. As the first wave of colonists were preparing to board ship, the Reverend John Cotton of Boston, Lincolnshire, reminded them to "forget not the wombe that bare you, and the breasts that gave you sucke." So before they left English waters, John Winthrop and his company took Cotton's advice by addressing a *Humble Request of his Majesties loyall Subjects . . . to the rest of their Brethren in and of the Church of England* to forestall any misreport of their intentions. "Consider us as your Brethren," they asked, "standing in very great need of your helpe, and earnestly imploring it." For despite the "disaffection, or indiscretion, of some of us, or rather, amongst us . . . we are not of those [separatists] that dreame of perfection in this world; yet we desire you would be pleased to take notice of the principals and body of our company, as those who esteeme it our honour, to call the *Church* of *England*, from whence wee rise, our deare Mother, and cannot part from our native Country, where she specially resideth, without much sadnes of heart, and many teares in our eyes, ever acknowledging that such hope and part as wee have obtained in the common salvation, we have received in her bosome, and suckt it from her breasts: wee leave it not therfore, as loathing that milk wherewith we were nourished there, but blessing God for the parentage and education. . . ." [2]

To their posterity it was memorable that the founders were

---

1. *Memoirs of Roger Clap* (Boston, 1731), pp. 1–4.
2. [Edward] *Johnson's Wonder-Working Providence, 1628–1651,* ed. J. Franklin Jameson (New York, 1910), p. 21; John Cotton, *Gods Promise to His Plantation* (London, 1630), p. 4; "The Humble Request" (London, 1630), in Edmund Morgan, ed., *The Founding of Massachusetts* (Indianapolis, 1964), pp. 187–89.

able to distinguish between the Church of England as it contained the "whole *Body of the Faithful,* scattered throughout the Kingdoms" and the Church as it was confined to a "certain Constitution by *Canons,* which pronounced *Ipso Facto,*" between the Church as keeper of the "true *Doctrine* of the *Protestant Religion,* with a Disposition to pursue the *Reformation* begun in the former Century," and the Church as merely a "certain Faction, who together with a *Discipline* very much *Unscriptural,* vigorously prosecuted the *Tripartite Plot* of *Arminianism* and Conciliation with *Rome,* in the *Church,* and unbounded Prerogative in the State." "We may easily perceive," said Cotton Mather, speaking for third-generation New England, "what *Church of England* it was, that our *New-England* Exiles called, *Their Mother;* though their *Mother* had been so harsh to them, as to turn them out of Doors, yet they highly honoured Her; believing that it was not so much their *Mother,* but some of their angry *Brethren;* abusing the Name of their *Mother,* who so harshly treated them." [3]

Thus spurned by their mother, the founders of New England began their errand into the wilderness to seek out a place of "Cohabitation and Consorteshipp under a due forme of Government both civill and ecclesiasticall," to build before the eyes of all people a "Citty upon a Hill" to beacon the living message of the Reformation to a dying Europe. The instrument of their mission was a special commission from God. "Wee are entered into Covenant with him for this worke," preached John Winthrop on the *Arbella* somewhere in the Atlantic, "wee have taken out a Commission, [and] the Lord hath given us leave to drawe our owne Articles." When God delivered them safe to New England "then hath hee ratified this Covenant and sealed our Commission, [and] will expect a strikt performance of the Articles contained in it. . . . But if wee shall neglect the observacion of these Articles . . . the

3. Cotton Mather, *Magnalia Christi Americana* (London, 1702), bk. 1, chap. 5.

Lord will surely breake out in wrathe against us, be revenged of such a perjured people and make us knowe the price of the breache of such a Covenant." [4]

The covenant with God could be broken only by his people, for as soon as God's ordinances cease, warned John Cotton, "your security ceaseth likewise; but if God plant his Or-dinances among you, feare not, he will maintaine them." The only way to ensure that the covenant would not be broken was to have a "tender care that you looke well to the plants that spring from you, that is, to your children, that they doe not degenerate as the Israelites did. . . . If men have a care to propagate the Ordinances and Religion to their children after them, God will plant them and not roote them up." It was advice not soon forgotten.[5]

"Why came you into this land?" asked Eleazar Mather of his congregation in 1671, *"was it not mainly with respect to the rising Generation?* And what with respect to them? was it to leave them a rich and wealthy people? was it to leave them Houses, Lands, Livings? Oh, No; but to leave God in the midst of them." The Reverend John Wilson was even more direct: "You came hither for your Children, Sons and Daughters, and for your Grandchildren to be under the Ordinances of God." In nascent New England, children were at the heart of the search for cultural identity.[6]

4. John Winthrop, "A Modell of Christian Charity," in Morgan, ed., *The Founding of Massachusetts,* pp. 201–03.
5. Cotton, *Gods Promise to His Plantation,* p. 19.
6. Eleazar Mather, *A Serious Exhortation* (Boston, 1671), p. 16; John Wilson, *A Seasonable Watchword* (Boston, 1677), p. 8. For a superb de-scription of "The Puritan Hegira," see Carl Bridenbaugh, *Vexed and Troubled Englishmen, 1590–1642* (New York, 1968), chaps. 11–12.

I

The Fair Schoolroom of the Sky

I shall know why—when Time is over—
And I have ceased to wonder why—
Christ will explain each separate anguish
In the fair schoolroom of the sky.

Emily Dickinson

A new society, like a child, craves an identity. It must reckon with its strengths and weaknesses, agonize over the choice of priorities, and strive to create for itself a defining uniqueness. Over time it will acquire a distinctive culture that expresses the common values and unvoiced assumptions of its heterogeneous members—the way they think, act, and feel. Since the cultural behavior of a society is transmitted socially rather than genetically, its children are initiated into its ways most effectively through its dominant symbols, the visual signs of its deepest commonality.[1]

The distinguishing mark of New England's cultural identity was symbolized by the one book that stood beside the Bible in their regard—the catechism. For the New English child the catechism not only symbolized his Protestant inheritance but tangibly inaugurated his education in the elements of his new faith. So powerful was the impress of this initiation upon the younger generations of New England that neither the cate-

1. Darrett Rutman, *American Puritanism* (Philadelphia, 1970), pp. 114–20; George Kneller, *Educational Anthropology* (New York, 1965), chap. 1; John Beattie, *Other Cultures* (London, 1964), chap. 5.

5

chetical form nor the credal content of religious education changed significantly over the first century and a half. Until and even after the American Revolution, the New English child was formed in the religious image of his Puritan ancestors. And even when the inner vitality of its founding ideals began to flag, New England continued to accord the catechism unstinting importance as the symbol of its distinctive errand into the wilderness.

The religious nurture of the New English child began at birth, when the potential saint was ushered into the spiritual maelstrom, to be fought for by Heaven and Hell. Church members were urged to bring their children to the meetinghouse within two weeks of birth for baptism, the sacrament in which they "give up their seed to the Lord" as they had promised in the covenant of grace.[2] This was primarily the father's duty because "the mother at that time by reason of her travell and delivery is weake, and not in case to have her head much troubled with many cares; much lesse able her selfe

2. The requirements for congregational church membership changed with time and distance from England. In England and Holland, they were an honest life, a profession of faith on the basis of Christian knowledge, and willingness to submit to the discipline of a properly founded church (by covenant). Upon arrival in New England, however, the Puritans further restricted membership in an attempt to equate the visible church with the invisible (Christ's elect). By 1636 a rigorous public narration of the experience of election based on an elaborate morphology of conversion was widely required by the Massachusetts and New Haven churches. So that much of the early English Puritan "household government" literature refers to a comprehensive church membership resembling the English parish, and most of the early New England literature refers to a very restricted membership in which only "full members" (those accepted as visible saints after a relation of their conversion) could vote in church affairs, participate in the Lord's Supper, and have their children baptized. After 1646 every New Englishman was required by law to attend church services on the Sabbath, thus at least bringing everyone *into* the church, if not enabling them to become members *of* it. It was not until 1662 in theory, and the 1670s in practice, that a Half-Way covenant began to open membership and to dispense with the public relation. For the history of Puritan church membership, see Edmund Morgan, *Visible Saints* (New York, 1963), and Robert Pope, *The Half-Way Covenant* (Princeton, 1969).

to take order for such weighty matters. Onely the husband is to make known to his wife (if she be not extraordinarily weake) what his purpose is concerning the place, time, manner, and other like circumstances of baptizing the childe, and to advise with her about the name, witnesses, and such like points." [3]

The correct performance of the ceremony required that a minister officiate during a regular worship service (the first Sabbath after birth "if at least it fall not out within two or three daies after, which is somewhat with the soonest both for mother and childe"), anoint the child's head with water while speaking the proper words, "In the name of the Father, and of the Son, and of the Holy Ghost," and announce its Christian name to the congregation. As an initiation to Christian life, baptism was appropriately rigorous. Merely being brought to meeting within days of birth denoted the overwhelming concern for the child's soul in spite of the more visible dangers of weather, disease, accidents, and hostile Indians. In a day of often alarming child mortality, it was deemed a greater risk to miss the sign and seal of baptism than to incur the high odds of natural death in obtaining it. In England even midwives were authorized to baptize infants in "jeopardy of life," as they still are today, or to carry them to a priest, despite the ubiquitous rural dangers of "bad roads, ditches, planks, places one must jump over, ice, bad weather, encounters with dogs, etc." [4]

The meetinghouse itself was little better. Often rudely constructed, crowded, dark, drafty, and unheated, it offered small creature comfort to the babes brought to its baptismal font by their fathers and midwives. Children born in the raw New England winter months were not treated to any warm water

---

3. William Gouge, *Of Domesticall Duties*, 3d ed. (London, 1634), pp. 526–27. Ministers were usually prompt in baptizing their own children, but members of their congregations often marched to different drummers. Despite the two-week ideal, actual baptisms occurred anywhere from one day to several months after birth. See, for example, the *Records of the First Church at Dorchester in New England, 1636–1754* (Boston, 1891).

4. Gouge, *Of Domesticall Duties*, p. 521; Thomas Forbes, *The Midwife and the Witch* (New Haven, 1966), pp. 128–30.

baptisms for fear of softening them for the hard religious life ahead. While ministers officiated in greatcoats and congregations huddled frozen on plank benches, the Christian generations of New England renewed their covenant with God and promised Him their seed. Samuel Sewall's seven-day-old son Stephen was recommended to the Lord in February 1687 between three and four o'clock in the afternoon on a day that was "louring [lowering] after the storm, but not freezing." His "child shrunk at the water but cryed not," to the transparent pride of the judge.[5]

The giving of a fit name to the child was an essential part of the baptismal service, and the Puritan literature of "household government" offered many suggestions. Biblical names (Habakkuk, Jerusha, Solomon), common names of the country (Henry, Edward, Robert, William), and the names of persons of note (Isaak, David, Peter, Mary, Elizabeth) were good and obvious choices. But especially appropriate were "names which have some good signification: and among them such as are warranted by the Scripture, as *John* (the grace of God), *Jonathan* (the gift of God), *Andrew* (manly), *Clement* (meake), *Simeon* (obedient), *Hannah* (gracious), *Prudens* (wise) and such like: that thus their name may stirre them up to labour after the vertue signified thereby." [6]

When a person's name is chosen so carefully, it may become a significant instrument of his education. Parents whose hopes and ideals are verbally pinned to their child may consciously mold the child's personality toward those ideals, cultivating those character traits that exemplify them and weeding out those that do not. This kind of conscious nurture was not widely promoted, for common English names occur far more frequently in New England records, but the very choice of

---

5. Ola Winslow, *Meetinghouse Hill, 1630–1783* (New York, 1952), chap. 4; Diary of Samuel Sewall, *Colls. MHS*, 6 February 1687, 5th ser., vol. 5 (1878), p. 167.

6. Gouge, *Of Domesticall Duties*, p. 530. See also John Dod and Robert Cleaver, *A godly forme of housholde governement* (London, 1612), sigs. Q1v.–Q2r., and Alice M. Earle, *Child Life in Colonial Days* (New York, 1899), pp. 14–17.

ideals in names is one useful key to New England's vision of itself and the direction in which it wished to grow.

Some names were chosen for their promise, others as simply descriptive. Judge Sewall named one son Joseph "in hopes of the accomplishment of the Prophecy of Ezekiel xxxvii. and such; and not out of respect to any Relation or any other Person except the first Joseph." After another christening he wrote: "I named my little Daughter Sarah. . . . I was struggling whether to call her Mehetable or Sarah. But when I saw Sarah's standing in the Scripture, viz. Peter, Galatians, Hebrews, Romans, I resolv'd on that suddenly." Eliphalet (from the Hebrew for "God is deliverance"), the son of the Reverend William Adams of Dedham, was born in March 1677 "2 or 3 hours before day" and "named from the Lord's special preservation and deliverance of him and his mother from the danger they were both in at his birth." And on a Sabbath morning in February 1697, Cotton Mather's wife presented him with "a very hearty and comely" daughter. He "gave her the Name of Hannah, with my Desires, that shee may bee a *gracious* Child, and imitate those of her Name, which are commemorated in the Oracles of God." [7] As one would expect, ministers were the most conscientious donors of biblical names.

The conditions under which children were born often received commemoration as a reminder of God's grace in preserving them. In 1653 Edward Johnson described the origins of one of the earliest of these names in his account of the transatlantic crossings that peopled New England. On shipboard, he said, you might see women "whose Wombes could not containe their fruit, being ready for the Worlds-light, travailed and brought forth upon this depthlesse Ocean in this long Voyage, lively and strong Children yet living, and like to prove succeeding Instruments in the Hands of Christ, for furthering this worke; among other[s] Sea-borne Cotten, now a young student in Colledge in Cambridge, being Son to that Famous and Renowned Teacher of Christ, M[r.] John Cotten."

7. Earle, *Child Life in Colonial Days*, pp. 15–16; *Sibley's Harvard Graduates*, 4 : 189; *Diary of Cotton Mather* (New York, n.d.), 1 : 218.

The widow of a physician who had perished in the snow while trying to visit a distant patient named her child Fathergone. Abiel—"God is my father"—was commonly given to children born after the death of their fathers. Parental feelings and expectations were frequently expressed in such names as Truegrace, Reform, Hoped For, Promise, More Mercy, Restore, Preserved, Thanks, Desire, Hope, Joy, Rejoice, Patience, and Love. Sometimes the choice was sadly appropriate, as for the infant girl who was delivered into the "Worlds-light" at Truro on Cape Cod on the first day of May 1748 and left it for the "Kingdom of Darkness" less than two months later. Her name was Silence Paine.[8]

Baptism was only the beginning. In the years that followed, the child felt the religious pulse of New England "even from his very cradle." Since "betimes" was none too soon for Puritan casuists, they urged that no chance to instil the message of Christ in the young be missed. Benjamin Wadsworth, teacher of the First Church in Boston and later president of Harvard, advised that "while you lay them in your bosomes, and dandle them on your knees, try by little and little to infuse good things, holy truths into them. When you are *dressing* and *undressing* your Children morning and evening, you might very properly say something to them about religion, for the good of their Souls." William Gouge, a popular English Puritan writer, added still further occasions for teaching them piety: "at table, by resembling the spirituall food of their soules to that corporall food, whereby their bodies are nourished; when they are walking abroad, by shewing them the stars, how they remained stedfast in their course; the trees, how they bring forth fruit in their season; how all things are for the use & Benefit of man, and thereupon make spirituall uses."[9]

Everyone agreed that "parents ought to begin to nurture

8. [Edward] *Johnson's Wonder-Working Providence, 1628–1651*, ed. J. F. Jameson (New York, 1910), p. 63; Earle, *Child Life in Colonial Days*, pp. 15–17; *Vital Records of Truro, Massachusetts, to the End of the Year 1849* (Boston, 1933), p. 27.

9. Benjamin Wadsworth, *The Well-Ordered Family* (Boston, 1712), pp. 60, 63; Gouge, *Of Domesticall Duties*, p. 549.

their children, as soone as they are capable of any instruction," but no full or formalized program was recommended at first. For "in giving this spiritual food," cautioned William Gouge, "parents [should] deale with their children, as skilfull nurses and mothers do in feeding Infants; they will not at once cram more into their mouths then their stomach is able to digest, but they will rather oft feed them with a little: for it is not meet, that parents be too tedious; that will dull a childes understanding and breed wearisomnesse, and make it loth to bee againe instructed. If a vessell have a little mouth, we use not to fill it by powring whole paile-fulls upon it." [10]

Cotton Mather, that most literal of Puritans, probably ran closer to tediousness, if not into it, than any of his brethren. When he said goodnight to his family and sang his "Song of the Night with them," he would enquire "how they spent their Time in the Day; but also contrive to utter some Sentence, which I may leave with them, as worthy to be remembred and applied, in the Conduct of their Lives." When any of his children were ill, he "would make it an Occasion to putt them in mind of the Evil in Sin [and] show them the analogous Distempers of their Souls." When they were well, he gave them spiritual examinations on such sensitive questions as "What Course do I take, and must I take, that I may have the Fatherly Providence of the Great God, and my Saviour, concerned for me, that I may not be abandoned of God unto the Miseries that some Orphans are left unto?" Even when they were at their "Games and Sports" he would "by way of occasional Reflection, as plainly as tis possible, mind them of those pious Instructions, which the Circumstances of their play may lead them to think upon." His children's patience must have been frequently tried by the unremitting didacticism of a father who made it a rule "rarely to lett one of my children to come anear me, and never to sitt any time with them, without some explicit Contrivance and Endeavour, to lett fall some Sentence or other, that shall carry an useful Instruction with it." [11]

Piecemeal moralizing was a necessary prelude to religious

10. Gouge, *Of Domesticall Duties*, p. 548.
11. *Diary of Cotton Mather*, 1 : 79, 104, 136, 144, 150–51.

maturity, but not an exemption from a more concentrated form of instruction. Although Man could do nothing to earn God's saving grace, piety was never a passive affair. On the contrary, it was strenuously active. The Puritans were positive that, although knowledge could not possibly guarantee salvation, salvation was impossible without it. "I deny not but a man may have much knowledge, and want Grace," admitted the learned John Preston, master of Emmanuel College, Cambridge, "but, on the other side, looke how much Grace a man hath, so much knowledge he must have of necessity. You cannot have more Grace than you have Knowledge." The patriarch of Stuart Puritans, Richard Baxter, agreed. "Education is God's ordinary way for the conveyance of his grace, and ought no more to be set in opposition to the Spirit than the preaching of the Word." [12]

Because children are born without the knowledge and fear of God, they must acquire it by the careful ministrations and instructions of parents and ministers. According to William Perkins, the most popular Elizabethan Puritan, one of the beliefs held by ignorant people was that "a man need not have any knowledge of Religion, because he is not book-learned." The danger of such a mistake was obvious: "where ignorance raigneth, there raines sinne; and where sinne raigns, there the divell rules: & where he rules, men are in a damnable case." English parents valued education "betimes" and good habits of mind and body for their children, but not to excess. They only wanted to "bring our children as neer to Heaven as we can." [13]

12. Peter Bulkeley, *The Gospel-Covenant,* 2d ed. (London, 1651), p. 162; John Preston, *The New Covenant* (London, 1629), p. 446; *The Autobiography of Richard Baxter,* ed. J. M. Lloyd Thomas (London, 1925), p. 10. See Richard Greaves, *The Puritan Revolution and Educational Thought* (New Brunswick, 1969), chap. 6, for the differing views of the sectaries and the moderate Puritans, such as Baxter and Preston, on the relation of reason and spirit in the acquisition of religious knowledge.

13. Samuel Willard, Boston sermon, 31 August 1679, quoted in Edmund Morgan, *The Puritan Family* (New York, 1966), p. 90; William Perkins, *The Foundation of Christian Religion Gathered into six Principles,* 2d ed. (London, 1641), sigs. A3v.–A4r.; Thomas Hooker, *The Application of Redemption* (London, 1659), p. 357.

So literacy was a universal prerequisite to spiritual prepared-
ness, the central duty of the covenant. As the minister of Boston's First Church, Thomas Foxcroft, explained: "the Word
Written and Preacht is the ordinary Medium of Conversion
and Sanctification. Now in order to obtaining these Benefits
by the Word, it is requisite, that Persons be diligent in *Reading and Hearing* of it." It followed, as New England knew,
that it was "one chief project of that old deluder, Satan, to
keep men from the knowledge of the Scriptures." The quickest
and most effective way of subverting the Devil's designs was,
"when children begin to read, let them read the holy Scripture. Thus will children sucke in Religion with learning." [14]

The Bible was an especially apposite choice for several
reasons. William Gouge, one of its constant readers, thought
"there is a secret vertue lurking in the holy Scriptures (which
is Gods own Word) more then in any bookes of men. No
bookes are more easie then many parts of Scripture; and no
histories more admirable and delightfull." Even Cotton Mather
thought it possible to entertain the children around the table
with "delightful *stories* out of the Bible." But despite the en-
joyable aspects of Scripture, the chief end of its reading was to
"incline and winne their affections to the word of God, to
inure and acquaint them in the phrase of the holy Ghost, by
little and little to learne the heavenly doctrine, to note the
examples of Gods vengeance powred upon the wicked and
disobedient; and of his blessings unto those that walke in his
feare." [15]

The ideal Puritan child had made a good start. He had
been promised to the Lord in baptism and had come under the

14. Thomas Foxcroft, *Cleansing our Way in Youth* (Boston, 1719), p.
176; *The Laws and Liberties of Massachusetts [1648]*, ed. Max Farrand
(Cambridge, Mass., 1929), p. 47; Gouge, *Of Domesticall Duties*, p. 548.
15. Gouge, *Of Domesticall Duties*, p. 548. Of godly books the Bible was
incomparably the best, but there were books of other kinds. New
English parents were warned to "keep a strict eye upon [their children],
that they don't stumble on *the Devil's library*, and poison themselves
with foolish *romances*, or *novels*, or *plays*, or *songs*, or *jests that are not
convenient*" (Cotton Mather, *Bonifacius, An Essay upon the Good*, ed.
David Levin [Cambridge, Mass., 1966], pp. 44, 46); Dod and Cleaver, *A
godly forme of housholde governement*, sigs. Q4v.–Q5r.

religious watch and ward of his parents, who nurtured him "in Gods stead." He had begun to read from the holy Scriptures and to appreciate on a simple level at least their stories and histories. But he was still a long way from a state of spiritual preparation. His soul was only awakening from the Adamic torpor of ignorance and sin in which it was born. To escape it, the Westminster Assembly of Divines told him, he had to turn seriously to the "outward & ordinary means whereby Christ communicateth to us the benefits of Redemption," to the "Word, Sacraments, & Prayer" of the visible church. Of these by far the most important was the Word, for "the Spirit of God maketh the Reading, but especially the Preaching of the Word an effectual Means of Convincing & Converting Sinners, and of building them up in Holiness & Comfort, through Faith unto Salvation." Most Puritans, from Elizabeth's Archbishop Edmund Grindal to Richard Baxter and John Bunyan, went even further in their verbal precision. They asserted that preaching was the *only* ordinary means of salvation and demanded that it become the duty of every minister in the land. So confident were they of its efficacy that they believed with John Preston that "there is not a sermon which is heard, but it sets us nearer heaven or hell." [16]

The full benefit of public preaching, however, was impossible without "diligence, Preparation & Prayer." Family prayers twice a day, daily Scripture readings, and plain explanations of the "mysteries of those outward rites which God hath ordain'd in his Church, as of *Preaching, Baptizing Children, administring the Lords Supper,* [and] *ceasing from worke on the Lords day,*" were unanimously recommended by Puritan writers. But the keystone of the whole religious effort that supported the preaching of the Word was catechizing, the familiar, personalized way of learning the "principles and foundations of the Christian religion." When the ministry realized that their sermons would be lost upon an uncate-

16. Christopher Hill, *Society and Puritanism in Pre-Revolutionary England* (New York, 1964), pp. 30–31; John Preston, *Riches of Mercy to Men in Misery* (London, 1658), p. 288.

chized people, they told their congregations, "The better you Instruct your Children at home, the more likely they'll be to profit by Publick Preaching." Like the relation of knowledge and salvation, catechism could not guarantee the full benefit of preaching, but that benefit was impossible without it. With it the child took a giant step toward religious maturity.[17]

Despite a promising beginning under Henry VIII and Edward VI, the English progress of the Protestant Reformation had petered out under Elizabeth. The English church's break with Rome appeared to its Puritan critics as only a partial success, a half-measure that failed to do justice to God's Word or Christ's promise. It was a cowardly "middle way" between the purity of Scripture and the whoredom of Rome, and the most damning evidence of its cowardice was sacramentalism.

William Perkins was one of those godly preachers who knew the enemy well. In 1590 he warned the ignorant readers of his popular catechism that one of the many errors they made, "as though [they] were in a most happy estate," was to believe that "God is served by the rehearsing of the ten Commandments, the Lords Prayer, and the Creed." Inevitably, he and his strenuous brethren disparaged the lazy masses who thought that "it was a good world when the old religion was, because all things were cheape" and peace of mind was easily obtained at the ceremonial altar instead of wrestled from the Devil. These were the kind of Christians who peopled Richard Baxter's parishes in Shropshire and Worcestershire before the Civil War:

> The generality seemed to mind nothing seriously but the body and the world; they went to church and would answer the parson in responds, and then to dinner, and then to play; they never prayed in their families, but some of them going to bed would say over the Creed, and the Lord's Prayer, and some of them Hail Mary:

17. Gouge, *Of Domesticall Duties*, p. 549; Mather, *Bonifacius*, p. 74; Wadsworth, *The Well-Ordered Family*, p. 81.

all the year long, not a serious word of holy things, or the life to come that I could hear of, proceeded from them. They read not the Scripture nor any good book or catechism. Few of them could read, or had a Bible.

It could go unsaid that their children were spiritually wasted.[18]

A "Preacher of the Word at Arley," Robert Sherrard, caught them in a similar pose for the readers of *The Countryman with his Houshold*. He despaired of ever having older folk taught the elements of faith, especially those victims of sacramentalism who "put a confidence in the *saying* and *rehearsing* of the words, as though there were some secret vertue or efficacie in the words, that of themselves and of the sounding or pronouncing of them do please God, and make them that can and do utter them to be Christians, as they doe superstitiously suppose." Sherrard was only confirming the common observation that the "prayers of the common people are more like spells and charms than devotions." [19]

This was the dismal situation Puritan ministers found when they set out to snatch the children of England from the jaws of inevitable perdition. Yet they were not without competition, for certain other elements in the English church were equally eager to stamp out religious ignorance and the disobedience that ignorance bred—but in their own way. Wishing to sustain the episcopal hierarchy, they could not countenance the unharnessed activities of preachers and lecturers or assign to preaching the supreme virtue of preparing men for salvation. Instead, to the great annoyance of the Puritans, they placed their hopes in the discipline and catechizing of the Church. But the view from London was not the view from the shires. Richard Baxter too wanted discipline in the Church, but his own experience in the country villages of the western Midlands had taught him that "the very frame of diocesan prelacy excluded it" and not

18. Perkins, *The Foundation of Christian Religion*, sigs. A3v.–A4r.; Richard Baxter, *The True History of Councils* (London, 1682), p. 90.

19. Robert Sherrard, *The Countryman with his Houshold* (London, 1620), p. 41; Hill, *Society and Puritanism*, p. 58.

"only the bishops' personal neglects." "What a sin it is," he lamented, "in the pastors of the church to make no distinction but by bare names and sacraments, and to force all the unmeet against their own wills to church communion and sacraments (though the ignorant and erroneous may sometimes be forced to hear instruction)." [20]

And force them they did. The Ecclesiastical Canons of 1604 required that

> Every Parson, Vicar, or Curate, upon every Sunday and Holy day before Evening prayer, shall for halfe an houre or more, examine and instruct the youth and ignorant persons of his Parish in the ten Commandements, the Articles of Beliefe, and in the Lords prayer: and shall diligently heare, instruct, & teach them the Catechisme set forth in the Booke of Common prayer. And all Fathers, Mothers, Masters, and Mistresses, shall cause their children, servants, and apprentices, which have not learned the Catechisme, to come to the Church at the time appointed, obediently to heare, and to bee ordered by the Minister, untill they have learned the same.[21]

But the English catechism fell far short of the high standards set by the Puritans for the essence of scriptural truth. In Puritan eyes it mistakenly emphasized a parrot-like memorization of the Creed, Ten Commandments, and the Lord's Prayer, at the expense of a full disclosure of Man's cosmic history and universal predicament. Nowhere in its small confines —only twenty-five questions—was the nature of a true church or the overwhelming burden of original sin described. Rather, the emphasis was on the social control of the parish through required catechizing each Sabbath and holy day, and a religiously enforced "duty towards my Neighbour," which included the obligation to "honour and obey the King, and all that are put in authority under him, to submit myself to all

---

20. *The Autobiography of Richard Baxter*, pp. 17, 116.
21. *Constitutions and Canons Ecclesiastical, 1604*, ed. H. A. Wilson (Oxford, 1923), sigs. L1v.–L2r.

my governors, teachers, spiritual pastors and masters, To order myself lowly and reverently to all my betters." [22] In the abstract, Puritans had few objections to such discipline, but in practice they knew that it was largely directed against their own proselytizing efforts. And the man most responsible for countering those efforts was no mean opponent.

William Laud, successively bishop of St. David's and London, and archbishop of Canterbury, was the most persistent episcopal advocate of church uniformity and diocesan control. For a man who had risen to prominence on the strength of his merciless opposition to Puritan "disobedience," Laud was understandably touchy about his public reputation. A citizen of Dorchester noticed a symptom of his extreme sensitivity in August 1633, just after he had been elevated to Canterbury upon the death of George Abbot. "A Gentleman went to Reading to see the house where Dr. Lawd was borne, and seeing the stocks, pillory, and whipping post stand before it, he noted it. The next weeke order was sent to the Mayor of Reading to remove them thence, and place them some where els. And in Michaelmas Terme following a Gentleman was fined 2,000 £. for saying the Archb[ishop] was an Arminian." This was the man whose policy of "Thorough" tried to corral the whole stock of Puritan activities within the official Church, where they would be removed from the susceptibility of the weak-minded English common man and his children. From St. David's to Canterbury, his visitation articles hammered home the same message: Trust your souls to the ship of state and don't rock the boat. From 1622 on he asked the churchwardens of his dioceses "whether any of your parish do not send their children, servants, and apprentices of either sex, being above seven years of age, and under twenty, to the minister, to be catechized upon such Sundays and holydays as are appointed?" He was obviously pleased in 1634 to receive the king's instructions "that in all parishes the afternoon sermons be turned into catechizing by question and answer; where and whensoever

22. "A Catechism," *The Book of Common Prayer . . . According to the Use of the Church of England* (London, 1620).

there is not some great cause apparent to break this ancient and profitable order," which was a reiteration of King James's "ancient" order of 1622. But he could not have been very happy with the news from his bishops that poured across his desk annually from 1633.[23]

Winchester reported in 1636 that "there are divers recusants in several parts of the country and that some of them have been seduced away from the Church of England within these two or three years," perhaps, Laud must have thought, because the "three or four ministers that are negligent in catechising, and observe it not at all, or but in the Lent only" had more company than his officers could ferret out. The tough bishop of Puritan-prone Norwich, Matthew Wren, "found a general defect of catechising quite through the diocese. And in Norwich, where there are thirty-four churches, there was no sermon on the Sunday morning, save only in four; but all put off to the afternoon; and so no catechising." Wales was worst of all, Laud told his king: "I find that catechising was quite out of use in those remote parts (the more the pity)." In 1638 the archdeacon of Gloucester, in another Puritan hotbed, certified that "there are divers, which as far as they dare, oppose catechising; and but for fear of losing the livings, would almost go as far as [Dr. Henry] Burton and [Dr. John] Bastwick did" in assailing the official church doctrine and discipline. Most Puritans, however, rejected a direct confrontation with their powerful adversary and turned inward to the home to shelter their children from the determined proselytism of the Laudian church.[24]

Household religion had long been a common Protestant tradition, but from the late sixteenth century it was elevated to an advance position in the Puritan strategy. Just as the English Church was prohibiting "all preaching, reading, catechism and other such-like exercises in private places and fami-

23. Thomas Murphy, "The Diary of William Whiteway of Dorchester, County Dorset, from the Year 1618 to the Year 1635" (Ph.D. diss., Yale University, 1939), p. 195; *The Works of William Laud* (Oxford 1847–60), vol. 5, pt. 2, pp. 307–08, 388; Hill, *Society and Puritanism*, p. 37.

24. *The Works of William Laud*, 5, pt. 2 : 339, 343, 359.

lies whereunto others do resort, being not of the same family," Puritan writers were describing the household as "a little Church," "a little Common-wealth," and a "schoole" of obedience and religion. They were certain that the religious reform of the nation had no chance if only legislated from above.

> For although there be never so good lawes in Cities, never so pure order in Churches, yet if masters of families doe not practise at home catechising in their houses, and joyne their helping hands to Magistrates and Ministers, they may in truth (but unjustly as many have done) complaine that their children and servants are disordered, and corrupted abroad, when in truth, they were disordered, and are still corrupted and marred at home.

Under such an assumption it was inevitable that Puritan parents would be warned, long before Laud's views were regnant, that "it is not enough to bring thy children to be catechized at the Church, but thou must labour with them at home after a more plaine and easier manner of instruction." [25] Their intention was to remedy the shortcomings of the state church by making godly households at least supplements and perhaps alternatives to the parish. In alliance with a rigid Sabbatarianism, they sought to complete the substitution, inaugurated by the Reformation, of the lay head of household for the priest.

But their success in insulating and spiritualizing the family was only partial. In the English countryside, where the vermiculate webbing of social relations firmly bound man to man, the textbook prescription for independent households of godly atoms was difficult to fill. A complete break with it all was the only feasible way to achieve true purity. As long as the Church would not countenance the existence of a sub-

25. Hill, *Society and Puritanism*, p. 468; Michael Walzer, *The Revolution of the Saints* (Cambridge, Mass., 1965), chap. 5, pp. 183–98; Dod and Cleaver, *A godly forme of housholde governement*, sigs. A4r., C7r. See also Deodat Lawson, *The Duty and Property of a Religious Householder* (Boston, 1693), pp. 50–51.

stantial number of teaching elders to oversee the proper religious education of children in the churches, and family religion was eyed so suspiciously by the hierarchy, a new start promised the only salvation. Not every Puritan could free himself from the natural ties that bound, but the search for purity of church and family did draw many to the tabula rasa of New England where the blueprints for "little Churches" could be translated into reality.

What the English Puritan family had wanted but been unable to do, the New England family was forced to do. In the face of a scarcity of ministers, wilderness demands for mere survival, and, after all, an ideal opportunity, the family could do little else but accept the educational role assigned to it by the Puritan casuists. As early as 1623, when the plantation was only in its third year, some critics of the Plymouth church charged that "Children [were] not Cattachised nor taught to Read," to which the church replied, "This is Not true in Neither parte therof for divers take pains with theire owne as they Can; Indeed wee have noe Comon scoole for want of a fit person or hitherto meanes to maintaine one." Neither the church nor the school was able at this time to lift any of the heavy responsibility for the child's development from the family's shoulders. When the Massachusetts Bay Company sealed its contract for ministerial services with Francis Higginson and Samuel Skelton on 8 April 1629, it was promised that they were willing "to doe their endeavour in their places of the ministery as well in preaching, catechizing, as also in teaching, or causing to be taught, the Companyes servants & their children, as also the salvages and their children." Reluctantly the church assumed the responsibility for the two groups of New Englanders who could not be expected to provide their own wholesome, ordered households for the proper religious education of their children.[26]

26. "Plymouth Church Records, 1620–1859," *PCSM* 22 (1920): 52; Edmund Morgan, ed., *The Founding of Massachusetts* (Indianapolis, 1964), p. 345.

In 1642 most churches still maintained a hands-off policy on catechizing, but, as Thomas Lechford observed, sustained it with a piece of spurious reasoning.

There is no catechizing of children or others in any Church, (except in *Concord* Church, and in other places, of those admitted, in their receiving [to full church membership]:) the reason given by some is, because when people come to be admitted, the Church hath tryall of their knowledge, faith, and repentance, and they want a direct Scripture for Ministers catechizing; as if, *Goe teach all Nations,* and *Traine up a childe in the way he should goe,* did not reach to Ministers catechizings. But, God be thanked, the generall Court was so wise, in June last, as to enjoyn, or take some course for such catechizing, as I am informed, but know not the way laid down in particular, how it should be done.[27]

The visiting lawyer was only half right. The Massachusetts General Court did pass the first of its famous education laws at that time, but not to enjoin church catechizing. On the contrary, it merely reinforced the family as the principal educator, after frowning upon "the great neglect in many parents and masters in training up their children in learning, and labor." The selectmen of each town were empowered "to take accompt from time to time of their parents and masters, and of their children, concerning their calling and impliment of their children, especiallity of their ability to read and understand the principles of religion and the capital lawes of the country, and to impose fines upon all those who refuse to render such accompt to them when required."[28]

As the years passed, the government's eye saw little cause for joy. In 1648 the General Court again reprimanded the family for its negligence of duty and ordered that

27. Thomas Lechford, *Plain Dealing: Or, Newes from New-England* (London, 1642), *Colls. MHS*, 3d ser., vol. 3, p. 79.

28. Marcus Jernegan, *Laboring and Dependent Classes in Colonial America* (New York, 1931), p. 87; *Mass. Records* 2 : 6–7.

all masters of families doe once a week (at the least) catechize their children and servants in the grounds and principles of Religion, and if any be unable to doe so much: that then at the least they procure such children or apprentices to learn some short orthodox catechism with book [by memory], that they may be able to answer unto the questions that shall be propounded to them out of such catechism by their parents or masters or any of the Select men when they shall call them to a tryall of what they have learned in this kinde.

Connecticut, New Haven, and Plymouth colonies followed suit in 1650, 1655, and 1671 with almost identical injunctions to insure that "such Children or Servants may [not] be in danger to grow barbarous, rude and stubborn, through ignorance." [29]

Individual towns, too, joined the state in keeping the family to the mark. In 1655 the selectmen of Dorchester, one of the older Bay towns with a vigorous church that could easily have subordinated the family in this matter, felt it necessary instead to remind "all parents, masters and any that have the Charge and oversight of any youth with in this Plantation" of the General Court's order and their own resolve "that they be diligent to observe this Injunction to Catechize there Cheldren, servants and other with in there severall Charge in some sound and Orthodox Catechisme that they may be able to render account hereof when they shall be hereunto required either in the Church or privatly." As the "Constituent Parts of Nations," families were responsible for the "Foundation of

---

29. Jernegan, *Laboring and Dependent Classes,* p. 91; *New Haven Col. Records,* 2 : 583–84. The law was seldom enforced, at least at first. Between 1642 and 1647 no court actions were taken against negligent towns. After that, presentments were few and confined to the remoter outposts. In 1649, for example, Kittery in Maine, then under the jurisdiction of Massachusetts, was presented to the General Court for not having its children taught the catechism and educated according to law (Geraldine Joanne Murphy, "Massachusetts Bay Colony: The Role of Government in Education," [Ph.D. diss., Radcliffe College, 1960], pp. 49–51); Joseph Felt, *The Ecclesiastical History of New England* (Boston, 1862), 2 : 28.

a whole People or Kingdoms Reformation, or Defection, Religion, or Rebellion"—but not wholly. The Puritan ministry, by instinct and training, leaped at the chance to assist the family in initiating its young into their religious culture.[30] In fact they had not even waited for the ships to land. On board the *Arbella* at sea the company "appointed Tuesdays and Wednesdays to catechize our people, and this day [27 April 1630] Mr. [George] Phillips began it." As soon as they did land, an earlier arrival, Francis Higginson of Salem, was informing the English interest in *New-Englands Plantation* that "Thankes be to God, we have here plentie of Preaching, and diligent Catechizing, with strickt and carefull exercise." To answer the educational critics of Plymouth, the Reverend John Reyner plied a singular "gift and propence upon his speritt to traine up children in a Cattikettical way" for eighteen years with such success that "by losse of him [in 1654] Ignorance Inseued in the Towne of Plymouth amonst the voulgare and alsoe much lysensiousnes[s] and prophanes[s] amongst the younger sort." [31]

Ezekiel Rogers enjoyed similar success during his twenty-two years in the Rowley, Massachusetts, pulpit. "He was a *Tree of Knowledge*,"said Cotton Mather,

> but so laden with *Fruit,* that he stoopt for the very *Children* to pick off the Apples ready to drop into their Mouths. Sometimes they would come to his House, A dozen in an Evening; and calling them up into his Study, one by one, he would *examine* them, *How* they walked with God? *How* they spent their Time? *What* good Books they read? *Whether* they pray'd without ceasing? And he would therewithal *admonish* them to take heed of such *Temptations* and *Corruptions,* as he thought most endangered them.[32]

30. Dorchester Town Records, *Fourth Report of the Record Commissioners of the City of Boston, 1880,* 2d ed. (Boston, 1883), p. 73; Lawson, *The Duty and Property of a Religious Housholder,* pp. 50–51.

31. *Winthrop's Journal,* 1 : 36–37; Francis Higginson, *New-Englands Plantation* [1630] (Salem, 1908), sig. D1r.; *PCSM* 22 (1920): 107–08.

32. Cotton Mather, *Magnalia Christi Americana* (London, 1702), bk. 3, pp. 103, 142–45.

The New England ministry's penchant for catechizing was not an unconscious residue of insecurity derived from the Laudian English past. It was often a simple continuation of the practices of Puritan ministers who had not been detected by the hostile Anglican hierarchy. While he was still in England in 1633, Richard Mather drew up a list of promises to God for the betterment of his ministry, which he renewed upon his arrival in New England three years later. The second promise was "to be more careful in *Catechising* Children, And therefore to bestow some Pains this way, *every Week* once; and if by urgent Occasion it be sometimes omitted, to do it twice as much another Week." [33]

John Cotton's catechetical eloquence produced some unexpected results. During his twenty years in Boston, Lincolnshire,

> on the *Lord's Days* in the *Afternoons,* he thrice went over the *Body of Divinity* in a *Catechistical way;* and gave the Heads of his Discourse to young Scholars [grammar students], and others in the Town, that they might answer to his Questions in the Congregation; and the Answers he opened and applied unto the general Advantage of the Hearers. Whilst he was in this way handling the *Sixth Commandment,* the Words of God which he uttered were so quick and powerful, that a Woman among his Hearers, who had been married sixteen Years to a *Second Husband,* now in Horror of Conscience, openly confessed her murdering her former Husband, by Poison, tho' thereby she exposed her self to the Extremity of being burned.

Though without such drastic results, Charles Chauncy foreshadowed some of his intellectual nimbleness as a future president of Harvard College by stepping around the detested *Book of Sports,* which Puritans thought invited the people "unto the Profanation of that *Sacred Rest*" of the Sabbath. "When he was inhibited from attending of other Exercises, on the Afternoons of the *Lord's Day,* he set himself to *Cate-*

33. Ibid., p. 127.

chise as many as he could, both *old* and *young;* which, as the *Bishop* in *Sheeps Cloathing* said, was *As bad as Preaching.*" Once in New England, therefore, it was no novelty for him to advise a ministerial candidate "to *Catechise* every Lord's Day in the Afternoon, so as to go through the *Catechise* once in a Year."[34]

Still, for the first half-century, Puritan preference and New England necessity conspired to minimize clerical catechizing and to maximize that of the family. Even when public catechizing was offered in the church, the home was expected to prepare the children for it, as the householders of Salem were reminded in 1660. On 10 September the church voted "that Mr. Cotton's Catechism should be used in families for teaching children, so that they might be prepared for public catechising in the Congregation." Other initial church efforts, instead of simply undercutting the family, sought its revitalization and rigorous performance. "At a publick church meeting on the 13th day of the 10th moneth [December] 1669 it was agreed on and concluded by a unanimous vote that the Elders [of Boston's First Church] should go from hows to hows to visit the familys and see how they are instructed in the grounds of religion." In the struggle with "old deluder Satan," the family was still believed to constitute the first line of defense.[35]

But by the late 1660s it was becoming increasingly clear that both the family and the ministry of New England were moving in directions far off their original religious course. The congregational churches, for better or worse, were slipping unconsciously into habits and practices they thought they had left behind on the English wharves. Drawn into the Half-Way Covenant by the English congregational Savoy Declaration of 1658 and by the imperatives of biology, some churches soon began to relax their restrictive requirements for membership. While most churches still required a full public narration of

34. Ibid., pp. 17, 135, 138.
35. Joseph Felt, *Annals of Salem* (Salem, 1827), 1 : 207; "Records of the First Church of Boston, 1630–1868," *PCSM* 39 (1961) : 64; Wadsworth, *The Well-Ordered Family*, p. 81; Cotton Mather, *Cares about the Nurserie* (Boston, 1702), pp. 44–45; *EIHC* 2 (1860) : 97–99.

saving grace, others began to offer the options of a private hearing before the minister and deacons or a written relation to be read by the minister before the congregation. More than a few churches, under the example of the congregations of the Connecticut River Valley, dropped the relation altogether as a condition of full membership. This in turn served to open admission to the Lord's Supper, the sanctity of which had been preserved by the Half-Way Covenant.[36]

Prompted by the Presbyterian-Congregational accord, after the restoration of the English church had put both sects on the defensive, the New England churches enlarged in practice the evangelical role of the ministry—which they had always maintained in theory—to include the unconverted. Ministers remembered that their function extended beyond their own particular congregations. From 1690 the spread of ministerial associations, in which the ministers of an area met regularly to discuss common problems, reminded some purists too much of Presbyterian synods. At the same time the churches and the college around Boston were slowly but perceptibly becoming anglicized, and kinder words were spoken for the Church of England. In 1725 a Boston minister could write to his friend, an Anglican bishop, of the "catholick Spirit" that had "these forty Years past" induced Harvard College and the surrounding churches to receive the "Writings and Gentlemen of the Church of *England* with most open Reverence and Affection." Perhaps the most galling sign of change was the appearance of wigs on the heads of New England's ministers, a blatant and unscriptural borrowing from what the orthodox regarded as the decadent English pulpit of the day.[37]

The New England family was equally susceptible to change.

36. Morgan, *Visible Saints,* p. 133.

37. Ibid., chap. 5; Benjamin Colman to White Kennett, *Sibley's Harvard Graduates,* 4 : 127. For the metamorphosis of the New England clergy, see Perry Miller, *The New England Mind: From Colony to Province* (Cambridge, Mass., 1953), chaps. 15–17, and David D. Hall, *The Faithful Shepherd: A History of the New England Ministry in the Seventeenth Century* (Chapel Hill, 1972). Samuel Sewall was the most famous critic of the new fashion of wigs (Sewall Papers, *Colls. MHS,* 5th ser., vols. 5–7).

With the elemental struggle for survival largely won, the colonists turned to the invariably human but spiritually hazardous
opportunity to improve and multiply their own. Ezekiel
Rogers expressed the mounting uneasiness of many of the
first generation in 1657:

> I find greatest Trouble and Grief about the *Rising
> Generation. Young People* are little stirred here; but they
> strengthen one another in Evil, by Example, by Counsel.
> Much a do I have with my own *Family;* hard to get a
> *Servant* that is Glad of *Catechizing,* or *Family-Duties:* I
> had a rare Blessing of Servants in *Yorkshire;* and those
> that I brought over were a Blessing; But the *Young Brood*
> doth much afflict me. Even the *Children* of the Godly
> here, and elsewhere, make a woful Proof. . . . We grow
> *Worldly* everywhere; methinks I see little Godliness, but
> all in a Hurry about the *World;* every one for himself,
> little Care of *Publik* or *Common Good.*[38]

But John Fiske's long experience in Chelmsford was an even
apter symbol of the tension that was shifting the locus of New
England's cultural identity.

In June 1646, two years after he had been ordained, his congregation "concluded in the church that the third day of [the]
week [Wednesday] at the time the cows go forth the children
[were] to come down to be catechized and to give account of
what they learned of the sermon [of the] sabbath before to
[the] pastor's house." This practice continued without incident
until 17 February 1660 when "upon some complaints brought
to the officer [deacon] it was proposed whether the church did
allow of the falling off of some from our week day catechising.
And if not what course to be taken with them that do intermit
or retain their children thereupon?" Brother Adams brought
up the case of his servants and children, and, "from his in-
ability to infuse grace" into them because of the "command
of God to work six days," pleaded to be made an exception

38. Cotton Mather to Zechariah Symmes, 6 February 1657, in Mather,
Magnalia, bk. 3, pp. 103–04.

and to have his children "attend on the Lord's day. The church seemed to be divided touching his case, divers speaking on his behalf. The officer only bore witness against the carnal reasonings as to the case and so dismissed the assembly."

A week later "the church stayed again," and the deacon arranged an accommodation with Mammon. The former times for catechizing were maintained on the first and second days of the week after the lecture. "Those that have discontinued as whose parents may have occasion to employ them about their outward business do come upon the 2nd day of the week as aforesaid in the afternoon at about an hour before sunset to the officer's house." And finally Brother Adams's children were invited to stay after the afternoon lecture on the Sabbath every third or fourth week to be catechized. Embarrassed by the trouble he had caused, Brother Adams weakly explained that he wanted no special treatment and that "his reasoning the [Sun]day before was for all and not his only on [the] Lord's day." [39]

In 1646 the children of New England could be catechized when the cows were put out to pasture. By 1660, however, the relative leisure of a primitive economy has dissipated before the demands of a diversifying market economy and a heightened desire to make a heaven on earth while preparing for the one beyond. If their "outward business" came in conflict with their inner duties, many New Englanders, being mortal, chose to become the victims of that "great backsliding" from the founding ideals the church and state were so ready to decry. The resulting malaise, as the Massachusetts General Court saw it, was a "great & generall neglect of instructing & governing the rising generation, both in familyes & churches." [40]

Against these currents the concerted entrance of the churches into public catechizing appears plausible if not in-

39. Rev. John Fiske's Notebook of Chelmsford Church Affairs, 1637–1675, Essex Institute, Salem, Mass., transcript by Robert Pope.

40. *Mass. Records*, 27 May 1670, 4, pt. 2 : 451. By 1702 the situation was so desperate that Cotton Mather advised masters to "*Hire* [their servants] to learn their *Catechisms* rather than that they should not" (*Cares about the Nurserie*, p. 45).

evitable. But it should not blind us to the close resemblance
it bore to Laud's determined and somewhat pathetic efforts to
keep his leaking ship of state afloat with "Thorough" Church-
ism. In a time of economic stress and leveling enthusiasm for
religious purity, the New England state, like its mother, stood
behind the churches to stem the tide as best it could, starting
on 10 March 1669 in a broadside order "To the Elders and
Ministers of every Town" in Massachusetts.[41] Despite the hope
that "sundry of you need not a spur" in overseeing religious
education, the governor and council had cause to fear "too
much neglect in many places, notwithstanding the Laws long
since provided therein." Thus they felt it their duty to desire
and require the ministers and elders

> to be very diligent and careful to Catechize and Instruct
> all the people (especially the Youth) under your Charge,
> in the Sound and Orthodox Principles of Christian Re-
> ligion; and that not only in publick, but privately from
> house to house, as blessed *Paul* did, *Acts* 20, 20 or at
> least three, four, or more Families meeting together, as
> strength and time may permit, taking to your assistance
> such godly and grave persons as to you may seem most
> expedient. And also that you labour to inform your selves,
> (as much as may be meet) how your Hearers do profit by
> the Word of God, and how their Conversations do agree
> therewith; and whether the Youth are taught to Reade
> the *Englishe* Tongue: Taking all occasions to apply suit-
> able *Exhortations* particularly unto them, for the Rebuke
> of those that do evil, and for the Encouragement of them
> that do well.

The order was a catalyst both to churches that had already
begun to catechize their members' children and to those that
had formerly done so or had wanted to but had been reluctant
to subordinate the family. The crucial difference was that now
"*all* the people," including the unconverted churchgoers who

41. *To the Elders and Ministers of every Town within the Jurisdiction
of the Massachusetts in New-England,* broadside, 10 March 1668/69.

were not full members, were subject to the church's oversight. For the first time the New English clergy was making its evangelical power felt. As we have already seen, the First Church of Boston empowered its elders on 13 December 1669 to "go from hows to hows to visit the familys and see how they are instructed in the grounds of religion." The previous November the newly ordained pastor of Plymouth, John Cotton, revived the public catechizing of his predecessor John Reyner, "(the Elder also accompanying him therein constantly) once a fortnight, the males at one time & the females at the other." Out in Roxbury John Eliot's congregation had to wait until 6 December 1674 when, he noted, "this day we restored our primitive practice for the training up [of] our youth." The hiatus may have been quite short, however, since Eliot "spent in [catechizing] a World of time" and left behind him "a *well-principled People*" immune to the "Contagion of such *Errors* as might threaten any peculiar Danger to them." [42]

Upon other churches the order had mixed effect. The First Church of Dorchester took full cognizance of the Council's instructions to catechize as early as 4 April 1669, but "the maner of doeing this was left to farther consideration." Although the church had moved far enough from its early family reinforcement policy by 30 July 1665 to call on the congregation "to send in the names of thos who they would have to [be] Cattechized the next lords day," it was still beset by indecision in 1672: on 26 May "something was said Concerning Cattechising but not concluded in what manner," even though Josiah Flint had been ordained teacher the previous winter. By June matters had little improved. "Mr Flint desiered the Church & Congregation to send in the names of all children & servants that weer under any famely government in order to catechising or some other way of instruction." Either the town was dominated by a tradition of family independence or beset by lackadaisical church leadership—or perhaps both

42. *PCSM* 39 (1961): 64; 22 (1920): 145, 154; Roxbury Church Records, *Report of the [Boston] Record Commissioners*, 2d ed. (Boston, 1884), 6: 191; Mather, *Magnalia*, bk. 3, p. 187.

—for in February 1676 a church meeting at Mr. Flint's house "judged that we fell short of our former Covenant engagement in wa[t]ching over one another and in famely instruction & Church dissepline & publique Catechizing." Unfortunately the vote on catechizing left it "to be furder considered off by Mr Flint & the rulling Elder & the Select men." It is small wonder that the governor and council had to renew their order in the spring of 1685 "to excit the Elders & minister to take Care of their flocks by goeing from hous to hous & see how the people [are] profitting by the word." [43]

Nevertheless, the trend was clear; the transition from family to church catechism was set irrevocably in motion, and no amount of wishful preaching could reverse it. In the religious freedom of New England, the Puritan home, long congested with the spiritual, economic, and political duties of a distinctive culture, opened its doors to a new world of human possibility, and inadvertently admitted many of the social forces that would sunder its unity. New England discovered the unhappy truth that living *in* the world sooner or later creates inhabitants *of* the world, and the necessity of adjusting its identity to that truth.

But adjustment came slowly, as the hardy ideals of the founders endured and even thrived in the hands of the ministry. Into the eighteenth century the family was still publicly hailed as the chief bulwark against Antichrist and the most proper place for catechizing, even though the ministry privately bemoaned "the Irreligion and Ignorance of many (professedly Christian) Families among us of this Country, notwithstanding the Care universally taken for their Instruction" in the churches.[44] So lamentable was the family's performance in securing New England's religious foundations that even grammar school masters were pressed into service in the unfamiliar role of catechists.

43. *Records of the First Church at Dorchester*, pp. 47, 58, 66–67, 70, 93.
44. The Diary of Ebenezer Parkman, 23 August 1726, *PAAS*, n.s. 71 (1961) : 155.

In England, where education was regulated if not supported by the state church, the ecclesiastical canons required all schoolmasters to be licensed and to

teach in English or Latine, as the children are able to beare, the larger or shorter Catechisme heretofore by publike authoritie set foorth. And as often as any Sermon shall bee upon Holy and Festivall dayes, within the Parish where they teach, they shall bring their Schollers to the Church where such Sermon shall bee made, and there see them quietly and soberly behave themselves, and shall examine them at times convenient after their returne, what they have borne away of such Sermons. Upon other dayes, and at other times they shall traine them up with such sentences of holy Scripture, as shall be most expedient to induce them to all godlinesse.

The law was no dead letter, at least under Laud's steady gaze. His visitation articles periodically asked "whether are your schoolmasters negligent in instructing their scholars in the catechism and grounds of religion, and in bringing them to the church to hear divine service and sermons?" We have already seen John Cotton giving "the Heads of his [Sabbath] Discourse to young Scholars" for their Monday examinations. Another New England colonist, John Sherman of Watertown, remembered that the only time he was chastized at school in Dedham, Essex, was "for his giving the *Heads of Sermons* to his Idle School-Mates, when an Accompt thereof was demanded from them." National uniformity in religion as in education was at least theoretically possible because there was one catechism and one grammar prescribed by law.[45]

But in the congregational diversity of New England, anything resembling a uniform *enforcement* of the articles of

45. *Constitutions and Canons Ecclesiastical, 1604*, sigs. N3v.–N4r.; *The Works of William Laud*, vol. 4, pt. 2, pp. 387, 408, 427; Mather, *Magnalia*, bk. 3, pp. 17, 162; Mark Curtis, "Education and Apprenticeship," *Shakespeare in His Own Age*, ed. Allardyce Nicoll (Cambridge, 1965), pp. 58–59.

belief—even though their *acceptance* may have been universal
—was resisted. Nuances were too important, as the very
existence of New England affirmed. The early grammar schools
confined themselves to equipping their pupils with the secular
tools for acquiring religious knowledge rather than the knowledge itself, content to leave the catechetical function to the
home and the dame school. But that was before the tumultu-
ous sixties and seventies, when New England felt that the family was in a percipitate decline. During those years town en-
gagements with young Harvard graduates to keep school began
to require some attention to formal religious education. In
1669 John Prudden agreed with the feoffees of the Roxbury
Latin School "to use his best skill, and endeavour, both by
praecept, and example, to instruct in all scholasticall, moral,
and theologicall discipline, the children [of the subscribers]
. . . All abcdarians excepted." Daniel Epps and the trustees of
the Salem grammar school agreed in 1677 that he would teach
the children the three classical languages as well as "good
manners" and "the principles of Christian Religion." Two
years later Richard Norcross agreed with Watertown to take
both English and Latin pupils and "once a week to teach
them the catechism." [46]

But the 1684 codification of its rules brought New Haven's
Hopkins Grammar School closer to its English antecedents
than any other New England school had ever come. The
trustees required the master to correct any of his students who
were observed to "play, sleep, or behave themselves rudely, or
irreverently, or be any way disorderly att Meeting on the
Sabaath dayes or any other tymes, of the Publique worship
of God," but also insisted that

46. Morgan, *The Puritan Family*, pp. 100–01; *PCSM* 35 (1951) : 251;
Felt, *Annals of Salem*, 1 : 434; Walter Small, *Early New England Schools*
(Boston, 1914), p. 7. In isolated communities the need for public catechizing may have arisen sooner. Hampton, New Hampshire, for example, engaged John Leget in 1649 to teach and to "instruct [the children] once in
a week, or more, in some orthodox catechise provided for them by their
parents and masters" (Felt, *Ecclesiastical History of New England*, 2 : 28).

all the Lattin Schollars, and all others of the Boyes of Competent age and Capacity give the Master an accompt of one passage or sentence at least of the sermons the foregoing Saboth on the second day morning [Monday]. And that from 1 to 3 in the afternoone of every last day of the week [Saturday] be Improved by the Master in Catechizing of his schollars that are Capable.

By the turn of the century practices such as these had become such a sturdy prop under the family that Cotton Mather could confidently assert that "a School-Master is indeed by way of Eminency to be a Catechist" and should make catechizing a *"frequent,* or at least, a *weekly,* exercise of the *school."* There would be few times in the future when the distance between homeland and colony was smaller.[47]

We have seen the full arsenal of reasons New England gave for catechizing their children except one, and that seldom appeared until the advent of the long wars with the French and the Indians. Especially sharp for the colonists was the realization that their battles constituted only the American theaters of essentially European wars of dynasticism and religion, conflicts that more often than not replayed a post-Reformation theme in pitting Catholic against Protestant. In urging diligent catechizing upon his brethren, the Protestant New Englishman often conjured up a tribe of devious Jesuits and diabolical priests attempting to corrupt the spiritual purity of the North. And over the tiniest child the battle was joined.

In *The Holy State* of Thomas Fuller, a leading English divine, one of the excellencies of "the Faithful Minister" was that he "carefully catechiseth his people in the elements of religion." For "by this catechising, the gospel first got ground of popery; and let not our religion, now grown rich, be ashamed of that which first gave it credit and set it up, lest

47. Thomas Davis, *Chronicles of Hopkins Grammar School, 1660–1935* (New Haven, 1938), pp. 158–59; Mather, *Cares about the Nurserie,* p. 46; Mather, *Bonifacius,* p. 84.

the Jesuits beat us at our own weapon." A warning from the security of an English parish was one thing, from the wilds of North America, where the Catholic presence was menacingly real, quite another. Capture by the Indians often meant redemption by the French in Quebec and a determined campaign of indoctrination and conversion. Under such possibilities a deep and early religious tincture of New England minds might mean salvation from later temptations. To lend authenticity to his *Repeated Warnings*, Cotton Mather appended a letter from a gentleman in Lyme, Connecticut, whose son had run away to sea while the father was attending the sessions of the General Court. For four years the boy ran a terrifying gauntlet—savage storms, pirates, press-gangs, Indians, smallpox, Spanish viceroys who almost sent him to the mines, sea fever, and, most significantly, the captain of a Spanish galleon who offered him £300 if he would convert to Catholicism. "Then the Pious Instructions of a Godly Mother, long since gone to a better World, were of Precious use to him" and he triumphantly resisted the temptation. "I might wish," concluded his father, "that such Experiences as these, might stir up Parents to be more careful in *Catechising their Children;* and that You, or Some Powerful Person," he told Mather, "would move the Authority, that if it be possible, some more Effectual Course may be taken, for the Instruction of Youth." [48]

As a strictly intellectual procedure catechizing was simple and straightforward. The first step was to choose a catechism from the more than 500 extant that was appropriate for the age, capacity, and particular circumstances of the child. In the early years of settlement the choice was likely to fall on William Perkins's *Foundation of Christian Religion,* but after midcentury the Westminster Assembly's *Shorter Catechism* or John Cotton's *Spiritual Milk for Boston Babes,* both at times

48. Thomas Fuller, *The Holy State and The Profane State* (London, 1840), p. 63; Cotton Mather, *Repeated Warnings* (Boston, 1712), pp. 13, 30–31.

appended to the hugely popular *New England Primer,* came into frequent use. As might be expected from staunchly independent Congregationalists, many ministers prepared catechisms for their own particular flocks, giving play to nuance and emphasis within the circle of accepted fundamental beliefs. Despite the great number of catechisms, John Eliot of Roxbury "gave himself the Travail of adding to their Number, by composing of some further *Catechisms,* which were more particularly designed as an Antidote for his own people, against the Contagion of such *Errors* as might threaten any peculiar Danger to them." Salem, Chelmsford, Newbury, Hampton, N.H., Boston, Norwich, Hartford, and Andover were only a few of the towns favored with individualized catechisms. Yet even when these were available, the coherence and universality of the Assembly's *Shorter Catechism* was largely preferred. Although John Fiske "did himself compose and publish a most useful *Catechism* [for Chelmsford], which he entituled, *The Olive-Plant watered,* yet he chose the *Assembly's Catechism* for his Publick-Exposition, wherewith he twice went over it, in Discourses before his Afternoon-Sermons on the Sabbath." [49]

The second step was to have the child memorize the catechism as soon as he was able, for mere repetition without understanding was held to precede true reverence for knowledge. But this was only a temporary means to a higher end. "Alas, we find, Many who can *Say* their *Catechism,* do *know* very Little of what they *Say.* But *this way* of coming at their *Understandings* will bring them into Goshen immediately; into a *Marvellous* Light." Until the child was seven or eight, his religious apprenticeship was confined to the home, where he was expected to parrot the answers to the catechetical questions posed by his parents at least once a week, usually on the Sab-

49. Wilberforce Eames, "Early New England Catechisms," *PAAS*, n.s. 12 (1899) : 76–182; Mather, *Magnalia*, bk. 3, pp. 143, 187. On 14 December 1655 John Fiske's Chelmsford congregation voted to order the Assembly's *Shorter Catechism* to be sold to the inhabitants of the town by one of the officers of the church (Rev. John Fiske's Notebook of Chelmsford Church Affairs).

bath. But beyond that age, as we have seen, he could also expect to feel the close embrace of the church in one of a variety of ways, whichever complemented his own congregation's peculiar style.

> Some of the *Pastors* do on the *Lord's Day,* in the *Afternoons,* before the Sermon, make the Young People publickly to Answer the *Catechism.*

> Others of the *Pastors* do on some *Week-Days,* publickly hear their Young People . . . and then they make a short *Sermon,* upon one of the *Questions.* Or, perhaps upon some Text, for the Animation of *Early Piety.*

> There are yet others who send for the Young People to their Houses, *numbring* and *sorting* of them as they think fit; and then, when they have Answered the *Catechism,* there are Pastoral and Personal Admonitions given unto them, *to Remember their CREATOR in the Days of their Youth.*

> Some of the Pastors chuse to do this Part of their Office after the *Pauline* way, *To teach from House to House.* And perhaps *no way more significant!* The Pastor may send aforehand unto such *Families* as he intends, an Intimation *that* he intends at such a Time to Visit them: And coming to the *Families,* he assays with as decent and as pungent Addresses as he is able, to treat each Person particularly about their Everlasting Interests. And unto the *Young People,* he puts Questions of the *Catechism,* from the Answers whereof he makes as lively Applications unto them as he can, for the Engaging of them in the Service of the Lord.[50]

The third and final step was to move as quickly as possible from mere tests of memory to enquiries testing true understanding, graduated according to the age and capacity of the child. Initially the catechist was advised to break the several

50. Cotton Mather, *Man of God Furnished* (Boston, 1708), in Paul L. Ford, ed., *The New-England Primer* (New York, 1897), pp. 263–73; Cotton Mather, *Ratio Disciplinae Fratrum Nov-Anglorum* (Boston, 1726), pp. 103–05.

questions of the catechism into smaller parts so that "a pertinent Word or two" from the child would be a sufficient answer. For instance, when the children had answered, "God has made me, He keeps me, and can Save me," he should then be asked, "What? Is there then a God, who made all things? Did you make yourself? Who then made you? Can you keep yourself? Should you not quickly fall into all Miseries, if God did not keep you?" With questions like these, a simple yes-or-no answer revealed the degree of the child's understanding whereas a straight parroting of answers might have concealed it.[51]

When they grew older, though, and advanced in subtlety, Cotton Mather

> would bring every *truth,* into some *duty* and *practice,* and expect them to *confess* it, and *consent* unto it, and *resolve* upon it. As we go on in *catechizing,* they shall, when they are able, turn to the [Scriptural] *proofs,* and *read* them, and say to me, *what* they prove, and *how.* Then, I will take my times, to put nicer and harder *questions* to them.

This was the occasion perhaps to give the growing youth more substantial fare, such as James Fitch's *First Principles of the Doctrine of Christ; Together with stronger Meat for them that are skil'd in the Word of Righteousness.* As Increase Mather explained in his prefatory puff, "here is not only Milk for Babes in respect of Principles, with much solid Dexterity asserted; but strong Meat in respect of rational explications, and Demonstrations of those Principles, that the ablest men, who have their senses exercised in discerning things of this nature, may be edified."[52]

Catechizing brought into the church a highly variable group of children, both in knowledge and age. In 1676, for example, 173 "children" of ages stretching from seven to thirty-one, presented themselves to the First Church in Dorchester for instruction. There were 88 under twelve, 85 over twelve, and

---

51. Ford, *The New-England Primer,* p. 270.
52. Mather, *Bonifacius,* p. 45; James Fitch, *First Principles of the Doctrine of Christ* (Boston, 1679), sig. A5r.

35 over twenty years of age, all groups about evenly divided between girls and boys. Obviously, to ensure some efficiency of instruction, each church had to divide its candidates into separate classes. The church in Norwich, Connecticut, directed all children between the ages of eight and thirteen to be cate-chized in the public congregation each Sabbath. Those over thirteen, while under family government, were provided with a private meeting for their instruction. Chelmsford saw fit to have those under sixteen attend catechetical sessions at the pastor's house on specified days of the week, girls on one day, boys on the next. Apparently girls completed their formal religious education at that age because only unmarried "young men" over sixteen were asked to volunteer to answer the catechism in public. Those who refused were catechized at the pastor's house with the younger boys. Almost universally, re-ligious education was conducted in sexually segregated classes.[53]

The catechetical process continued unaltered and unim-paired through the eighteenth century. Even the religious up-heavals of the Great Awakening did nothing to change it. For the emphasis of the revival, as Peter Thacher of Middle-borough said, was on "the *experimental* Part of *Piety*," not the logically earlier stage of rational religious learning that was thought to underlie true religious experience. Therefore, we should not be disappointed when we hear little of cate-chizing and religious education in the literature of the revival: the Great Awakening *presupposed* that elementary stage of religious growth. When the people asked their ministers what they must do to be saved, the answer given was to attend to the means of conversion, "as *reading* GOD's *Word, hearing* it *preached, and Prayer.*" Nothing had really changed in the essential Puritan message; spiritual life and power merely suf-fered at different times until they were rekindled. As the Rev-

53. *Records of the First Church at Dorchester*, pp. 183–85; Frances Caulkins, *History of Norwich, Connecticut* (Hartford, 1874), pp. 123–24; Rev. John Fiske's Notebook of Chelmsford Church Affairs, 6 February 1665.

erend George Griswold of East Lyme, Connecticut, wrote in April 1744, "We as well as the rest of the Country were grown very careless and stupid in Matters of Religion: but little of the Life and *Power* of Godliness was to be observed among us; yea as to sundry, the *Form* was wanting." The people who were least liable to take religious forms for granted and most susceptible to the touch of the "Life and *Power*" of godliness were the young, those who had made some headway in their religious education as to fundamentals but had not yet been exposed to the *"experimental* Part of *Piety."* In many instances across New England it was the children and youth of the towns who were first and most visibly touched by the religious quickening of spirit. Although some ministers were doubtful of the lasting results of this affective phenomenon upon the majority of children, the fact that children were so central to the Great Awakening strongly suggests that the experimental, experiential side of religion was being emphasized over the rational, epistemological side and the catechizing that was the heart of it.[54]

As the form of religious education perdured, so too did its content. A strong sign of continuity was the common form of covenant made by new congregations in the eighteenth century. One of the promises made was to raise their children and servants according to God's holy ordinances, and "in special by the use of Orthodox Catechism" to maintain "the true religion." And without question, the Westminster Assembly's *Shorter Catechism* was the touchstone of orthodoxy in colonial New England, so much so that it was vested with the aura and power of a cultural symbol quite distinct from its credal content.[55]

Whenever a party at law in religious matters, for example,

54. Thomas Prince, Jr., ed., *The Christian History* . . . *For the Year 1743* (Boston, 1744), pp. 238, 412–13; *The Christian History* . . . . *For the Year 1744* (Boston, 1745), pp. 82, 98, 105, 107, 167, 171, 347, 392.
55. See, for example, F. C. Pierce, *History of Grafton* (Worcester, 1879), p. 168; Henry Nourse, ed., *The Early Records of Lancaster, Massachusetts 1643–1725* (Lancaster, 1884), p. 170; Heman DeForest, *The History of Westborough, Massachusetts* (Westborough, 1891), p. 83.

wished to claim the side of truth and justice for its cause, it would pledge unwavering allegiance to an archetypically orthodox catechism. This is what Edward Woodman's party of Newbury church members did in 1671 in their fight with their Presbyterian pastor, Thomas Parker. Although judgement was eventually brought against them, the Woodman party claimed that they "stood unmovable" for "mr [Richard] Mathers Catechisme" and "those principles proved by the scriptures . . . in cattechisms by the synod by the Eccleseastical lawes confirmed, & approved of by the practise of all churches in Gen[eral]." Indeed, they believed they were prosecuted for the very reason that they did "abide constant to those principles & [would] not turne Presbeterians." Twenty years later some citizens of Lancaster made a similar use of the catechism in presenting George Newby to the Middlesex Grand Jury for "high handed contempt of God's Word, Reproaches of the ministers . . . and for a practice of high handed Debauching." "Since he came to our Town," read his indictment, "he has endeavored to Pervert all thats Good and has been a Leader of all maner of evill, Paying nothing to church nor state. . . . But that which I most would signifie to your Honors is said Newbys most profainly sp[e]aking & sli[gh]ting of that most worthy Peice of worke the Assembly of divines, *even the Catechism,* sli[gh]ting the holy Bible & the Ambassadors of Jesus Christ." For his blasphemy of the highest cultural symbol of this "Little Israel," Newby received twenty stripes on his naked body and was ordered to pay court costs and £20 bond for good behavior.[56]

During the Great Awakening, when doctrinal issues were argued at length and in depth, the catechism resumed its primary character as credal repository. Whatever their differences, Separatists, New Lights, and Old Lights all rushed to affirm their fidelity to the principles of the Westminster Assembly. Many congregations felt a *"great shaking among the Dry Bones,"* as did John Seccomb's in Harvard, Massachusetts, whereby "the BIBLE hath appeared to some to be a *new Book;*

56. *Essex Co. Court Records,* 4 : 364–65; Nourse, ed., *Early Records of Lancaster,* p. 129 (my emphasis).

and the *Catechism* of the *Assembly of Divines* to be a *new* and *most excellent* Composure, tho' before they saw no great Excellency to be in the one or the other." To ensure that they would never again find those particular books so novel, Seccomb instituted a monthly lecture to preach upon "the Assemblies Catechism; and to Catechise and Instruct children and youth after service."[57] There were similar "shakings among Dry Bones" throughout New England, and it was always the Westminster *Catechism* that fell out.

Yet, when the religious fervor of the Awakening ebbed into lassitude, the catechism became once again a cultural symbol, though often at times when the debate was on questions of religious doctrine. The unforgettable turmoil of the previous decade clearly inflected the question that the Reverend John Bass put to his Ashford, Connecticut, congregation in 1751: whether they were of the opinion that "Original Sin as explained in our Shorter Catechism of the Westminster Assembly of Divines be an Essential Term of Christian Fellowship & Communion." Although it was "resolved in the Affirmative by a great Majority," it may be hazarded that as many voted for the catechism itself as for the concept of original sin.[58]

If there was any doubt in New English minds about the locus of orthodoxy throughout its history, Thomas Prince laid it to rest in 1744 in the concluding article of his popular serial, *The Christian History*. Having explained that even the separatist congregations adhered to "the *Assembly's Confession of Faith*," he went on to describe the "doctrinal Principles of those who continue in our Congregations and have been the Subjects of the late Revival." They are, he said, "the same as they have been all along instructed in, from the *Westminster Assembly's shorter Catechism*: which has been generally receiv'd and taught in the Churches of *New-England* from its first Publication for these *hundred Years* to this Day; and which is therefore the System of Doctrine most generally

57. Henry Nourse, *History of the Town of Harvard, Massachusetts, 1732–1893* (Harvard, 1894), pp. 190–92.
58. Ashford Church Records, Conn. Archives, Eccles. Affairs, 1st ser., 10 : 291.

and clearly *declarative* of the *Faith* of the *New-England* Churches." [59] As symbol and as doctrine, the catechism was to countless generations of New English children the talisman of religious maturity, the key that unlocked the cultural heart of the New England experience.

As a rule a New English youngster could not expect to be free from formal catechizing, either in the home or the church, until his sixteenth birthday. But that was no magical passport to independence, for, if anything, the church now tucked him even farther under its wing—as a privilege, though, and not as punishment. Catechizing, it must be remembered, was only a means to a means to an end. It brought the child only to the threshold of church membership, which in turn only maximized—but never guaranteed—his chances of salvation. Before he could enter the communion of saints, he had to pass a test of his religious knowledge, such as John Fiske administered to "the children of the church grown up to years of discretion" in Chelmsford. After the evening services on the Sabbath and the fortnightly meetings in the summer of 1663, the minister, with an assistant, began with his own family and then followed "as the houses in order do stand [in the town] till he hath gone through." His journal recorded the initial results:

> Moses Fiske his knowledge competent touching experience.
> Sarah Fiske she were taken into full communion.
> John Fiske merely as to understanding.
> Anna Fiske more in the letter then as to understanding.
> Jonathan Bates this very ignorant.
> Nathaniel Butterfield and Jonathan Butterfield. They answered beyond expectation as to understanding, though short of what is required
> Jonathan Wright his knowledge comfortable and a good

59. Prince, ed., *Christian History . . . For the Year 1744*, pp. 374, 413–14.

relation of a work of grace, only not clear as to the work of closure with Christ. He upon consideration and to come again upon trial. Benjamin Spalding answered in part well, though his memory seems better than his understanding.[60]

On 19 February 1678 in the Dorchester congregation "Nathanell Mather was Called forth to give Satisfaction for his slighting & neglect in Coming up to the Order of the Church at which time he did give some account publikly of his knowlidg out of a Cattechisme but falling short of what he should be attained unto, & he promising to doe his best to attain more, he was dismissed & was appointed to Come to the Elders againe about a fortnight after." An exasperating number of cases like young Mather's prompted the church to vote in 1685 that "two of the tithing mens Squadrons" should, in addition to catechizing those eight to sixteen years old, call the young persons sixteen to twenty-four years old together "to be discoursed with, all the maids by themselves & the men by themselves." [61]

Preparation for church membership was not always initiated from the outside by parents and ministers. Often, especially during the Great Awakening, the children themselves sought each other's company for mutual support and edification— and, one suspects, for a momentary escape from the largely adult existence they led. Admittedly, the substance and style of their religious gatherings was precociously mature, but they did provide one of the rare occasions for young people to get together without their ubiquitous elders standing over them.

As early as 1726 the children of New Milford, Connecticut, felt the "warming presence of Christ" in their midst. "They set up private Meetings, which they carried on by praying, reading good Books, singing, etc. The Meetings were chiefly of the younger Sort of People; of Children about five or six

60. Rev. John Fiske's Notebook of Chelmsford Church Affairs.
61. *Records of the First Church at Dorchester*, pp. 80, 93. For "The Brotherly Watch of Fellow-Members," see Winslow, *Meetinghouse Hill*, chap. 11.

Years of Age, and so upwards to about twenty one, or two:
And there were among them two or three of thirty Years, or
more; tho' they were mainly of the more youngerly Sort."
The tone of such meetings was uniformly serious. "All Frolic-
ing and Carousing, and Merry Meetings were laid aside;
Foolish talking and Jesting seem'd terrible to the young
People; they would not endure it; they desir'd to hear nothing
but what was serious and solemn; they took more Delight in
going to a Meeting than ever they did to a Frolick." [62]

Curiously, the apprehension most frequently voiced by ministers and parents did not concern the religious maturity of the
participants—"they behaved with a great deal of Seriousness
and Regularity, and the Manner of the Performances was
beyond what could be expected from such Children"—the
fear was rather for the sexually mixed character of the meetings. In sharp contrast to the seventeenth century, when all
catechizing, church attendance, and even cattle-tending was
segregated, the youthful effusions of the eighteenth century
spirit were coeducational. Almost all the children of Halifax,
Massachusetts, "both male and female," attended meetings in
the 1740s. In Plymouth, Connecticut, "a doubt at once arose
with respect to the propriety of encouraging so young a class,
of the different sexes, meeting by themselves, for religious purposes," but it was soon assuaged by the propriety and visible
seriousness of the young. Children in Chester, Connecticut,
from nine to fifteen years of age met "frequently in mixed
assemblies" where they prayed, sang, and exhorted one
another "in a serious and solemn manner. And it is supposed,"
their pastor wrote, "that a number of them became truly
friends to Christ." [63]

All this, however, was only a preparation for the main business of the Puritan religion, the child's rite of passage into
spiritual adulthood as a full member of the church. With

62. Prince, ed., *Christian History . . . For the Year 1743*, pp. 238–39;
Christian History . . . For the Year 1744, pp. 45, 120–25, 171, 347–50;
Sanford Fleming, *Children and Puritanism* (New Haven, 1933), pp. 146–
52.
63. Fleming, *Children and Puritanism*, pp. 146–52.

uncustomary conciseness, Cotton Mather pinpointed the issue when he said, "Our whole religion fares according to our Sabbaths. Poor Sabbaths make poor Christians." Attendance upon the outward ordinances of the "Word, Sacraments, & Prayer" was the *sine qua non* of church membership and visible sainthood. So as soon as children were old enough "to be benefited themselves and the Congregation not disturbed by 'em," they were taken to church and taught to "Hallow the LORDS Day." The latter was no easy task, for the Puritan Sabbath began at 3 o'clock on Saturday afternoon and ended late Sunday night; in between, every manner of worldly activity was looked on with a cold eye. Cooking, washing, trading, sailing, farming, smoking, shaving—the Puritan God was a jealous God, and nothing escaped His commandment to rest on the seventh day and prepare for the reception of His Word. The innocent as well as the wilful felt the lash of church and state, as in 1670 when two lovers of New London were tried for "sitting together on the Lord's Day under an apple tree in Goodman Chapman's Orchard." Others, like sixteen-year-old Nathaniel Mather, merely suffered from their own consciences.

> When very young I went astray from God, and my mind was altogether taken with vanities and follies; such as the remembrance of them doth greatly abase my soul within me. Of the manifold sins which then I was guilty of, none so sticks upon me, as that being very young, *I was whittling on the sabbath-day;* and for fear of being seen, I did it behind the door. A great reproach of God! a specimen of that atheism that I brought into the world with me.[64]

Staying out of trouble until the Sunday services was only half the problem; getting there was often the other. The

64. Winslow, *Meetinghouse Hill*, p. 179; Joseph Belcher, *Two Sermons Preached at Dedham* (Boston, 1710), p. 12; Alice M. Earle, *The Sabbath in Puritan New England* (Boston, 1891), chap. 17; Fleming, *Children and Puritanism*, p. 21. For the rise of Sabbatarianism, see Hill, *Society and Puritanism*, chap. 5.

rivers, hills, marshes, and forests of New England proved a suitable trial to the religious zeal of many pious families, especially the younger members. Many river towns encountered formidable obstacles that were faced to some extent by every New England community. Hadley, Massachusetts, isolated on the far western edge of the colony, spoke for many in 1667:

> Sometimes we come in considerable numbers in rainy weather, and are forced to stay till we can empty our canoes, that are half full of water, and before we can get to the meetinghouse, are wet to the skin. At other times, in winter seasons, we are forced to cut and work them out of the ice, till our shirts be wet upon our backs. At other times, the winds are high and water rough, the current strong and the waters ready to swallow us—our vessels tossed up and down so that our women and children do screech, and are so affrighted that they are made unfit for ordinances, and cannot hear so as to profit by them, by reason of their anguish of spirit; and when they return, some of them are more fit for their beds than for family duties and God's services, which they ought to attend.[65]

When they did arrive at the severely appointed meetinghouse, with its noises, smells, and creeping chill, armed guards were stationed at the entrance in time of war to watch for Indians. Dogs roamed freely (despite paid "dog-beaters"), pews creaked endlessly with bodies shifting against the cold and the hours, and the children, segregated in their own pews or the gallery, did their best to stay entertained when they could no longer be enlightened. They let their imaginations wash over the stained knots in the woodwork, day-dreamed into spiders' webs, waited hopefully for the sounding board over the pulpit to drop on its occupant, and fidgeted and fussed as the minister inverted the hourglass once, twice, even three times. When their discomfort erupted into deviltry, the appointed

65. Winslow, *Meetinghouse Hill*, p. 138.

overseer of the children whipped into action to restore decorum and order, if not concentration.[66]

Yet for all its unpalatable features, the church was the vital center of New England life. In the absence of theater, it provided a form of weekly drama, austere yet sentient, like its congregations. When newspapers were scarce, it was the community center of information and entertainment. In an age which knew the tension of a new printed culture and an older oral one, the minister was the personal link between the homely conversation of rural New England and the literary sophistication of Boston, New York, and London. Most important, the church was the locus of the deep layer of common values shared by New Englanders, the physical center that gave point and structure to their various lives. The children of New England came to know it almost from the day of birth, and many grew up to welcome its awesome embrace. Without risk of a major loss of identity, there was no other course. America was yet too young to live without the King of Kings.

New England was built to last. Its founders were men of uncommon steel, its blueprints were drawn by God, and its foundations were laid on the "word of his Promise." Not surprisingly, the process of religious education in colonial New England changed very little over a century and a half. The New English child on the eve of revolution was still largely shaped after the religious model of his Tudor ancestors, for duty did not allow his parents to disguise for him the terror they lived by. Life was deadly serious, predestination inhumanly grim, and New England prepared its children accordingly. No change would mar the stark reality of the Puritan vision until a gentle man of mediocrity, himself the son

66. Earle, *Sabbath in Puritan New England,* pp. 17–18; Pierce, *History of Grafton,* pp. 166–67; *NEHGR* 15 (1861) : 193–204, 305–15; Hezekiah Sheldon, ed., *Documentary History of Suffield, . . . 1660–1749* (Springfield, 1879), p. 228; *Watertown Records* (Boston, 1906), p. 9.

of Calvinist parents, would convince his countrymen that the Adam in their children was the initial creature of innocence and purity, not the fallen wretch of Paradise Lost. Until John Locke's rejection of original sin was heard, the children of New England were condemned to replay painfully adult roles in the drama of salvation.

2

The Perdurable Milieu

A man and a woman that before were members of another family, do therefore joyne together in marriage, that they become the rootes of a new family, and begetting children and training them up.

William Whately

The book that helped to popularize a gentler conception of childhood had its genesis in 1684 in Holland, where John Locke was avoiding the unhealthy political and climatic airs of England. *Some Thoughts concerning Education* (1693) represents an important yet traditional stride forward in European thought on education. It builds on the work of many predecessors and gains its importance largely from its intimate association with Locke's more innovative thoughts on human understanding. In this sense, it is a conservative work, seeking reasonable accommodation with social change, but desiring no peremptory disjunction from the best efforts of the past.[1]

But another of Locke's works does represent a considerable break with historical modes of thought, his *Two Treatises of Government* (1690), which he had written substantially in 1679–80. The immediate occasion of Locke's essay in political philosophy was the republication in 1680 of a collection of tracts by Sir Robert Filmer, an early Stuart defender of the patriarchal basis of absolute monarchy. Locke, the intellectual companion of Lord Shaftesbury, the leader of the Whig

1. *The Educational Writings of John Locke,* ed. James Axtell (Cambridge, 1968), chap. 3.

opposition to King Charles II in Parliament, sought to refute
Filmer by establishing the forms and authority of government
on the basis of the rational consent of every individual in
society. For Locke, the family as well as the state depended
for their being and continuity on conscious thought. They
were, in short, human artifacts, *"voluntary* and *conventional"*
constructs of the human mind.[2]
The appearance of a liberal theory of politics in the late
seventeenth century, however, flew in the face of centuries of
European social experience and thought. From Aristotle to
Filmer, men had believed—and rightly—that their association
in civil society was *"natural* and *native"* to the human condition, not the consequence of logical argument. "Man is born
into society," wrote Montesquieu, one of the philosophers who
reasserted the naturalistic tradition in the eighteenth century,
"and there he remains." He is "by nature, the member of a
community" because, as Aristotle had seen, "the individual,
when isolated, is not self-sufficing." "He is only part of a
whole." For the naturalistic tradition, the least common de-
nominator of civil society was not the consenting individual
but the perdurable family, "the association established by nature for the supply of men's everyday wants." And over the
family stood the father.[3]
"Adam was the Father, King and Lord over his family,"
argued Filmer, and from that authority derived the authority
of the state over its subjects—naturally, smoothly, inexorably.
The natural duties of a king were all one with those of a
father, for political society was nothing but "a general family
or household wherein good governors do put on the same
carefree affection to the advancement of their subjects, which

2. John Locke, *Two Treatises of Government,* ed. Peter Laslett (Cam-
bridge, 1960), chap. 3. The final phrase is from Edward Gee, *Divine
Right and Original of the Civill Magistrate* (London, 1658), quoted in
Sir Robert Filmer, *Patriarcha,* ed. Peter Laslett (Oxford, 1949), p. 38.
3. Adam Ferguson, *An Essay on the History of Civil Society, 1767,* ed.
Duncan Forbes (Edinburgh, 1966), p. 57; Aristotle, *Politics (The Basic
Works of Aristotle,* ed. Richard McKeon), 1253a 27, 1252b 11–12.

wise and dear fathers use to their entirely beloved children."
For men in early seventeenth century England, as for their
ancestors, the state was merely an extended patriarchal family,
bound by the childlike "humility, frank obedience and perfect
love" of its subjects and governed by the paternal "wisdom,
love and zeal" of its magistrates.[4]

One group of Englishmen, however, were considerably uneasy in the presence of the naturalistic tradition of social
polity. The leading Puritan spokesmen, long imbued with the
lessons of Adam's curse, distrusted nature and the natural to
such an extent that in theory they often disapproved of personal connections made by local loyalty, kinship, familial alliance, and marriage. Instead their tendency was to politicize
the family by trying to substitute the legal bonds of a contractual relation for the natural ties of a sacramental community. In the large Puritan literature on "household *government*"—a characteristic emphasis—there is very little talk of
love or trust or emotional affinity among the prolix legalistic
discussions of the reciprocal rights and duties of family members. There was obviously little room for such things in a
group invariably regarded as an institution.

"A family is a little Church, and a little Common-wealth,"
said William Gouge, "at least a lively representation thereof,
whereby tryall may be made of such as are fit for any place of
authority, or of subjection in Church or Commonwealth. Or
rather it is as a schoole wherein the first principles and grounds
of government and subjection are learned." The idea of the
family as a school reveals "the overbearing Puritan sense of
purpose, directed towards ends beyond or, at any rate, not
identical with the needs and feelings of ordinary men." The
contrast with the traditional idea of the "old fashioned family
founded on nature and love" could not be starker.[5]

4. Filmer, *Patriarcha*, p. 188; Geoffrey Fenton, *A Forme of Christian
Policy* (London, 1574), p. 13, quoted in Michael Walzer, *The Revolution
of the Saints* (Cambridge, Mass., 1965), p. 184.

5. William Gouge, *Of Domesticall Duties* (London, 1634), p. 17; Walzer,
Revolution of the Saints, pp. 191, 197.

But if Puritan social thought anticipated the contractual legalism of liberal political theory, it nevertheless retained the family as the common element of the state. And in the end the transformation of the family remained incomplete. For "as long as children were born, instead of appearing voluntarily like colonists in a new country, the family could not become a purely political society," either at home or in New England. In addition to its evident value for the individual life histories of New Englishmen, then, just how children were born and raised in the perdurable milieu of the natural family assumes considerable importance for our understanding of their society.[6]

Before there are children, there must be parents. Whether the nights were cold and long in December or warm and sweet scented in May, New Englishmen were confident that "great conjunctions betwixt the male & Female Planets of our sublunary Orb" would occur with unfailing regularity, "the effects whereof may be seen about nine months after." In the seventeenth century, conception patterns appear to have followed "the rhythm of the seasons" as in Europe, with low peaks during harvest time and renewed vigor from November to January, and especially from April to June, but in the eighteenth century, the pattern began to spread out over the year. Still, despite the largely unseen force of demographical change, the belief in the amorous potential of New England winters persisted. As one lady who had proudly resisted the trend remarked, "Pray what do you think every body marrys in, or about Winter for: Tis quite merry, isn't it? I realy believe tis fear of laying cold, & for want of a bedfellow." [7]

But not all parents were married when their orbits con-

6. Walzer, *Revolution of the Saints,* p. 196. See below, chap. 4, for the family's role in educating children to a sense of social place.

7. *NEHGR,* February 1688, 8 (1854) : 21–22; Kenneth Lockridge, "The Population of Dedham, Massachusetts, 1636–1736," *Economic History Review,* 19 (August 1966) : 318–44; Esther Burr to Sarah Prince, [winter 1754/55], Journal of Esther Burr, p. 45, Yale University Library, New Haven, Conn.

joined. The colonial courts recognized the varieties of parental condition when they fixed the penalties for "fornication." Plymouth Colony was typical in classifying the crime under three headings: "Without Contract," that is, before formal engagement; "If they be or will be married" but without being contracted; and "After contract" but before marriage. The fines accordingly were £20, £10, and £5, as two Plymouth men discovered in 1664. On 7 March Thomas Cushman was assessed £5 for carnal relations with his wife before marriage "but after contract," but Thomas Totman, because he could not prove that he and his wife had been engaged at the time of their offensive behavior, paid £10, "but if soe cleared," granted the court, "to pay but five pounds." Something like 85 percent of the married defendants in fornication cases that came before the Plymouth court from 1633 to 1691 shared with Mr. Totman the misfortune of conceiving children out of contract.[8]

The majority of those prosecuted for fornication were usually well married, and only the untimely arrival of a child spoiled their secret. At a General Court session in 1652, for instance, two Cape Cod fathers were arraigned for fornication on the basis of their children's birth dates. (Why mothers were not always equally guilty is one of the mysteries of the English judicial mind.) Thomas Laundus of Sandwich was found guilty of "haveing a child born within thirty weeks after marriage," and Nicholas David of Barnstable of "haveing a child five weekes and foure daies before the ordinary time of woemen after marriage," which seems to have been a minimum of thirty-two weeks. But time could cut both ways. On another occasion, a young man—though unmarried—narrowly escaped being branded as a fornicator and assessed child support with the help of the same providential timing that often fingered less fortunate husbands. On 1 March 1670, while the Plymouth court was considering Bethyah Tubbs's paternity suit against

8. In the early years of settlement, public stocking or whipping was often added to the fines, but the frequency of violation presumably softened the magisterial view of its heinousness (*Plymouth Records*, 4 : 83; 11 : 95). Of 34 cases of premarital fornication, only five (15 percent) were "after contract."

John Prince, Jr., "it soe fell out by the ordering hand of God" that she was delivered, too early on her own testimony for John to have been the father.[9] Premarital pregnancy was more common in New England than the court records indicate, a situation not unlike that of rural England and perhaps attributable to the same causes. In the years from 1540 to 1835, between one-third and one-half of the women who went to the altar in seventy-seven rural English parishes were "great with child." The American score appears to have been hardly better. Though there are no precise figures, the historian of seventeenth century Plymouth Colony found the number of "early children" there to be "extremely high," even in the best of families. In eighteenth century Bristol, where statistics are available, the incidence of premarital conception was between 44 percent and 49 percent in the forty years after 1740. In all likelihood, New England as a whole experienced a loosening of restrictive standards of sexual morality in the eighteenth century, which would help to explain why the judicial and ecclesiastical exposure of fornication gradually ceased at the same time.[10]

Though the vagaries of human behavior in the past are seldom clear, there are two likely explanations for the incidence of premarital pregnancy among the English in the early modern period. The first is the nature of the betrothal contract itself, which was not officially abolished until 1753 by Hardwicke's Marriage Act. According to William Gouge, "Contracted persons are in a middle degree betwixt single persons and married persons. . . . Many make it a very marriage, and thereupon have a greater solemnity at their contract than at their marriage: yea many take liberty after a contract to know their spouse, as if they were married: an unwarrantable and dishonest practice." Dishonest or not, the practice must have

9. *Plymouth Records*, 2 March 1652, 3 : 6; 5 : 32; *Suffolk Co. Court Records*, p. 22.
10. P. E. H. Hair, "Bridal Pregnancy in Rural England in Earlier Centuries," *Population Studies* 20 (November 1966) : 233–43; John Demos, "Notes on Life in Plymouth Colony," *WMQ* 22 (April 1965), 273–74; Demos, "Families in Colonial Bristol, Rhode Island," *WMQ* 25 (January 1968) : 56–57.

enjoyed more than local favor since so many ministers felt obliged to inveigh against it, both at home and abroad. William Perkins, the leading Puritan spokesman, was only one of many who were strongly of the opinion that the espoused couple should "not presently upon the Contract, seeking to satisfie their own fleshly desires," hop into bed.[11] In New England, especially in the eighteenth century, the ministry waged a persistent if losing battle against this "wicked practice of young people in their courtships." So topical had the issue become by 1721 that a Harvard society debated "whether it be lawful to lie with one's sweetheart before marriage." Even young ministers flushed with Harvard degrees had to confront the temptation. In 1729 the Reverend Ebenezer Parkman of Westborough stopped his daily labors to make a list of evidences of "Divine Benignity and Providence" toward him in his still short life. One was his marriage to Mary Champney of Cambridge on 7 July 1724, the year he received his master's degree and ascended the pulpit. His addendum is revealing, perhaps especially since Mary was four years his senior. "And here I would bless God for his wondrous Grace in restraining me from the Sin of Fornication, and carrying me through so many Temptations as Those pass'd in the Time of Courtship." Not all of his contemporaries were so favored.[12]

Another custom which must have led to "early children" was "tarrying," a common practice in certain parts of England in the late sixteenth century. In 1760 Andrew Burnaby, a visiting Anglican minister, described the New England version of this "singular custom" of courtship among "the lower people of this province," which at first appeared to be "the effects of mere grossness of character" but, upon "deeper research," was shown to "proceed from simplicity and innocence."

11. Peter Laslett, *The World We Have Lost* (London, 1965), pp. 141–44; Gouge, *Of Domesticall Duties,* p. 203; William Perkins, *Christian Oeconomie* (London, 1618), p. 72.

12. *Sibley's Harvard Graduates,* 4 : 80; 6 : 512; *PCSM* 12 (1911) : 229; *PAAS,* April 1729, n.s., vol. 71 (1961). John Adams, another Harvard man, expressed similar relief at having emerged from an amorous youth with his innocence intact (*Diary and Autobiography of John Adams,* ed. L. H. Butterfield (New York, 1964), 3 : 260–61).

When a man is enamoured of a young woman, and wishes to marry her, he proposes the affair to her parents, (without whose consent no marriage in this colony can take place); if they have no objection, they allow him to tarry with her one night, in order to make his court to her. At their usual time the old couple retire to bed, leaving the younger ones to settle matters as they can; who, after having sate up as long as they think proper, get into bed together also, but without pulling off their undergarments, in order to prevent scandal. If the parties agree, it is all very well; the banns are published, and they are married without delay. If not, they part, and possibly never see each other again; unless, which is an accident that seldom happens, the forsaken fair-one prove pregnant, and then the man is obliged to marry her, under pain of excommunication.

Either the good pastor walked on the gullible side, or his informants were far more saintly than their countrymen.[13]

Some children were not only conceived in sin but born there as well. It is nearly impossible to plumb the emotional effects of having been born out of wedlock in children so distant from us in time and culture, but perhaps we are not helpless to imagine the plight of the bastard son of Dorothy Temple, "a mayde servant," and Arthur Peach, "who was executed for murther and roberry by the heighway before the said child was borne." Such children—and the court records are heavy with them—never knew the warmth of belonging to a natural family or the security of the knowledge that they were really wanted. And in a culture that placed supreme importance upon the family, that deprivation must have been costly.[14]

When a woman was ready for pregnancy, an ample medical

13. Andrew Burnaby, *Travels through the Middle Settlements in North-America* (Ithaca, 1960), pp. 102–03; Laslett, *World We Have Lost*, pp. 141–42; George Howard, *A History of Matrimonial Institutions* (Chicago, 1904), 2 : 169–95.

14. *Plymouth Records*, 8 February 1639, 1 : 113. On 4 June Dorothy was "censured to be whipt twice; but shee faynting in the execucion of the first, thother was not executed" (Ibid., 1 : 127).

and religious literature was available with advice. Of primary concern to most parents in a patriarchal society was the sex of the child, which at least some doctors believed could be regulated. Jacques Guillemeau counseled that to produce a boy the man "must know his wife as soone as her courses [menstruation] are stayed, and then try the utmost of his strength," having tied his left testicle "as hard as he can endure it" to allow only the semen from the right to flow. To obtain a girl, the right "stone" was bound and the union consummated several days after the woman's period, or during it. This was not only a significant departure from the normal prohibition of intercourse during menstruation, but a characteristic indication of the way the female was regarded.[15]

The normality of "rightness" and the predominant physiology of "humors" placed the female at a disadvantage from birth. Women carrying boys enjoyed fair complexions, red nipples, and white milk, while girls gave their mothers "a pale, heavy, and swarth countenance, a melancolique eye," black nipples, and watery bluish milk. Boys always stirred on the right side of the belly, girls on the left. And "the Male child lyeth high above the Navell by reason of his heate, and the Female at the bottome of the belly, because of her coldnes and weight." Naturally, any sane parent should want a boy, "for the Female, through the cold and moistness of their Sex, cannot be endowed with so profound a judgment. We find indeed," observed Nicholas Culpepper, "that they talk with appearance of knowledge in slight and easie matters, but seldom reach any further than to a slight superficial smattering in any deep Science."[16]

Perhaps Lucy Hutchinson's English mother could be excused

---

15. Alan Macfarlane, *The Family Life of Ralph Josselin* (Cambridge, 1970), pp. 200–01; Jacques Guillemeau, *Child-Birth; or, The Happy Deliverie of Women* (London, 1612), chap. 2.

16. Guillemeau, *Child-Birth*, chap. 2; Nicholas Culpepper, *A Directory for Midwives* (London, 1651), pp. 129–30; John Pechey, *The Compleat Midwife's Practice Enlarged* (London, 1698), p. 275. For the scholastic physiology of women, see William Costello, *The Scholastic Curriculum at Early Seventeenth-Century Cambridge* (Cambridge, Mass., 1958), pp. 97–98.

for being "very desirous of a daughter" after having "had 3
sons," even in the heyday of the scholastic view of women. But
many years after the scholastic basis for female inferiority had
been demolished, many men were still under the sway of its
original conclusion. Aaron Burr, the second president of
Princeton, is a good example. According to his wife, he was
perfectly capable of great affection toward his firstborn daughter, Sally, when she was a toddler. "You my dear," she wrote a
friend, "cant immagine how much pleased of late Mr Burr is
with his little Daughter. He begins to think she is good to kiss,
& thinks he sees a great many beauties in her, that he used to
be perfectly blind to. He complains she is another temptation
to him, to spend two much time with her—he does love to
play with her dearly." But three years later, when they were
"about sending her to School" to confront the serious things
of life for the first time, Mr. Burr expected her to prove a
"Numbhead." He may have been simply a good judge of character, but her mother, the daughter of Jonathan Edwards and
no mean intellect herself, thought "her about Middling on all
accounts," perhaps because they now had a "little dirty Noisy
Boy very different from Sally almost in every thing," who
would one day surpass their highest expectations as vice-
president of the United States.[17]

The second kind of advice for pregnant women concerned
the regulation of sexual relations. Unlike some peasant societies,
seventeenth century England seems to have had no taboo on
intercourse during pregnancy except for medical reasons. In
a popular manual on *Child-Birth,* Jacques Guillemeau recommended that "in the first foure moneths she must . . . aban-

17. Lucy Hutchinson, *Memoirs of the Life of Colonel Hutchinson,* ed.
Julius Hutchinson (London, 1810), 1 : 24; Journal of Esther Burr, p. 53
and 2 September 1757. Esther's husband was not the only male suprema-
cist in the vicinity. On 12 April 1757 she had a heated exchange over
women's intellectual capabilities with a Mr. Ewing, who was, after an
hour, talked "quite silent" by Mrs. Burr. "One of the last things that he
said," as he blushingly departed, "was that he never in all his life knew
or heard of a Woman that had a little more lerning then but it made
her proud to such a degree that she was disgusfull to all her acquaintance."

don Venus for feare of shaking the child, and bringing down her courses, which must also be observed in the sixth and eight[h] moneth, but in the seventh and ninth she may boldly use it, especially toward the end of the ninth moneth, which some are of opinion will help and hasten the delivery." [18]

There were other prohibitions for English women. "Disordinate appetite" for "Coles, Chalke, Ashes, Waxe, Salt-fish raw, [and] Vinegar," riding in coaches and wagons, and the frightening effects of "Thunder, Artillery, and great Bells" (which were thought to mark the child *in utero*) were frowned upon. But among their gentle clientele there was one practice that even the unanimous legions of the medical profession could not exorcise, and that was tight lacing to attain a fashionable figure. In 1612 Guillemeau was adamant that women "must leave off their Busks as soone as they perceive themselves with child, not lacing themselves too straight, or crushing themselves together, for feare lest the child be mishapen and crooked, or have his naturall growth [impeded]." At the end of the century doctors were still butting their heads against the inexorable power of fashion, but with obviously little success. It was not until the late eighteenth century that Dr. Hugh Smith could talk in the past tense of a time when "no one denies that [women's] shapes were greatly injured by the stiffness of their stays, and by being laced so exceedingly close," causing frequent miscarriages and fainting in public places.[19]

Conversely, New England women do not seem to have been afflicted by this particular custom until late in the eighteenth century. Puritan standards of modesty in dress simply forbade such excesses as silken accessories and unnatural shapeliness. In 1603 the wife of the pastor of the separatist English church

18. Guillemeau, *Child-Birth,* p. 23, whose advice was followed by Pechey, *Compleat Midwife's Practice Enlarged,* p. 65, one of the "most vendible books in England" (William London, *A Catalogue of the Most Vendible Books in England* [London, 1658]).

19. Guillemeau, *Child-Birth,* pp. 20–26; Pechey, *Compleat Midwife's Practice Enlarged,* p. 68; *Educational Writings of John Locke,* pp. 123–24; Hugh Smith, *Letters to Married Women on Nursing and the Management of Children* (Dublin, 1777), p. 55.

in Amsterdam was reproved and admonished for her apparel
by his brother, who cited as one of her extravagances "Whale-
bones in the bodies of peticotes Contrary to the former rules
[of modesty], as also against nature, being as the Phisitians
affirme hinderers of conceiving or procreating children." Until
a few fashion-conscious ladies from the growing affluence of
New England's capital cities began to ape prevailing European
styles in the latter half of the eighteenth century, the women
of New England enjoyed uncorsetted comfort and health.[20]

Another form of advice, usually designed by ministers to
"Prepare a Pious Woman for Her Lying in," gives us our
first clue to some of the attitudes women must have held
toward pregnancy and childbearing. Labor pains, Cotton
Mather told his female readers, are woman's curse for Eve's
transgression and should "very properly lead you to bewail
your Share in the *Sin of your first Parents;* and to bewail with
Bitter Tears, that *Corrupt Nature,* which by a Derivation from
your *Next Parents* you brought into the World with you.
Think, *Lord, I was conceived in Sin; I was born a Leper; And
my poor Child will be so too!*" With their souls in such eternal
peril, women obviously needed more spiritual preparation
than "if they only get Linnen and other necessaryes for the
child, a nurse, a midwife, entertainment for the women that
are called to the Labour, a warm convenient chamber etc."
Much more should they turn to prayer and confession, seeking
their own rebirth in Christ, for "all these [domestic prepara-

20. George Johnson, *A discourse of some troubles and excommunica-
tions in the banished English Church at Amsterdam* (Amsterdam, 1603),
p. 135. My impression of New England's long devotion to unconfining
apparel for women is derived from formal contemporary portraits (where
one would expect women who cared to appear at their shapeliest), news-
paper advertisements for imported items of fashion (which generally
do not appear in provincial papers until the 1760's, except in Boston,
where the transition was made somewhat earlier), and Alice M. Earle's
discussion of children's dress (which was usually cut from adult patterns)
in *Child Life in Colonial Days* (New York, 1899), chap. 2. By 1829 an
American physician was obliged to add a long letter to a reprint of
Hugh Smith's *Letters to Married Women* warning American women away
from the then "universal" habit of wearing constricting "Corsets" and
"stays."

tions] may prove miserable comforters; they may perchance need no other linnen shortly but *a Winding Sheet,* and have no other chamber but a *grave,* no neighbours but *worms.*" To the extent that a mother shared these beliefs with the orthodox ministry, she must have looked on the birth of her child with mixed emotions.[21]

Colonial women have left little direct evidence of their feelings about childbearing, but two casual remarks by Esther Burr to her close friend Sarah Prince reveal something of one New English woman's attitude. In July 1755, after paying a visit to a new mother and child, she wrote, "Mrs Sergeant is very hearty, well & in good Spirits, not so vapory as she used to be—This having Children does good some times." Having visited many mothers in her husband's congregation who had lost children at birth or been seriously ill themselves, she obviously found the isolated example of the medicinal value of childbearing worthy of comment. And on the arrival of her own second child, she commented, "When I had but one Child my hands were tied, but now I am tied hand & foot (how I shall get along when I have got ½ dzn. or 10 Children I cant devise)." Like the great majority of New English mothers, Esther Burr, intelligent, respected, and well-to-do, saw for herself only a future of hobbling prolificity.[22]

Nor within the normal course of events would she be wrong. Without effective methods of contraception—*coitus interruptus* was regarded as a sin—colonial women could not hope to confine their childbearing to the first few years of marriage. Although they tended to marry somewhat later than their modern counterparts, they could usually anticipate twenty years of uninterrupted though declining productivity before menopause. With two years between each child, Esther Burr could have had her ten children.[23]

21. Cotton Mather, *Elizabeth in Her Holy Retirement* (Boston, 1710); John Oliver, *A Present for Teeming American Women* (Boston, 1694); *Diary of Cotton Mather* (New York, n.d.), 2 : 618.

22. Journal of Esther Burr, pp. 108, 132.

23. For the sin of Onan, which seems to have enjoyed some currency in seventeenth century England, see Culpepper, *Directory for Midwives,*

When the New English mother finally felt the first pangs of
labor, her husband went for help, much as Ebenezer Parkman
did on the day after Christmas 1738. "A little after 4 in the
morning my Wife called Me up by her extreme pain prevailing
upon her and changing into signs of Travail. I rode over to
Deacon Forbush's and brought her [Mrs. Forbush] over as our
midwife. Sister Hicks, old Mrs. Knowlton, Mrs. Whipple, Mrs.
Hephzibath Maynard, Mrs. Byles and Mrs. Rogers were call'd
and brought and stay'd all Day and Night." Unfortunately it
was a false alarm, so the following morning "the Women
Scattered away to their several Homes except Mrs. Forbush
who did not leave us." But the next morning—again at 4:00
A.M.—"Mrs. Forbush call'd me up with great earnestness to
gather some women together. It was very Cold, and I ran on
foot to sister Hicks and to old Mrs. Knowlton—sent to Mrs.
Maynard and rode to Mrs. Byles, all which came together by
Daybreak. We were in the Article of Distress," he admitted,
presumably employing the editorial "we" to cover his own
paternal discomposure, but "about Seven o'Clock my Fourth
Daughter was born." [24]

p. 84, and E. A. Wrigley, "Family Limitation in Pre-Industrial England,"
Economic History Review 19 (1966), 82–109. Menstruation, and therefore
fertility, normally began at 14 years among the English in the seventeenth
century, and menopause between 40 and 50 (Culpepper, *Directory for Midwives*, p. 86; *A Rational Account of the Natural Weaknesses of Women*
[London, 1716], p. 1; John Graunt, *Natural and Political Observations
made upon the Bills of Mortality* [London, 1662], ed. Walter Willcox
[Baltimore, 1939], p. 58; Macfarlane, *Family Life of Ralph Josselin*, p. 99,
n. 2). The average age of first marriage in seventeenth century England
was between 26 and 28 for men and 22 and 24 for women. In New
England the averages seem to have dropped slightly to about 24 to 26
for men and 21 to 23 for women (Laslett, *World We Have Lost*, p. 83;
Philip Greven, Jr., *Four Generations: Population, Land, and Family in
Colonial Andover, Massachusetts* [Ithaca, 1970], pp. 33–36; John Demos,
A Little Commonwealth: Family Life in Plymouth Colony [New York,
1970], p. 193; *Economic History Review* 19 (August 1966) : 330). On birth
intervals, see Greven, *Four Generations*, pp. 30, 112, 210; Demos, *Little
Commonwealth*, pp. 68–69; Macfarlane, *Family Life of Ralph Josselin*,
pp. 82, 199–204; *NEHGR* 14 (1860) : 222; Graunt, *Natural and Political
Observations*, p. 68; Alex McNeil, "Sudbury, Massachusetts, 1639–1739,"
(Seminar paper, Yale University, 1968).
24. Diary of Ebenezer Parkman, *PAAS*, n.s. 71 (1961): 447–48. The
gathering of the village women was a symbolic as well as functional part

Besides a houseful of neighborhood women, the new mother often had her own mother, who would stay for as long as a month or two. Mrs. Parkman's mother came for at least a month to help with the birth of her first grandchild. And shortly after Esther Burr had arrived for a long visit at her parents' home in Stockbridge, her mother left for Northampton because "my sister Dwight is near her time. So I never said one Word against it, altho' I am come 150 Miles to see my friends & am apt to think I shall not come again in many years if ever." Although her mother was gone "about a Month," she knew from personal experience how important it was to a delivering woman to have her mother present. Only seven months before, upon the birth of her second child, "it seemd very gloomy when I found I was actually in Labour to think that I was as it were destitute of Earthly friends—No Mother-No Husband & none of my petecular friends that belong to this Town, they happening to be out of Town." As a custodian of the lore of childrearing, a mother provided an important link in a long generational chain.[25]

The other party present at most births was the midwife, usually a respectable woman with more experience than medical knowledge. In Tudor and Stuart England, midwives were examined and licensed by the Church, partly because they were allowed to baptize infants "in the time of necessity." But in New England regulation was impossible without a hierarchical church or professionalized medicine, and perhaps unnecessary, given the low estate of midwifery in England. Despite a large number of manuals addressed to them by competent physicians, English midwives did not inspire confidence, often

---

of the childbearing ritual. When Samuel Sewall's wife was delivered of a daughter on 12 August 1690, she "had not Women nor other preparations as usually, being wholly surpris'd, my wife expecting to have gone a Moneth longer." On some occasions, perhaps only in substantial homes, they were all dined, as at Sewall's, "with rost Beef and minc'd Pyes, good Cheese and Tarts," or with special "groaning cakes" and "groaning beer" (Arnold van Gennep, *The Rites of Passage* [Chicago, 1960], chap. 5; Macfarlane, *Family Life of Ralph Josselin*, pp. 85–86; *Colls. MHS*, 5th ser., vol. 5 [1878], pp. 328, 394; Earle, *Child Life in Colonial Days*, pp. 17–18).

25. Macfarlane, *Family Life of Ralph Josselin*, p. 116; *PAAS*, n.s. 71 (1961) : 119; Journal of Esther Burr, pp. 102–03, 154–55.

because they were illiterate to begin with. Percival Willughby said that he wrote his "Observations in Midwifery" (1670) in English because "few of our midwives bee learned in severall languages. For I have been with some, that could not read; with severall, that could not write; with many, that understood very little of practice." [26]

The consequences of such ignorance could be felt with chilling directness in the weekly bills of mortality, even by contemporaries inured to the ubiquity of death. In 1547 Dr. Andrew Boorde complained that half of the miscarriages and stillbirths in England could be prevented if the midwives were only better educated in such matters as uterine prolapse. A century and a half later the situation had not improved, and may even have declined, in the congested heart of London. In 1687 the expert and articulate midwife Elizabeth Cellier petitioned the crown for the founding of a royal hospital, to be maintained by a corporation of one thousand skilled, dues-paying midwives. Her reasons were compelling, although her venture was unsuccessful.

> Within the space of twenty years last past, above six-thousand women have died in childbed, more than thirteen-thousand children have been abortive and about five-thousand *chrysome* infants [those in their first month of life] have been buried within the weekly bills of mortality; above two-thirds of which, amounting to sixteen thousand souls, have in all probability perished, for want of due skill and care, in those who practice the art of midwifery.

26. Thomas Forbes, *The Midwife and the Witch* (New Haven, 1966), chap. 10, p. 140. As many a father must have known, a midwife was not absolutely necessary. Seventeenth century women frequently delivered themselves. See Macfarlane, *Family Life of Ralph Josselin,* p. 85, and the Roxbury baptism records for 5 May 1644: "Peniel Brown . . . [his father] living at a farme nearer to us then to Boston, his wife was delivered of this child by Gods mercy without the help of any other woman. God himself helping his pore servants in a straight," and 15 September 1650: "Joseph Weld, son of John Weld. There was no help present when the mother was delivered of this child" (*Report of the [Boston] Record Commissioners,* 2d ed. [Boston, 1884], 6 : 115, 119).

It was small wonder that, as one midwife lamented to her daughter-successor in 1698, "Now adays, Women use [midwives] as meer Hirelings." [27]

If the quality of New English midwifery was higher, no contemporary bothered to leave his testimony to it. On the contrary, the church records and diaries of their ministers continued to echo the same disheartening notes throughout the colonial period. In 1642, for instance, John Eliot of Roxbury recorded that "2 infants dyed in the birth," the loss of whom "was conceived to be through the unskilfullnesse of the midwife." And nearly a century later, in the enlightened provincial town of Westborough, only a short day's ride from Boston, "Mr. Samuel Fry juniors Infant Child [was] bury'd which bled to Death at the Navel." [28]

When all the attending women were present, or more precisely and in the contemporary idiom, when Nature decreed that her time had come, the mother was "brought abed" of her child. Actually a bed was not the only place of delivery, though it may have been the most popular. "All women," wrote an experienced physician, "are not delivered after one fashion: for some are delivered in their bed; others sitting in a chaire, some standing being supported and held up by the standers by; or else leaning upon the side of a bed, table or chair; others kneeling being held up by the armes." Samuel Sewall's wife used another means, which he discovered when he "Went home with the Midwife about 2 o'clock" one morning, "carrying her Stool, whose parts were included in a Bagg." [29]

27. Forbes, *Midwife and Witch*, p. 140; *The Harleian Miscellany*, ed. William Oldys (London, 1744–46), 4 : 142–46; Pechey, *Compleat Midwife's Practice Enlarged*, pp. 345–51.

28. [*Boston*] *Record Commissioners*, 6 : 170; *PAAS*, 5 February 1739, n.s. 72 (1962) : 36. See *Winthrop's Journal*, 1, 45, for the courage of New England's first midwife: "A woman in our ship fell in travail, and we sent and had a midwife out of the *Jewel*," undoubtedly in a very precarious gam-chair which was slid on a cable suspended between the masts of the two ships.

29. Guillemeau, *Child-Birth*, p. 88; *Colls. MHS*, 2 April 1677, 5th ser., vol. 5 (1878), p. 40. See Forbes, *Midwife and Witch*, pp. 114, 144, and title page for contemporary views of "borning stools" in use.

Perhaps most young New English mothers had a relatively "quick & good time" of delivery because they were physically fit from hard work and adequate diet. Older women, of course, worn out by successive pregnancies, and lazy society women who "seldom use their bodies to any exercise, unless it be playing with their Dogs," must often have been "in great Extremity" though seldom in mortal danger. On the whole New English women appear to have weathered the childbearing years in remarkable health, even to the extent of living longer on the average than their husbands.[30]

What a difficult delivery might have contributed was physical justification for the long periods of lying-in after the birth, which are inexplicable on any other grounds save custom. Women like Mary Parkman who were bearing their last children in their late forties may have truly needed a substantial period of rest when they fainted "in going from the bed to the Table" a week after delivery and could only "take a step or Two with Help" at the end of a month. Yet the physicians of the time talked of a universal "Month" of recovery, and many women were bedridden and house-bound even longer. It is doubtful that a healthy, twenty-four-year-old mother like Esther Burr, who had had "a fine time" in delivering only her second child, required anything like the seven weeks she took to work up the strength to write a letter. Indeed, she may have entertained similar doubts herself during the third week, when she "had the Canker very bad" from an excess of bed-sitting.[31]

30. Journal of Esther Burr, pp. 102–03; Culpepper, *Directory for Midwives*, p. 157; *PAAS*, n.s. 71 (1961): 119; Greven, *Four Generations*, pp. 27–28, 109–10, 195–96. John Demos estimates that in Plymouth Colony "a bit less than 20 per cent of the deaths among adult women were owing to causes connected with childbirth. Or, to put it another way, something like one birth in thirty resulted in the death of the mother" (*Little Commonwealth*, p. 66). John Graunt was hardnosed about his definition of mother mortality when he analyzed the London bills of mortality in 1662. He concluded that "not one woman of an hundred (I might say of two hundred) dies in her Labour; for as much as there be other Causes for a woman's dying within the Moneth, then the hardness of her Labour" (*Natural and Political Observations*, pp. 42–43).

31. *PAAS*, n.s. 72 (1962): 32, 36; Guillemeau, *Child-Birth*, p. 189; Culpepper, *Directory for Midwives*, bk. 8; Journal of Esther Burr, pp. 102–03.

The other inhabitants of New England suffered their women no such luxury. "I have often knowne," wrote Roger Williams, "in one Quarter of an houre an [Indian] Woman merry in the House, and delivered and merry againe: and within two dayes abroad, and after four or five dayes at worke." Ezra Stiles, an assiduous collector of information about his country and its various peoples, was "often told that a pregnant Squaw will turn aside & deliver herself, & take up the Infant & wash it in a Brook, & walk off. They do not lye by the Month; but make little more about Pregnancy & lying in than the Cows." In fact they may even have turned the sexual tables. The French chirurgeon, Jacques Guillemeau, had learned from "they that write the History of *America*" that, as soon as Indian women "be delivered, (they are so kind to their husbands, which tooke the paines to beget the child) that they presently rise up and lay their husbands in their roome; who are used and attended, like women in childbed. And in this manner they be visited of all their friends, and kinsfolk, who bring them gifts and presents." [32]

English women could have learned much from their native neighbors about the recuperative value of early exercise and moderate bed rest after delivery, and indeed several did. Mrs. Adams of Wells, Maine, "had Lain in about Eight Days" when she was captured by a war party and ordered to march. "She could not stir. By the help of a Stick she got half a step forward. She look'd up to God. On the sudden a new strength entred into her. She travelled that very Day Twenty Miles a Foot: She was up to the Neck in Water six times that very Day in passing of Rivers. At night she fell over head and ears, into

---

In 1628 William Leigh, the rector of Groton, Sussex, informed his patron John Winthrop that, eleven days after giving birth, "my wife is not soe soare weakned of this child as she was on the last (blessed be god) but as yet she is not able to feele her leggs to stepp from her couch to her bedd but with help of others" (*Winthrop Papers*, 1 : 395).

32. *The Complete Writings of Roger Williams* (New York, 1963), 1 : 170–71; *Extracts from the Itineraries . . . of Ezra Stiles*, ed. F. B. Dexter (New Haven, 1916), pp. 145–46; Guillemeau, *Child-Birth*, pp. 90–91. See Stiles' list of "Indian Usages Extensive:" "Easy Parturition—a day or two by—more usually travel same day" (*Itineraries*, p. 411).

a Slough in a Swamp, and was hardly got out alive. She got not the least Cough nor Cold by all this." Another hapless pioneer, Hannah Dustin, of remote Haverill, "having lain in bed about a week, attended by her nurse, Mary Neff," was forced to rise "in her weakness" to watch her newborn child dashed to death against a tree and then to march about 150 miles. She survived her interrupted "month" well enough to wreak revenge on ten of her twelve captors with their own tomahawks one night as they lay sleeping and to become thereby a New England legend.[33]

Perhaps the prostrating effort of giving birth to New English babes was worth the price. Literature promoting emigration to America boasted that "the Christian Children born here are generally well-favoured and Beautiful to behold." Gabriel Thomas, for one, "never knew any come into the World with the least blemish on any part of its Body, being in the general, observ'd to be better Natur'd, Milder, and more tender Hearted than those born in England." In New England, promised Francis Higginson of Salem, children would be healthier than they were at home, for "a suf of *New-Englands* Aire is better then a whole draft of old *Englands* Ale. I have one of my Children that was formerly most lamentably handled with sore breaking out of both his hands and feet of the King's Evill, but since he came hither he is verie well over hee was, and there is hope of perfect recoverie shortly, even by the verie wholesomness of the Aire, altering, digesting and drying up the cold and crude humors of the Body." For medical cures, God's land was apparently better than the King's hand.[34]

33. *A Memorial of the Present Deplorable State of New-England* (Boston, 1707), p. 33; Cotton Mather, *Magnalia Christi Americana* (London, 1702), bk. 7, pp. 90–91; *Colls. MHS*, 5th ser., vol. 5 (1878), pp. 452–53.

34. Gabriel Thomas, *An Historical and Geographical Account of the Province and Country of Pensilvania* (London, 1698), pp. 42–43 (Thomas was speaking of Pennsylvania, but his reference extends to all New World children); Francis Higginson, *New-Englands Plantation*, [1630] (Salem, 1908), sig. CIV. New England's pure air must have been something of a family preoccupation with the Higginsons, for at the age of seventy nine Francis's son John told *his* son, an English merchant, that

Although their claims for New World beauty had scant basis in biology, the colonial promoters may have hit upon a demographic truth regarding health. New Englishmen in the seventeenth and early eighteenth centuries appear to have survived childhood in larger numbers and lived longer than their Old World contemporaries. In London, for example, one-third of all recorded deaths before 1660 were of children under six years of age, and after 1730 fully one-half were under five. In the third quarter of the eighteenth century, about two of every three children born in Dublin did not live to see their fifth birthday, while in Ipswich, Massachusetts, on the other hand, only one in six, and in Hingham, one in three, was so unfortunate. Even in the seventeenth century, when the primitive conditions of frontier existence might be expected to have increased mortality, Plymouth Colony children had three chances in four of reaching the age of twenty-one, and those of Andover even more; between 83 and ninety per cent of those born before 1700 survived their nineteenth year. In general, the chances of raising most of one's children to adulthood were far greater in colonial New England than in most of England and Europe.[35]

Those children who did die were usually the victims of man's three universal scourges: war, pestilence, and carelessness. The

he did not know how long he would live, but boasted that "many have lived to above eighty in this pure and healthful aire" (*Colls. MHS*, 1697, 3d ser., vol. 7 [1838], p. 200). For just how many, see James Cassedy, *Demography in Early America* (Cambridge, Mass., 1969), p. 270, and Greven, *Four Generations*, p. 192.

35. To judge from Andover's experience and the increased mortality due to epidemical disease throughout New England, it is likely that New England's unique healthiness diminished in the mid eighteenth century (Graunt, *Natural and Political Observations*, p. 28); Ivy Pinchbeck and Margaret Hewitt, *Children in English Society* (London, 1969), 1 : 300; Smith, *Letters to Married Women*, preface; Cassedy, *Demography in Early America*, pp. 252, 270; Demos, *Little Commonwealth*, p. 66; Greven, *Four Generations*, pp. 25, 191–92; E. A. Wrigley, "Mortality in Pre-Industrial England," *Daedalus*, Spring 1968, 546–80. Boston and some of the seaport towns, of course, had mortality rates that were higher but were still less than those of comparable European cities (John Blake, *Public Health in the Town of Boston, 1630–1822* [Cambridge, Mass., 1959], pp. 247–49).

exposure of most New England towns to the ravages of hostile Indians made life hazardous for all settlers, but especially for very young children and infants. For if they were captured, unlike their parents and older brothers and sisters who would be adopted, sold to the French, or held for ransom in Canada, their chances of surviving the long treks northward and the unpredictable behavior of their captors were very small. Cotton Mather wrote that

> when the children of the English captives cried at any time, so that they were not presently quieted, the manner of the Indians was to dash out their brains against a tree. And very often, when the Indians were on or near the water, they took the small children and held them under water till they had near drowned them, and then gave them unto their distressed mothers to quiet'em. And the Indians in their frolics would whip and beat the small children, until they set them into grievous outcries, and then throw them to their amazed mothers for them to quiet them again as well as they could.

Hannah Bradley of Haverhill knew the heartache not once but twice of watching her children's skulls crushed by Indian "Head-breakers." After her second capture, when she was "within Six Weeks of her Time," she was forced to snowshoe for three weeks to their winter headquarters before delivering her own child, "having the help of only one Woman, who got a little Hemlock to lay about her, and with a few sticks made shift to blow up a little Fire." When they finally moved to a camp for spring planting in late May, "she was put unto a hard Task, so that the Child extreamly Suffered. The Salvages would sometimes also please themselves, with casting *hot Embers* into the Mouth of the Child, which would render the Mouth so sore, that it could not Suck for a long while together. So that it Starv'd and Dy'd." [36]

A large and popular literature of captivity narratives sup-

36. Mather, *Magnalia*, bk. 7, p. 71; *A Memorial of the Present Deplorable State of New-England*, pp. 33–36.

plied the imagination and supplemented the personal experience of generations of New English mothers. Esther Burr, born and raised in the exposed frontier town of Stockbridge, spoke for their apprehension when she wrote a friend in the security of provincial Boston: "You cant conceive my dear friend what a tender Mother under goes for her children at such a day as this, to think of bring[ing] up Children to be *dashed against the Stones by our barbarous enemies*—or which is worse, to be inslaved by them, & obliged to turn Papist—it seems to me some times if I had no Child nor was likely to have any that I should not be much distressed, but I must leve the subject tis two dreadful to think off. . . . *Wo* to them that are *with Child,* & to them that give Suck in these days!" [37]

By far the greatest killer of New English children was disease. Virulent waves of dysentery ("bloody flux"), smallpox, diphtheria ("throat distemper"), whooping cough, and scarlet fever periodically ravaged the homes of rich and poor alike in a way that even hostile Indians could not match. Especially fatal was the "throat distemper" epidemic of 1735–40, when, in a population of approximately 200,000, over 5,000 people, about 80 percent of whom were children under ten years, died. Death was often so sudden that "children while sitting up at play would fall and expire with their playthings in their hands." In Kingston, New Hampshire, where the epidemic began, more than a third of all children died, a pattern that recurred in numerous towns with tragic regularity. The most characteristic feature of this epidemic was the occurrence of multiple deaths in families. At least six families lost eight children at a single stroke, as did the family of John and March Wilson of Andover. Within one week, in November 1738, their three sons and five daughters, aged two to seventeen years, were carried off by the disease. Fortunately, the continuity and cohesion of all families was not so broken. At least John Preston had something to build on when the epi-

---

37. *Journal of Esther Burr*, pp. 133, 185. On the captivity narrative as a literary genre, see Roy Harvey Pearce, "The Significance of the Captivity Narrative," *American Literature* 19 (1947): 1–20.

demic left Danvers in 1751. "My son Joshua was born [on 22 March]," he recorded in his diary, "and he died May 11th with the throat distemper. My other children very bad with the same distemper, but they recovered." [38]

If "the Loss of so many Children" by horrible disease was comprehensible to the New English only as "a Frown of Providence upon the Land in general, as well as a sore Affliction to the Parents in particular" for their worldliness, still less bearable were the deaths of their children by accident or carelessness. Hardly a year passed without a report of a child fatally burned from playing with candles or gunpowder or from falling into an open fire. More were drowned by falling off wharves or into open wells or by swimming in treacherous streams. Still more were seriously, if not fatally, scalded from falling into, or spilling, large caldrons of boiling milk or water. Because they involved some spark of human will, even these deaths, in their own way, could be explained by divine providence. But few parents must have been capable of wringing sense from the loss of "a new borne infant . . . [who] dyed by falling out of [the] lap of a girle that had it & slep[t], so leting it fall." Perhaps only the consuming guilt of a Cotton Mather could have given meaning to such senseless catastrophies.

38. Ernest Caulfield, "A History of the Terrible Epidemic, Vulgarly Called the Throat Distemper, as It Occurred in his Majesty's New England Colonies between 1735 and 1740," *Yale Journal of Biology and Medicine* 11 (1938–39): 219–72, 277–335; Ernest Caulfield, "Some Common Diseases of Colonial Children," *PCSM* 35 (1951): 4–65; *EIHC* 11 (1871): 260. The effects of nonfatal disease and illness on family relationships are revealed by Esther Burr. After a recent illness her daughter was "very cross. I am afraid this illness will cost [her] a whiping Spel." Two weeks later she had a relapse which brought her near death. But "she has been extreamly tendsome, would go to no Stranger, so Sukey [a young girl servant] & I have been obliged to watch every Night ever since her sickness that I am almost got to be as bad as the Child." After a slight improvement the young girl, aged eleven months, was "extreamly cross, crying all day *Mam-Mam* if I hant her in my Arms, that she is more troublesom than when she was sicker altho' tis not so distressing" (Journal of Esther Burr, pp. 86, 94–95, 163).

This morning, in my study, praying for each of my Children by Name (as I use to do) I left the Name of my *Mehetabel* unmentioned. I wondred at this Omission, in myself and blam'd and chid myself, that I should bee so sottish, as having but *three* children to forgett *one* of them. Now, I had no sooner done my prayers, but the messenger gave mee to understand that the Child had been for above an Hour before, by its Death, gone beyond the reach or use, of our *Prayers*. (Alas, the Child was overlaid by the Nurse!) [39]

When a New English child was born, its parents began the conscious process of rearing it according to one of a choice of methods culturally acceptable to their particular society. The first concern of most mothers was feeding, which was done primarily in one of two ways: at the breast of the mother, or of a hired substitute. The ideal Puritan family being as insular as it was, Puritan ministers could be expected to favor the first alternative, but they were ably seconded by a host of physicians and even an occasional member of the English nobility, who as a rule relied upon wet-nursing.

Besides the ever-present arguments from Scripture and Design, there were several reasons—two positive and many negative—advanced in favor of maternal nursing which offer some insight into English society of the time. The positive reasons were that it was better for the mother. "Commonly," argued William Gouge, "such children as are nursed by their mothers, prosper best. Mothers are most tender over them, and cannot

39. John Graunt found in a period of twenty years 529 deaths of children who were "Overlayd or starved at Nurse" in pre-Restoration London (*Natural and Political Observations*, folding chart); Cassedy, *Demography in Early America*, pp. 104–05; [*Boston*] *Record Commissioners*, 11 February 1678, 6 : 182; *Diary of Cotton Mather*, 28 February 1696, 1 : 186. See the *Plymouth Records*, 6 : 45, for the death of a six-month-old child, "being found dead in the morning, in the absence of its parents, lying in bed with Waitstill Elmes and Sarah Hatch, the childs sister." An inquest found that it was either "stiffled by lying on its face or accidentally over layd in the bed."

indure to let them lie crying out, without taking them up and stilling them. . . . [They] are for the most part more cleanly and neatly brought up, freer from diseases; not so many die; I am sure, not so many through negligence cast away." Mothers also "love such children best, as they have given sucke unto," and vice versa, as Lucy Hutchinson well knew. "After my mother had had 3 sons she was very desirous of a daughter, and when the weomen at my birth told her I was one, she receiv'd me with a great deal of joy." But when the nurses thought, "because I had more complexion and favour than is usuall in so young children, that I should not live, my mother became fonder of me and more endeavour'd to nurse me." [40]

Mothers, too, benefitted from nursing, for "such children as have sucked their mothers brests, love their mothers best." Dr. Hugh Smith was certain that "such as the mother is, generally speaking, such will be the first, and most probably the most durable impression received by the child." Consequently, only children "whose minds are early accustomed to agreeable objects, and whose expanding ideas are gratified with pleasing sensations . . . will possess that generous gratitude" required of children. In short, early neglect of the child leads to later neglect of the parents.[41]

The other kind of argument for maternal nursing was negative, based upon the unacceptability of the alternative—hired wet-nurses. Why any gentlewoman would send her newborn child "into the Country, to be rear'd in a leaky House, that lets in Wind and Rain from every Quarter" was beyond the comprehension of the mother-nurse advocates. Such a practice was doubly difficult to fathom for reasons of social class, since

40. Gouge, *Of Domesticall Duties*, pp. 519–20; Hutchinson, *Life of Colonel Hutchinson*, 1 : 24. Jacques Guillemeau's argument from design was that "nature hath bestow'd two Paps upon her, onely for that purpose [i.e. breast-feeding]" (*The Nursing of Children* [London, 1612], sig. Kkr). See also Perkins, *Christian Oeconomie*, p. 93, and John Dod and Robert Cleaver, *A godly forme of housholde governement* (London, 1612), sig. P5v.

41. Gouge, *Of Domesticall Duties*, p. 519; Smith, *Letters to Married Women*, pp. 67, 81, 184; Dod and Cleaver, *A godly forme of housholde governement*, sig. P5v.

most wet-nurses were "poore country women which have much worke to doe, and little helpe" and take "other folkes children" solely to "maintaine their house." "Be not accessory," pleaded the Countess of Lincoln in 1622, "to that disorder of causing a poorer woman to banish her own infant, for the entertaining of a richer woman's child, as it were, bidding her unlove her own to love yours." Maternal nursing would simply "prevent the temptation which poor women are laid under of abandoning their children to suckle those of the rich for the sake of gain: by which means society loses many of its most useful members and mothers become in some sense the murderers of their own offspring." [42]

Unfortunately, the nurse's children were not the only victims of the system. Placed children were switched, infected with the nurse's diseases (and, in the days of humoral physiology, it was believed, her disposition and base temperament as well), or accidentally "devoured, spoiled or disfigured by some wild beast, Wolfe, or Dogge," a danger that was known even in the city. "On Monday last," a London correspondent informed the readers of *The New England Courant*, "a Hog went into Turnmill Street, and very much mangled a Child, and 'tis judg'd would have eaten it, the Nurse being asleep, had not a Neighbour who heard it cry, run in to its Relief." [43]

Another frequent abuse emerges from Dr. William Cadogan's prescription for nurses "to keep the Children awake by Day, as long as they are disposed to be so, and to amuse and keep them in good Humour all they can; not to lull and rock them to sleep, or to continue their Sleep too long; which is only done to save their own Time and Trouble, to the great Detriment of the Childrens Health, Spirits and Understanding." The abuse was a real one, as the Countess of Lincoln found "by grievous experience." In placing her eighteen children she had discovered "such dissembling in nurses, pre-

42. William Cadogan, *An Essay upon Nursing* (London, 1749), p. 9; Gouge, *Of Domesticall Duties*, pp. 520, 523; *The Countesse of Lincoln's Nurserie* (Oxford, 1622), in *The Harleian Miscellany*, 4 : 32.

43. Guillemeau, *Nursing of Children*, sig. Ii2v.; *The New England Courant*, no. 8, 18–25 September 1721.

tending sufficiency of milk, when indeed they had too much scarcity; pretending willingness, towardness, wakefulness, when indeed they have been most wilful, most froward, and most slothful; as I fear the death of one or two of my little babes came by the default of their nurses." As she hinted, nurses would also become pregnant and not tell the mothers who employed them. Sir Hugh Cholmley ascribed his weak and stunted growth as a child to the fact that he had been put out to a nurse who was pregnant, whose milk was consequently poor. His sorry experience did not, however, prevent him from putting his own son to a forty-year-old nurse whose son was two years old.[44]

The final consequence of wet-nursing, however, was regarded as the strongest argument for maternal nursing, and that was the alienation of affection from the natural mother. "Wee may observe, many who have sucked others milke," William Gouge noted, "to love those nurses all the daies of their life." One European physician thought he could "tell that an infant has been sent away from home to nurse by its eyes: for the strong affection for the mother is slowly and gradually extinguished and is centered alone upon her who nurses the child, which has no further inclination or love for the one who gave it birth." According to Jacques Guillemeau, the reason was physiological. "Manners and conditions of the mind, do follow the temperament of the bodie, and the temperament ariseth out of the nourishment: so that commonly, such as the humours are, such prove the manners. Hence must we conclude, that the child that suckes a Nurse, that is vitious, and wicked; sucketh also from her, her faults and vices." By the same token, "when the child comes to understanding, and

44. Cadogan, *Essay upon Nursing*, p. 29; *Countesse of Lincoln's Nurserie*, 4 : 32; Lawrence Stone, *The Crisis of the Aristocracy, 1558–1641* (Oxford, 1965), p. 592; Smith, *Letters to Married Women*, p. 79. John Locke noted another common practice among wet-nurses when he urged parents not to allow their children to drink liquids at every turn, "it being the Lullaby used by Nurses, to still crying Children. I believe Mothers generally find some Difficulty to wean their Children from *Drinking* in the Night, when they first take them home" (*Educational Writings of John Locke*, p. 129).

observes what the Nurse speakes and doth, he retaines that, saies it after her, and imitates her: and that which is imprinted from the infancie, will hardly, or never be rooted out." Such prolonged influence on the child was possible in a day when children were put out to nurse for anywhere from one to three years and only saw their parents at infrequent intervals, if at all. One of the younger sons of Sir Hugh Cholmley was nursed out in 1630 and was not seen by his mother for six months. Robert Boyle, the fourteenth child of the first earl of Corke, was put out to an Irish nurse for nearly three years, at the beginning of which, Aubrey tells us, he was nursed "after the Irish manner, wher they putt the child into a pendulous satchell (instead of a cradle), with a slitt for the child's head to peepe out." Perhaps more usual was the experience of Lucy Winthrop, the Massachusetts governor's sister, who "came home from her Nurce" after almost exactly one year away from her family.[45]

As every parent knows, a one-year-old can be a surprisingly independent creature, a fact many seventeenth century families must have reckoned with achingly and often. One physician, though a fifty-year-old bachelor, knew that farming out impressionable infants to wet-nurses for prolonged periods could breed trouble. In 1693 John Locke told the readers of *Some Thoughts concerning Education* of "a prudent and kind Mother" of his acquaintance who was "forced to whip her little Daughter, at her first coming home from Nurse, eight times successively the same Morning, before she could master her *Stubbornness*, and obtain a compliance in a very easie and indifferent matter." Over such children wet-nurses must have exerted a disconcerting amount of personal influence.[46]

45. Gouge, *Of Domesticall Duties,* p. 519; Sebastian Oestereicher, *De puerorum morbis* (Leyden, 1549), in John Ruhräh, ed., *Pediatrics of the Past* (New York, 1925), p. 137; Guillemeau, *Nursing of Children,* sigs. Ii3v.–Ii4r.; Stone, *Crisis of the Aristocracy,* p. 592; A. B. Grosart, ed., *Lismore Papers,* 1st ser. (Blackburne, 1886), 2 : 207; 3 : 107; John Aubrey, *Brief Lives,* ed. Andrew Clark (Oxford, 1898), 1 : 120; *Winthrop Papers,* 1 : 72, 75.
46. *Educational Writings of John Locke,* p. 178.

But whether the nurse's influence was good or bad, the practice of wet-nursing had an important social consequence: it drove a wedge into the emotional cement of the natural family, something that contemporaries saw clearly. "Those who abandon their infants, who thrust them from themselves and give them to others to bring up, cut and destroy the spiritual bond and the affection by which nature binds parents to their children." At a time when a distinct concept of childhood was emerging in western Europe, and with it the privacy of the natural family, wet-nursing represented a conservative force of considerable strength for the retention of the older view of the child as a social cipher. For despite all the impassioned pleas and logical arguments of the mother-nurse advocates, the practice retained and perhaps increased its ancient popularity among the gentle classes throughout the seventeenth and eighteenth centuries.[47]

The nobility were the greatest offenders against maternal responsibility, and, because of their social position, they were capable of adversely influencing others. "This unthankfulness and unnaturalness," accused the Countess of Lincoln, "is oftener the sin of the higher and richer sort, than of the meaner and poorer; except some nice and proud idle dames, who will imitate their betters, till they make their poor husbands beggars. And this is one hurt which the better rank do by their ill example; egg and embolden the lower ones to follow them to their loss. Were it not better for us greater persons to keep God's ordinance, and to show the meaner their duty in our good example? I am sure we have more helps to perform it, and have fewer probable reasons to alledge against it, than women that live by hard labour, and painful toil." [48]

Yet allege reasons they did, to judge from the persistent rebuttals of the champions of maternal nursing. One objection was that "mothers that are of great wealth and high place, cannot endure the paine of nursing, not take the paines in handling young children as they must be handled," a less gen-

47. Ruhräh, ed., *Pediatrics of the Past*, p. 137; Philippe Ariès, *Centuries of Childhood* (New York, 1962); Stone, *Crisis of the Aristocracy*, p. 593.
48. *The Countesse of Lincoln's Nurserie*, 4 : 30–32.

erous interpretation of which was that they preferred to "more freely ride abroad, and meete their Gossips." Secondly, it was objected that "it is troublesome; that it is noisome to one's clothes; that it makes one look old &c," which to the Countess of Lincoln argued only "unmotherly affection, idleness, desire to have liberty to gad from home, pride, foolish fineness, lust, wantonness, and the like evils." Then there were some women who objected because of "fear, saying they were so weak, and so tender, that they were afraid to venture to give their children suck, lest they endanger their health thereby." To them, William Gouge could only reply that "drying up a womans milke will more breake her, then her childes sucking of it. . . . Barren women and bearing women which put forth their children to sucke, are most subject to sicknesse and weakenesse." And finally, as was to be expected in a patriarchal society, wet-nursing was advocated by some because "husbands are disturbed in the nighttime, and hindered of their sleep by their wives giving sucke to their children." Perhaps it was the Earl of Lincoln to whom his wife pointed when she admitted that she had nursed none of their eighteen children because "I was over-ruled by another's authority." [49]

The practice of giving children over to wet-nurses for their initial care and feeding was probably restricted to the upper ranks of society for simple economic reasons. In Tudor and Stuart England, where farmers and laborers ordinarily earned no more than a shilling a day, few families could afford even the £3 1s. 6d. that Adam Winthrop, a Suffolk gentleman, paid his "Sister Weston" in 1593 for nursing his daughter Jane for forty weeks and five days. Since this amount may represent a discount for relation's sake, perhaps more typical was the expense a century later of "Anthony Fallshort," who, well endowed with estate, had come from old to New England in search of business opportunities, which in the eighteenth

49. Ibid.; Gouge, *Of Domesticall Duties*, pp. 521–25; Dod and Cleaver, *A godly forme of housholde governement*, sig. P5v.; Smith, *Letters to Married Women*, pp. 76, 82–83; Cadogan, *Essay upon Nursing*, p. 24. For a noble male advocate of maternal nursing, see Henry Percy, Ninth Earl of Northumberland, *Advice to his Son*, ed. G. B. Harrison (London, 1930), p. 58.

century often meant suitable marriages to wealthy widows. He met a charming American lady calculated to have £1,000, married her, and then discovered that her "estate" consisted of "rough uncultivated Lands, Rocks, Trees, Bushes and Quag-Mires" worth £350. In ten years of marriage, however, his expenses for Madam Fallshort totalled £1,836 4s. 4d., including £153 0s. 8d. "To the Nursing of 4 Children." [50]

If New England did not know the widespread use of wet-nurses during the first century of settlement—and it seems it did not—the reason may well have been primarily an economic one, reinforced by the Puritan advocacy of the fortified nuclear family. In the late seventeenth century, when both reasons were minimized by growing commercial wealth and the despiritualization of the family, an urban aristocracy may have resorted to wet-nurses on a somewhat larger scale, and perhaps initially on a somewhat different basis. On 2 April 1677, for instance, Samuel Sewall wrote in his diary at the birth of his first child, "The first Woman the Child sucked was Bridget Davenport." Five days later, the attending women "first laboured to cause the child suck his mother, which he scarce did at all," but finally in the afternoon "my Wife set up, and he sucked the right Breast bravely." Eleven years later, on 29 September 1688, he noted that "Lydia Moodey comes hether to dwell, helping my wife to nurse the Child Joseph," who was born six weeks before. In both instances wet-nurses came into the Sewall home to perform their services, which might have obviated any lingering religious objections to the practice.[51]

50. Carl Bridenbaugh, *Vexed and Troubled Englishmen, 1590–1642* (New York, 1968), pp. 79, 148, 211; *Winthrop Papers*, 1 : 42; *The New England Courant*, no. 34, 19–26 March 1722.

51. *Colls. MHS*, 5th ser., vol. 5 (1878), pp. 40, 228. Of the twenty-seven women who placed advertisements for wet-nursing in the *Boston Gazette* between 1743 and 1756, twelve were willing to go into the mother's home, ten wished to have the child in their own homes, two would go either way, and three did not give sufficient information. Whether this pattern was the residue of an earlier in-family preference is impossible to tell. See Ernest Caulfield, "Infant Feeding in Colonial America," *Journal of Pediatrics* 41 (1952), 673–87.

But certainly by the turn of the century the women of Boston had no compunction about resorting to wet-nurses either at home or in the country. In *The New England Courant* for 2 April 1722, Silence Dogood (Benjamin Franklin's distaff half) told her readers that when she arrived fatherless in New England, having been born on shipboard, she "was put to Nurse in a Country Place, at a small Distance" from Boston, this just above an advertisement which read: "Any Person that wants a Wet Nurse into the House, may hear of one by enquiring of the Printer hereof." Boston had clearly come of age socially, following at a respectable distance ancient London, and preceding by her age advantage the newer provincial capitals of New England.[52]

The nursing patterns of English mothers—natural and surrogate—are difficult to discover and probably varied as much as the mothers' health and situation. But there is some indication that a large part of the nursing population fed at the demand of the child, rather than on any predetermined adult schedule. In 1612 Jacques Guillemeau spoke for the majority of physicians in Europe when he said, "it is fit [the baby] should have the teat, as often as he crieth." By the middle of the next century some physicians were trying to move mothers toward a more regular feeding pattern, but they had to contend with tenacious folkways. William Cadogan noted that "it is generally supposed, that whenever a Child cries, it wants Victuals; and it is accordingly fed ten, twelve, or more times in a Day and Night." And when Hugh Smith recommended,

52. *The New England Courant*, no. 35, 26 March–2 April 1722. Advertisements for wet-nurses first appeared in the newspapers of Portsmouth and Providence in 1767, always close upon the heels of the appearance of announcements for imported items of fashion, dancing and finishing schools for girls, and requests for live-in maids. One of the most poignant advertisements was placed by "A young married woman, whose child is dead, and has a fine breast of milk" who "would either go into a family, or take a child in her own house to suckle." This was probably an emotionally effective way a disappointed mother could satisfy some of her more immediate maternal needs (*The New Hampshire Gazette*, no. 571, 11 September 1767; *The Providence Gazette*, no. 182, 27 June 1767; *The Boston Gazette*, no. 23, 8 September 1755).

as Cadogan had done, only four or five feedings a day, he could hear the outcry from the "dear ladies" in his readership: "O barbarous man! Under a pretence of correcting us he intends to starve the little helpless creatures! Was there ever such a cruelty heard of before? Allow a child only a pint of milk a day! Why it would eat two quarts of pap and still cry for more." Since few parents were as free as their children were demanding, most mothers probably nursed on a pattern somewhere between the ideal medical prescription and the reality of their own daily lives.[53]

The other immediate concern of new mothers was the dressing of their infants. In the seventeenth century, a time of widespread rickets, physical dangers about the household, poor heating, and busy parents, most mothers turned fortuitously to swaddling as soon as the child was born, "to give his little body," they thought, "a strait figure." A fifteenth century Italian professor of medicine gave directions that were essentially repeated by generations of English physicians, midwives, and mothers:

> First with its arms raised above, she should wrap its breast and bind its body with a band, by three or four windings. Next the midwife takes another piece of linen or little cloth and draws the hands of the infant straight forward towards the knees and hips, shaping them evenly, so that the infant acquires no humpiness. She then, with the same assisting band, binds and wraps the infant's arms and hands, all of which will be correctly shaped.
>
> Then she should turn the infant over on its breast with its back raised upward and, taking hold of the infant's feet, make its soles touch its buttocks to the end that its knees might be properly set. Thereupon she should straighten the infant's legs and with another band and

53. Guillemeau, *Nursing of Children*, p. 23; Cadogan, *Essay upon Nursing*, p. 16; Smith, *Letters to Married Women*, p. 131. David Hunt indicates that in seventeenth century France the pattern was just the opposite, despite universal medical prescription of demand feeding. (*Parents and Children in History* [New York, 1970], p. 115).

little cloths bind and wrap up the hips. Next take the entire infant and roll it in a woolen cloth or after our manner in a cape lined with sheep skins; and this in winter, but in summer a linen cloth simply.

Thus the child remained until its arms were freed around three weeks; it was finally put into "coats" at about nine months.[54]

Swaddling gradually disappeared in the eighteenth century, when the condemnation of physicians and philosophers brought it into disrepute. But until that time it had the sanction of English culture, old and New. At a time when children were seen as creatures of original sin, education was regarded as the primary means of their salvation; in a society that saw education as a conscious "molding" of the child's original instincts, the physical molding of swaddling was an appropriate initiation of the educational process. It was therefore no coincidence that swaddling passed away just as a new concept of innocent childhood emerged in full force. By 1772 Dr. Hugh Smith could write, "that any children are born with vicious inclinations, I would not willingly believe," without the fear of educated reprisal. By then the voice of John Locke had clearly been heard.[55]

54. François Mauriceau, *The Diseases of Women with Child, and in Child-Bed* (London, 1697), pp. 293–94; Ruhräh, ed., *Pediatrics of the Past*, pp. 34–36; Hunt, *Parents and Children in History*, pp. 126–32. "Coats" were petticoats worn by children below two to three years of age, of the kind William Cadogan recommended as an alternative to the common infant garb of "Flannel, Wrappers, Swathes, Stays, etc.": "A little Flannel Waistcoat without Sleeves, made to fit the Body, and tie loosely behind; to which there should be a Petticoat sew'd, and over this a kind of Gown of the same Material, or any other that is light, thin and flimsy. The Petticoat should not be quite so long as the Child, the Gown a few inches longer." In the seventeenth century, young boys, until the age of four or five, dressed exactly as girls. From "coats" a boy progressed to a robe, skirt, and apron, and then, at five or so, into breeches and a robe which resembled a priest's cassock (Cadogan, *Essay upon Nursing*, p. 11). For the history of children's dress in Europe, see Ariès, *Centuries of Childhood*, pp. 50–62, and in America, Alice M. Earle, *Child Life in Colonial Days*, chap. 2.

55. Smith, *Letters to Married Women*, p. 182. Presumably in New England, where the older view of the Adamic child perdured among the

For about the first year of his life, a New English child had a relatively comfortable and easy existence: warmed by swaddling, "Creadle Ruggs," and hearth fires, rocked to sleep by the easy motion of a cradle, and reassured and nourished by regular access to his mother's breast. And then in his second year his world began to change, partly as a result of his parents' conscious design for his education. The first significant change came when he was forced to substitute the scheduled use of dish and cup for the unlimited access to the breast. This usually occurred between the ninth and the eighteenth month; most physicians thought a year was long enough, "itt being ordained by nature no longer than the child is weak, and cannot digest anything else." The crusty Doctor Culpepper went so far as to pronounce nineteen of every twenty London mothers unfit to nurse their own children because "they give them Suck too long." [56]

The reasons for weaning at any particular time obviously varied from family to family and with each child. Physical and emotional maturity were probably most pertinent, but illness, teething, and pregnancy also counted on occasion. When Ebenezer Parkman's wife, Mary, fell ill during his afternoon service on 10 July 1762, he "concluded it to be issue proceed-

---

orthodox well into the nineteenth century, swaddling also occurred, but it is very difficult to document. In the absence of pediatric manuals written in America, only the listing of "swathing Bands" in an occasional inventory yields any clue. By 1810, when a Jesuit scholar toured the country, "the custom of binding babies [had] altogether been given up in the United States" (Bernard Wishy, *The Child and the Republic* [Philadelphia, 1968], chap. 2; *Essex Co. Court Records*, June 1647, 5 : 329; Oscar Handlin, ed., *This Was America* [New York, 1964], p. 141).

56. *The Diary of the Rev. John Ward*, ed. Charles Severn (London, 1839), p. 254; Cadogan, *Essay upon Nursing*, p. 21; Culpepper, *A Directory for Midwives*, pp. 213–14; Smith, *Letters to Married Women*, p. 113. John Winthrop's sons were weaned at thirteen months, two of Samuel Sewall's at ten and eighteen months, and six of Ralph Josselin's children between twelve and nineteenth months (*Winthrop Papers*, 1 : 391; *Colls. MHS*, 5th ser., vol. 5 [1878], pp. 70, 310; Macfarlane, *Family Life of Ralph Josselin*, p. 202). Sometimes weaning was best delayed. On May Day 1628 Margaret Winthrop wrote her husband in London that "wee are all heare in health, onely little Sam who hath bin very sick. . . . I am glad I did not weane him for he will now take nothinge but the breast" (*Winthrop Papers*, 1 : 391).

ing from the Procidantia Uteri which she had been troubled
with. This accident puts us upon Weaning the Child [Mary,
aged ten months] which this Night began." Similarly, Hannah
Sewall "began to wean little Hull," their ten-month-old son
on 28 April 1685 "to see if that might be a means to free him
of Convulsions; he had one yesterday." Although most children were not weaned until after they possessed a full comple-
ment of teeth, mothers certainly knew, if most physicians did
not, that the appearance of the baby's sharp eyeteeth was often
good cause to bring out the cup. As John Pechey acknowledged, one sign of teething was that "the Nurse perceives the
Infant to gripe her breasts hard." The knowledge of her
pregnancy might also persuade a mother to give up breast-
feeding, for fear that her milk would turn. Although Ralph
Josselin's wife, Jane, did not always stop when she thought herself pregnant, the time of weaning and the date of conception
coincided almost exactly for her first three children. The difficulty in appraising such instances, of course, is in deciding
whether a woman weaned her child because she thought herself pregnant, or became pregnant because she stopped breast-
feeding, which normally provides a certain amount of contraception.[57]

A child could be weaned in several ways. The New England
poet and mother Anne Bradstreet knew that "some children
are hardly weaned; although the teat be rubbed with worm-
wood or mustard, they will either wipe it off, or else suck
down sweet and bitter together." Although he was unusual in
allowing the child to go two years before weaning, Jacques
Guillemeau recommended that, if a gradual withdrawal did
not still the child's cries for the breast, it should be swabbed
with mustard and the nipples with aloes, "and likewise make
him ashamed of it." Whatever method was employed, physicians universally agreed that weaning should proceed "not all
at once, but by insensible Degrees; that they may neither feel,

57. *PAAS*, n.s. 71 (1961) : 147; *Colls. MHS*, 5th ser., vol. 5 (1878), p. 70;
Macfarlane, *Family Life of Ralph Josselin*, pp. 90, 202–03; Pechey, *Compleat Midwife's Practice Enlarged*, p. 252; Demos, *Little Commonwealth*,
p. 133.

nor fret at the want of the Breast." One method, however, seems to have ignored this advice. Children were sometimes given to their grandparents to be weaned by abruptly separating them from their mother's breast. On 2 February 1690, Samuel Sewall noted, "Little Joseph sucks his last as is design'd, his Grandmother taking him into her Chamber in order to wean him." The practice seems to have been an old English one, for two of Ralph Josselin's grandchildren "went homewards well weaned" in the 1670s.[58]

Whatever its emotional effects, weaning was believed—with adult approval—to render the child helpless before parental superiority. One of the best expressions of that belief was John Winthrop's description of his religious conversion, which spoke for a cultural attitude toward children not confined to the Puritan community.

> I was now about 30 yeares of age, and now was the time come that the Lord would reveale Christ unto mee whom I had long desired, but not so earnestly as since I came to see more clearly into the covenant of free grace. First therefore hee laid a sore affliction upon mee wherein hee laid mee lower in myne owne eyes then at any time before, and showed mee the emptines of all my guifts, and parts; left mee neither power nor will, so as *I became as a weaned child . . .* I knew I was worthy of nothing for I knew I could doe nothing for him or for my selfe.

In such a setting, the seemingly innocuous act of weaning assumed considerable educational importance.[59]

58. *The Works of Anne Bradstreet,* ed. Jeannine Hensley (Cambridge, Mass., 1967), p. 279; Guillemeau, *Nursing of Children,* p. 27; Cadogan, *Essay upon Nursing,* p. 21; Smith, *Letters to Married Women,* pp. 113–16; *Colls. MHS,* 5th ser., vol. 5 (1878), p. 310; Macfarlane, *Family Life of Ralph Josselin,* p. 87. To judge by parental comments, weaning was a period of considerable anxiety. Ebenezer Parkman, for example, noted the day after "we began to Wean Sarah" that "the Child weans without Trouble." Esther Burr was not as fortunate: on 18 April 1757 she wrote, "I am weaning Aaron & he makes a great Noise about it" (*PAAS* n.s. 72 [1962] : 199; Journal of Esther Burr).

59. *Winthrop Papers,* 1 : 158–59. See Philip Greven, Jr., ed., *Child-Rearing Concepts, 1628–1861: Historical Sources* (Itaska, Ill., 1973).

The child's second and later years also marked the emergence of increased mobility and self-assertion, which, in the intimate confines of the colonial household, inevitably led it into trouble. "Joseph threw a knob of Brass," his father wrote, "and hit his Sister Betty on the forhead so as to make it bleed and swell; upon which, and for his playing at Prayertime, and eating when Return Thanks, I whip'd him pretty smartly." But Samuel Sewall continued, revealing a characteristic Puritan view of the child, "when I first went in (call'd by his Grandmother) he sought to shadow and hide himself from me behind the head of the Cradle: which gave me the sorrowful remembrance of Adam's carriage." The difficulty, as even a physician writing *A Directory for Midwives* saw, was the child's innate wilfulness, which became particularly visible in the second year. "Adams sin we know was Pride, he would fain have been a little God-almighty, and his Wife a Goddess, and this he left hereditory to all his Posterity, so that the first sin that you can perceive a Child guilty of, is Pride, and this is so bred in the bone, that 'twill never out of the flesh." [60]

Since "there is in all children . . . a stubbornness, and stoutness of mind arising from natural pride," it must in the first place "be broken and beaten down; that so the foundation of their education being laid in humility and tractableness, other virtues may, in their time, be built thereon." "For the beating, and keeping down of this stubbornness," counselled John Robinson, Plymouth's staunch minister, "parents must provide carefully . . . that children's wills and wilfulness be restrained and repressed. . . . Children should not know, if it could be kept from them, that they have a will in their own, but in their parents' keeping: neither should these words be heard from them, save by way of consent, 'I will' or 'I will not'." [61]

60. *Colls. MHS*, 6 November 1692, 5th ser., vol. 5 (1878), p. 369; Culpepper, *Directory for Midwives*, pp. 40–41.
61. *The Works of John Robinson*, ed. Robert Ashton (Boston, 1851), 1 : 246–47. Anne Bradstreet had similar thoughts on early education: "Some children (like sour land) are of so tough and morose a disposition that the plough of correction must make long furrows on their back and

The practical application of this advice can be seen in Esthur Burr's handling of her young daughter Sally. On 28 February 1755 the mother wrote to her close friend Sarah Prince: "I had almost forgot to tell you that I have begun to govourn Sally. She has been whip'd once on *Old Adams* account, & she knows the difference between a Smile & a frown as well as I do; when she has done any thing that she suspects is wrong, will look with concern to see what Mamma says, & if I only knit my brow she will cry till I smile, and altho' she is not quite Ten months old, yet when she knows so much, I think 'tis time she should be taught. But," she added with obvious feeling, "none but a parent can conceive how hard it is to chastise your *own most tender self*. I confess I never had a greater tryal await me—O to be fitted for Gods holy will & pleasure in every thing!" For the daughter of Jonathan Edwards, the final ejaculation was not an idle reflex, nor was it unrelated to the whole evangelical conception of the Christian experience. Just as John Winthrop saw himself in the state of spiritual preparation "as a weaned child," so Esther Burr could chastize herself for an unchristian attitude with words normally reserved for children. "I wish I could be willing to *be* & *do*, & *suffer* just what God pleased without any will of my own, but I am Stubborn, Willful, disobedient—how far these tempers from the Christian temper!" For evangelical Protestants at least, the education of the young child was not unlike the education of the adult Christian.[62]

---

the harrow of discipline go often over them before they be fit soil to sow the seed of morality much less of grace in them. But when by prudent nurture they are brought into a fit capacity, let the seed of good instruction and exhortation be sown in the spring of their youth, and a plentiful crop may be expected in the harvest of their years" (*Works of Anne Bradstreet,* p. 285).

62. Journal of Esther Burr, pp. 72, 117. Sally apparently learned her lessons well, for a year and a half after her brother was born, her mother compared them for Sarah Prince: "Aaron is a little dirty Noisy Boy very different from Sally almost in every thing; he begins to talk a little, is very Sly & Mischevious. He has more Sprightliness then Sally & must say he is handsomer, but not so good Tempered; he is very resolute & requires a good Governor to bring him to terms" (2 September 1757).

Although parental supremacy and the submission of the child was the *ideal* for the embattled Puritan family, whether in the sinful surroundings of old England or the hazardous wilderness of New England, it is more difficult to assess the nature of the *actual* relationships between parents and children as the social context of the family changed over time and space. For something so infinitely variable and complex, it should be no surprise that only tantalizing clues remain.

Before the Civil Wars, English family relationships among the gentle classes were extremely stiff. "In those dayes," testified John Aubrey, "fathers were not acquainted with their children." So when John went home from Oxford to recover from a bout of smallpox, he had the conversation of "none but servants and rustiques and soldiers quartred, to my great griefe." From the time of Erasmus until the Interregnum, "the gentry and citizens . . . were as severe to their children as their schoolmasters; and their schoolmasters as masters of the house of correction. The child perfectly loathed the sight of his parents as the slave his torture." The reason was not hard to find. "Gentlemen of thirty and forty years old were to stand like mutes and fools bare headed before their parents; and the daughters (grown women) were to stand at the cupboard-side during the whole time of their proud Mother's visit, unless (as the fashion was) leave was desired, forsooth, that a cushion should be given them to kneel upon, brought them by the servingman, after they had done sufficient penance in standing." [63]

If there was at one time no love lost in some gentle English families, the wars appear to have brought a change by weakening the religious sanction traditionally given to patriarchal au-

63. Aubrey, *Brief Lives,* ed. Clark, 1 : 38; ibid., ed. Anthony Powell (London, 1949), pp. 9, 11. Sir John Danvers told Aubrey that "when he was a young man the principal reason of sending their sons to travel, was to weane them from their acquaintance and familiarity with the servingmen: for their parents were so austere and grave that the sonnes must not be company for their father; and some company man must have—so, contracted a familiarity with the servingmen who got a hank upon them they could hardly clawe off" (ibid., ed. Powell, p. 9).

thority. In a nostalgic passage the Earl of Clarendon, the great Royalist historian, complained that, during the Interregnum, "all relations were confounded by the several sects in religion, which discountenanced all forms of reverence and respect as relics and marks of superstition. Children asked not blessing of their parents; nor did they concern themselves in the education of their children. . . . The young women conversed without any circumspection or modesty." In sum, "Parents had no manner of authority over their children." Even if we allow for exaggeration, Clarendon may have perceived a subtle change in social mores, but it does not seem to have much outlasted the restoration of king and church in 1660. When, toward the end of the century, John Locke wrote on education for the gentle classes, he gave witness to the persistence of the older ways that Aubrey so disliked. "Methinks," he wrote, "they mightily misplace the Treatment due to their Children, who are indulgent and familiar, when they are little, but severe to them, and keep them at a Distance, when they are grown up." Contrariwise, Locke advised fathers, on the basis of his own childhood experience, to be strict, austere, and thoroughly patriarchal while their children were young, but not forever. "I think it should be relaxed, as fast as their Age, Discretion, and Good-Behaviour could allow it; even to that degree, that a Father will do well, as his Son grows up, and is capable of it, to *talk familiarly* with him; nay, *ask his advice, and Consult* with him, about those things wherein he has any knowledge, or understanding." [64]

Even in the eighteenth century many upperclass parents continued to maintain starchly distanced relationships with their children, supported in part by the rise of Wesleyanism and evangelicalism in general. But increasingly the rising middle classes, possessed of more wealth to build houses for family

64. Edward Hyde, Earl of Clarendon, *The Continuation of the Life* (London, 1759), 2 : 39; Christopher Hill, *Society and Puritanism in Pre-Revolutionary England* (New York, 1964), chap. 13; Keith Thomas, "Women and the Civil War Sects," in Trevor Aston, ed., *Crisis in Europe, 1560–1660* (London, 1965), pp. 317–40; *Educational Writings of John Locke*, pp. 145, 201.

privacy from servants, visitors, and relatives, held more familiar attitudes toward their children. Many went so far as to "cocker" them in a fashion that many writers, as early as the Interregnum, felt compelled to warn against. But in so doing, the respectable classes were only approaching what seems to have been a more prevalent attitude among the "common people," who, it was said, "express more fondness for their children than persons of rank." [65]

The change towards greater familiarity in the family may have come to New England somewhat sooner than to England. If in seventeenth century New England the easy availability of land, more equitable division of estates, shorter terms of apprenticeship, and earlier marriages placed men at an earlier age "very near upon a level" with their parents—and there is evidence that it did—the emotional center of the family may have been strengthened in ways unperceived by contemporaries. For as Tocqueville later observed, with his keen eye for social nuance and European perspective: "perhaps the subdivision of estates that democracy brings about contributes more than anything else to change the relations existing between a father and his children. . . . In proportion as manners and laws become more democratic, the relation of father and son becomes more intimate and more affectionate; rules and authority are less talked of, confidence and tenderness are often increased, and it would seem that the natural bond is drawn closer in proportion as the social bond is loosened." [66]

Certainly the change in New England was not abrupt, especially in the few gentle families of old English stock. At the age of twenty-three, Fitz-John Winthrop wrote to his father, John Jr.: "My dew and strict observiance to such commands

65. Pinchbeck and Hewitt, *Children in English Society*, 1 : 304–07; *The Gentleman's Magazine*, January 1732.

66. Alexis De Tocqueville, *Democracy in America*, ed. Phillips Bradley (New York, 1945), 2 : 194–95; Thomas Hutchinson, *The History of the Colony and Province of Massachusetts-Bay*, ed. Lawrence Mayo (Cambridge, Mass., 1936), 1 : 370; Jackson T. Main, *The Social Structure of Revolutionary America* (Princeton, 1965); Darrett Rutman, "The Mirror of Puritan Authority," in George Billias, ed., *Law and Authority in Colonial America* (Barre, Mass., 1965), pp. 149–67.

and directions as you shall please to order me to observe shall
be punctually obayed. I have soe perfictly learnt the obediance
of a child that I dare not in the least scruple that ready performance of any imposition you shall please to laye upon me."
The Winthrops obviously subscribed to Fuller's description
of "The Good Child": "Having practised them himself, he en-
tails his parents' precepts on his posterity." [67]

Yet change did come, and other men of English experience
worried publicly about the course of the New English family.
Thomas Cobbett, who left England for Lynn, Massachusetts
in 1637, wrote some years later of the unfortunate lack of respect shown many English parents, old and new. "How over
familiar do too many children make themselves with their
parents? as if hail-fellow well met (as they say) and no difference twixt parent and child: too many there are who carry it
proudly, disdainfully and scornfully towards parents." Cobbett
was soon joined by a chorus of clerical jeremiahs who lamented in the darkest tones the dissolution of family order in
the solvent of materialism and irreligion. According to Daniel
Lewes of Pembroke, one of the most common *Sins of Youth*
was disobedience to parents. "Too many there are in the
World now a days who herein follow [Eli's sons'] Example:
They can't bear to be under the Government of their Parents,
nor even to be so much as check'd by them when they have
done amiss; they think it beneath them to stoop to their Authority, obey their Commands, and to pay them that deffer-
ence, respect and honour that a Parent may justly claim from
his Child, and which therefore is his Duty to give unto
him." [68]

It would appear that, in the levelling ambiance of forest and
farm, familiarity between New English parents and children
grew steadily, even to the point of reversing the roles upon oc-

67. *Colls. MHS*, 23 December 1661, 5th ser., vol. 8 (1882), p. 270;
Thomas Fuller, *The Holy State and The Profane State* (London, 1840), p.
12. Fitz-John was born in Ipswich, Massachusetts, in 1638.

68. Thomas Cobbett, *A Fruitfull and Usefull Discourse* (London, 1656),
p. 94; Daniel Lewes, *The Sins of Youth, Remembred with Bitterness*
(Boston, 1725), p. 7.

casion. On her way to New York in 1704, Sarah Knight of
Boston took the Groton-New London ferry with an eighteen-
year-old girl and her old father and horses. A high wind tossed
the boat and frightened the horses and "sett us all in a fright;
especially poor Jemima, who desired her father to say 'so jack'
to the Jade, to make her stand. But the careless parent, taking
no notice of her repeated desires, She Rored out in a Passionate manner: Pray suth father, Are you deaf? Say 'so Jack'
to the Jade, I tell you. The Dutiful Parent obey's; saying 'so
Jack, so Jack,' as gravely as if hee'd bin to saying Catechise
after Young Miss, who with her fright look't of all coullers
in the Rain Bow." Although it is unlikely that parents and
children became so familiar that they could ever exchange
places, new notes of affability and affection were sounded in
New English homes by the eighteenth century.[69]

As the colonial period was giving way to the search for in-
dependence, a transplanted Frenchman, Hector St. John de
Crèvecoeur, was writing a series of *Letters from an American
Farmer* in an attempt to explain the derivation of the "new
American man" he had found. While visiting the island of
Nantucket, he observed the education young Quaker children
received in their families. His description, which could have
been taken from the uninhibited letters of Esther Burr, bears
eloquent witness to the commingling of the old and the new in
New English child rearing. "At home," he wrote, "their tender
minds must be early struck with the gravity, the serious
though cheerful deportment of their parents; they are inured
to a principle of subordination, arising neither from sudden
passions nor inconsiderate pleasure; they are gently held by an
uniform silk cord, which unites softness and strength. . . .
They are corrected with tenderness, nursed with the most affectionate care, [and] clad with that decent plainness, from
which they observe their parents never to depart: in short, by
the force of example, which is superior even to the strongest

69. Sarah Knight, *The Private Journal of a Journey from Boston to
New York in the Year 1704* (Albany, 1865), p. 44.

instinct of nature, more than by precepts, they learn to follow the steps of their parents. . . ." For the generations of children who were born, bred, and loved there, the New English family was without doubt a perdurable milieu.[70]

70. J. Hector St. John de Crèvecoeur, *Letters from an American Farmer* (London: Everyman, n.d.), p. 113.

3

A Place for Each . . .

*Whatever qualifies any person to fill with propriety the rank and
station in life that may fall to his lot, is education.*

Jonathan Boucher

A Stuart Englishman did not have to believe literally that
"all the world's a stage" to know that "one man in his time
plays many parts, His acts being seven ages." It was a commonplace among Shakespeare's contemporaries that the human
life cycle, especially its first, more predictable half, was punctuated about every seventh year by occasions of often dramatic
transition. The first seven years were given over to childish
things, usually in the bosom of the natural family. A modicum
of religious instruction, a few household chores, and the arrival of new siblings were the only ripples on the placid existence of most English children. Despite their incessant anxiety
over idleness, even the Puritan ministry allowed that "the
first seven years are spent in pastime, and God looks not much
at it." [1]

But about the age of seven, children became the object of
altered adult expectations and standards of behavior, and the
life of the child slowly sank behind them. Instead of playing
idly at "handball, football or hockey," Tudor boys were required by law to practise the long bow to prepare them to de-

1. William Shakespeare, *As You Like It,* act 2, sc. 7, lines 139–66; John
Cotton, *A Practical Commentary . . . upon the First Epistle Generall of
John* (London, 1658), p. 125.

97

fend the sceptr'd isle.[2] Some boys took themselves to the sexually segregated study of Latin at seven, but their more
numerous peers who stayed at home were also no longer allowed to sleep with their sisters and the female servants. In
New England, illegitimate children were supported by their
putative fathers—the persons named by their mothers in the
throes of labor—until the age of seven, when they were considered by law able to work toward their own support. At the
same age they came under the watchful eye of the state. A
1653 Massachusetts law made the "Parents and Governours of
all Children above seaven years old (not that we approve
younger Children in evil)" liable to fines if they winked at
their "playing in the Streets and other places" on the Sabbath.
Most English children, especially boys, must have felt at least
a small twinge of regret at reaching their eighth year, much
as Lord Chesterfield's son must have felt upon reading a birthday greeting from his father in 1741: "This is the last letter I
shall write to you as a little boy, for tomorrow you will attain
your ninth year, so that for the future I shall treat you as a
youth. You must now commence a different course of life, a
different course of studies. No more levity. Childish toys and
playthings must be thrown aside, and your mind directed to
serious objects. What was not unbecoming to a child would
be disgraceful to a youth . . ." With his "first act" irrevocably
behind him, the new young man hitched up his recently acquired breeches and began to learn his new role.[3]

It must not be understood that the seven-year-old was
abruptly and rigorously forced into an adult mold and denied

2. Massachusetts boys from ten to sixteen years were ordered in 1645
to be instructed by an officer of the local trainband "upon the usuall
training dayes, in the exercise of armes, as small guns, halfe pikes, bowes
& arrowes . . . provided that no child shalbe taken to this exercise
against their parents minds" (*Mass. Records*, 14 May 1645, 3 : 12).

3. Ivy Pinchbeck and Margaret Hewitt, *Children in English Society*
(London, 1969), 1 : 10, 298; Walter Ong, "Latin Language Study as a
Renaissance Puberty Rite," *Studies in Philology* 56 (April 1959) : 103–24;
Alan Macfarlane, *The Family Life of Ralph Josselin* (Cambridge, 1970),
p. 91n.; John Demos, *A Little Commonwealth: Family Life in Plymouth
Colony* (New York, 1970), p. 140, n. 18; *The Colonial Laws of Massa-
chusetts*, ed. William Whitmore, (Boston, 1890), p. 132. For breeches, see
above chap. 2, n. 54.

the rest of his youthful heritage. On the contrary, most children, though they might have been expected to drop their "childish toys and playthings" for more "serious objects," managed to combine much of the insouciant playfulness of their childhood with some of the less onerous duties of their new status. For until the age of fourteen or sixteen, they were not supposed to know better. It was not until they were sixteen—the "age of discretion"—that the young people of Plymouth Colony were held responsible by law for lying and slander, though they had been allowed to choose their own legal guardians two years before. In Massachusetts, fourteen was the age at which Sabbath violaters were themselves fined, rather than their parents, and sodomists incurred the death penality instead of being "severely punished." At sixteen, Bay Colony children were held to have arrived at "sufficient years of understanding" and were therefore held responsible for acts of arson, heretical religious beliefs (particularly Quaker and Anabaptist), and "stubborn and rebellious" carriage toward their natural parents. And, as if to accentuate the seriousness of their third new role, they were also obligated to commit their lives in military service and their consciences in an oath of allegiance to the king.[4]

If the transition from child to adult was not abrupt, it was nevertheless steady. Once the child had begun to assume an adult role and style, around the age of seven, the way ahead was clearly marked by cultural signposts. Growing up then became a gradual, largely instinctive passage unbroken by serious discontinuities. There was no awkward adolescence, no predictable time of "storm and stress"—only the "steady lengthening of a young person's shadow" until it filled his father's.[5]

One of the most important signs on the road to maturity offered directions to the young person in choosing a career or,

4. Demos, *Little Commonwealth,* pp. 147–48; *Colonial Laws of Massachusetts,* pp. 15, 52, 59, 109, 133, 262. Maine children were held accountable for lying at fourteen (*Maine Records,* 1 : 148–49).

5. Demos, *Little Commonwealth,* p. 150; Ruth Benedict, "Continuities and Discontinuities in Cultural Conditioning," *Psychiatry* 1 (1938) : 161–67.

as contemporaries knew it, a "calling." William Perkins described it in 1603: "A vocation or calling, is a certain kind of life, ordained and imposed on man by God, for the common good." Of callings there were two basic kinds. "The generall Calling is that wherby a man is called out of the world to bee a child of God, a member of Christ, & heire of the kingdome of heaven." As Joseph Green told his young pupils at the Roxbury Latin School in 1696, man's efforts to seek "the Glory of God and the enjoyment of him forever" required such duties as "praying, reading the scriptures, honouring our parents, keeping strictly the Sabbath, and . . . a continual watch over our thoughts, words, & actions." The second or "personall calling is the execution of some particular office; arising of that distinction which God makes betweene man and man in every societie." Men are distinct, as William Perkins' contemporaries well knew, "in regard of the inward gifts which God bestowed on every man, giving to severall men severall gifts according to his good pleasure" and "by order, whereby God hath appointed, that in every society one person should bee above or under another; not making all equall, as though the bodie should bee all head and nothing else." Because God himself had placed the distinctions between men, it was especially foolhardy to break two general rules laid down for their guidance: first, "every person of every degree, state, sexe, or condition without exception, must have some personall and particular calling to walke in," and second, "every man must judge that particular calling, in which God hath placed him, to be the best of all callings for him." For in a word, "the good estate of the Church and common-wealth, is when every person keepes himselfe to his owne calling." Envy of other men's callings or estates only breeds "confusion and disorder in every society." As Isaac Ambrose, the minister of Preston, Lancashire, warned the parents and governors in his readership, "presume not above [your] Callings . . . [or your] Gifts." [6]

6. William Perkins, *Works* (London, 1626–31), 1 : 750–58; "Commonplace book of Joseph Green," *PCSM* 34 (1943) : 200–01; Isaac Ambrose, *The Well-Ordered Family* (Boston, 1762), p. 8.

The positive reason for choosing serviceable callings was, as for every human activity, "the Glory of God," but there was a negative reason as well: the fear of idleness. A good calling, argued William Gouge, is "the best ordinary meanes that can be prescribed to keepe a childe from the vanities of youth, from immoderate pursuit of pleasures, from unlawfull games, from idlenesse, from ill company, and such like evils." The sad truth for Puritans was that "men will ordinarily fall into horrible *Snares,* and infinite *Sins,* if they have not a *Calling,* to be their *preservative.*" Margaret Cheany was a depressing example. On 24 May 1674 the widow Cheany, "having long been bound by Satan under a melancholick distemper, (above 10 or 11 yeares) w[hi]ch made her wholly neglect her Calling & live mopishly, . . . gave thanks to God for loosing her chain, & confessing & bewailing her sinful yielding to temptation." Even more displeasing in Puritan eyes were the idle rich, the "mere gentlemen" of England, who followed no calling because of their inordinate pride. "Who are the wasters of patrimonies?" asked Dod and Cleaver, and would not stay for an answer. "Who are the robbers and rovers in the Commonwealth? Who are the deflowrers of maidens? Who are the defilers of matrons? Who are the corrupters of youth? and to speake in one word, who are the seeds-men of all mischiefe in our country, but these children of Gentlemen, who have not beene taught and trained up in learning, or some occupation, while they were young?" [7]

Few men regard the choice of vocation lightly, but the additional burden of religious imperative made the Puritan's choice all the more momentous, especially since it was felt that "every man [should] abide in that Calling, wherein he was called." The actual process of choosing was further burdened

7. Wiliam Gouge, *Of Domesticall Duties* (London, 1634), p. 541; Cotton Mather, *A Christian at His Calling* (Boston, 1701), p. 41; "Roxbury Land and Church Records," *Report of the [Boston] Record Commissioners,* 2d ed. (Boston, 1884), p. 212; John Dod and Robert Cleaver, *A godly forme of housholde governement* (London, 1612), sig. R7r.–v. The signers of the original Salem church covenant resolved to "approve our selves to the Lord in our particular callings, shunning Idleness as the bane of any State" (*EIHC* 1 [1859] : 37–39).

by a certain blurring of authority over the final choice. Most Puritan casuists urged parents to carefully "observe both the inclination and the natural gifts of body and mind that are in the child, & accordingly to bestow it in some honest calling and course of life." [8] And this many parents did, sometimes after an initial bout with filial willfulness.

Adam Martindale, the son of a Lancashire yeoman and carpenter, was sent to a series of schoolmasters until he contracted the smallpox around the age of thirteen. When he had recovered, several "neare relations were very importunate with [my father] to take me off learning, and set me to somewhat that might be [to] me a subsistance; alledging too many instances of such as made no advantage of their learning, though they had been brought up so long to it as to be fit for nothing else.[9] My father, overcome with their importunity, set me for a while to worke at his own calling, to which I submitted, and framed well enough; but he guessed right which way my mind still went, and thinking it pittie I should lose all I had got, he frankely put it to my choice, whether I would go on as I did at present, or returne to schoole againe. . . . I never stood considering the matter, but thankfully embracing his offer, repaired to mine old master." [10]

Some boys were unfit for the hard physical work of farming,

8. Perkins, *Works*, 1 : 759; 3 : 693; Mather, *Christian at His Calling*, p. 45; Hezekiah Woodward, *A Childes Patrimony* (London, 1640), in *British Journal of Educational Studies* 9 (May 1961) : 139; Gouge, *Of Domesticall Duties*, p. 542.

9. See James Howell, *Familiar Letters*, ed. Joseph Jacobs, ca. 1646 (London, 1892), 2 : 525: "The extravagant Humour of our Country is not to be altogether commended, that all Men should aspire to Book-learning: There is not a simpler Animal, and a more superfluous Member of State, than a mere Scholar, than only a self-pleasing Student," and the diary of Samuel Dexter of Dedham, Massachusetts, 6 July 1720: "I took my first Degree, and as it was the Desire of my Parents, so it was my own also, to be Improv'd in Business, & not to live Idlely, as some Schollars do," he kept school for two years (*NEHGR* 13 [1859] : 305–10).

10. *The Life of Adam Martindale*, ed. Richard Parkinson, *Chetham Society Remains*, 1st ser., vol. 4 (1845), pp. 24–25. Another yeoman's son, Ralph Josselin, also ran into some initial parental opposition to his plans for a ministerial career, but "at last God putt it into my fathers head to listen to me" (Macfarlane, *Family Life of Ralph Josselin*, p. 16).

so they were given over to higher learning. Another English boy whose scholarly career was foreshortened by the smallpox was John Brock, who caught the dread disease in 1639 after moving from Suffolk to Dedham, Massachusetts. Fortunately his minister, John Allin, took a paternal interest in him and in 1643 asked him "how far I was learned in my Youth, & would have me to think of it, whether God might not call me to study, to recover all again." Understandably, after a four-year absence from Latin grammar, John "had no Heart to it," but Master Allin "followed me with Encouragements for so much as I had but a weak body & so not able to follow Husbandry." At the advanced age of twenty-three he entered Harvard to study for the ministry. Similarly John Barnard, Boston-born son of pious parents, was devoted to "the service of God, in the work of the ministry, from my very conception and birth." Undoubtedly his parents' resolve was strengthened as John grew up, for they thought him "to be weakly, because of my thin habit and pale countenance." [11]

An even more exceptional parent was the father of Michael Wigglesworth, who brought the boy from England to New Haven at the age of six. There young Michael attended Ezekiel Cheever's school for two years and "began to make Latin & to get forward apace." But God visited lameness upon his father, who "wanting help was fain to take me off from school to follow other employments for the space of 3 or 4 yeers until I had gained in the Latine Tongue. But when I was now in my fourteenth yeer, my Father, who I suppose was not wel satisfied in keeping me from Learning whereto I had been designed from my infancy, & not judging me fit for husbandry, sent me to school again, though at that time I had little or no disposition to it, but I was willing to submit to his authority therein and accordingly I went to school. . . ." Michael more than justified his father's hopes by making up his lost ground in less than three years, graduating from Harvard, staying on to teach, and becoming the famous author of *The Day of Doom*. But he never forgot his father's "act of great self

11. *PAAS*, n.s. 53 (1943) : 97–99; *Colls. MHS*, 3d ser., vol. 5 (1836), p. 178.

Denial." "Notwithstanding his own Lameness and great weakness of Body w[hi]ch required the service & helpfulness of a son, and having but one son to be the staff of his age & supporter of his weakness he would yet for my good be content to deny himself of that comfort and Assistance I might have Lent him." [12]

With resolute and talented children like these, English parents did not have to think further on the best calling for them and could acquiesce with all good conscience in their children's choices. But then as now, few parents were blessed with such exceptional children, and the choice of an appropriate calling could not be left entirely to the young. So the Puritan spokesman insisted that, in the final analysis, the parents "ought to have an over-ruling influence in this Affair." [13] This was not a surprising stand to take because parental choice was already the reigning custom, particularly among the lower ranks of society where "the choice of a calling was scarcely a choice at all; instead it was something assumed, something everywhere implicit in the child's surroundings and in the whole process of growth." Among the husbandmen and yeomen of both old and New England, it was convenience and limited opportunity, rather than aptitude or ability, that determined most choices.[14]

During the long days and nights that parents and children spent together, there were many occasions and ways for the children to learn to accept the "over-ruling influence" of their parents' choice, which, as we have seen, was often made at their birth or even conception. In a slowly changing agricultural world, such an early choice would not have been superannuated by the time the child was ready to be "placed forth." On the contrary, time is a great educator, and the longer the parents had to prepare the child to accept their choice, the

12. *NEHGR* 17 (1863) : 137–38.
13. Samuel Willard, *A Compleat Body of Divinity* (Boston, 1726), p. 602; Perkins, *Works*, 3 : 695.
14. Demos, *Little Commonwealth*, p. 147; Mildred Campbell, *The English Yeoman under Elizabeth and the Early Stuarts* (New Haven, 1942), p. 276.

more successful they were likely to be. Not unlike the choice of Christian name at baptism, the early choice of calling was potentially an effective instrument of education. But its effectiveness depended to a large degree upon the continued presence of the child's parents, especially the father, which, among the uncertainties of seventeenth century life, could not be taken for granted.

Eliphalet Adams recalled his early life: 26 March 1677, "I was born a sinner into an evil world;" 24 June 1679, "My Mother died;" 17 August 1685, "My Father left this evil world and left me an orphan to God's Providence and a wide world." In a day of war, famine, and pestilence, many English children would have recognized something familiar in the poignant brevity of these memories. In the village of Clayworth, Nottinghamshire, for instance, fully 35 percent of all children were orphans in 1688, having lost either one parent or both. And in the decade 1650–59, six out of every ten brides who were being married for the first time in Manchester were fatherless, as were half of the grooms; both partners were typically still in their twenties.[15]

Another index of the prevalence of orphans among the youthful English population—of whom 45 to 50 percent were under the age of nineteen—is the rate of remarriage, since divorce was rare and people tended to remarry whenever they found themselves without a spouse to help them care for their children. In Clayworth, twenty-one of the seventy-two husbands (29 percent) had been married more than once as of 1688, as had nine (12 percent) of their wives. Between 1650 and 1659 a third of all marriages in Manchester were remarriages for at least one partner and 11.5 percent were for both; thus, for forty of the brides never before married, there was a good chance that they would become the stepmother of one

15. *Colls. MHS*, 4th ser., vol. 1 (1852) : 27; Peter Laslett, *The World We Have Lost* (London, 1965), pp. 95, 260–61n. In ten villages in the years between 1599 and 1796, between 12 and 37 percent of the child population were orphans, the average being 22 percent (Cambridge Group for the Study of Population and Social Structure, unpublished information supplied by Peter Laslett).

or more children. In New England the situation was much the same; between 25 and 40 percent of the men and women who lived to the age of fifty in Andover, Massachusetts and in the Plymouth Colony married more than once.[16]

When a widow remarried, her children were sometimes taken in by her new husband, but often they found themselves placed in another home. Occasionally their natural father had anticipated this problem before his death. Anthony Bessey's will stipulated that, in the event that his widow remarried, "the five bigest [children were] to bee put forth and theire Cattle with them according to the Descretion of the overseers." Likewise, in 1711, at the age of forty-eight, Cotton Mather began "providing *Patrons* for my children, when they shall be *Orphans.* For my Daughter *Lizzy,*" he announced to his diary, "I particularly have my Thoughts on a religious and ingenious Woman in our Neighbourhood; which has no Children of her own. I will visit her, and I will do what I can to engage her, that she will deal with that Child as her own." [17]

If the children did remain with their mother, there was a division of authority between the parents over the family's youngsters. Thomas Fuller thought that a good stepmother treated all the children equally, but "she is severest to her own, over whom she hath the sole jurisdiction. And if her second husband's children by a former wife commit a fault, she had rather bind them over to answer for it before their own father, than to correct them herself, to avoid all suspicion of hard using them." The normal parental authority over the choice of calling was also held in check on occasion. When Jonathan Morey was about to marry the widow Mary Foster in 1659, he contracted to "bring up" her son Benjamin "without looking for any satisfaction for the same or for any Charge

16. Laslett, *World We Have Lost,* pp. 99, 103, 260–61n.; Philip Greven, Jr., *Four Generations: Population, Land, and Family in Colonial Andover, Massachusetts* (Ithaca, 1970), pp. 29, 110–11; Demos, *Little Commonwealth,* p. 194.
17. *The Mayflower Descendant* 14 (1912) : 152; *Diary of Cotton Mather* (New York, n.d.), 2 : 95.

hee or his heires . . . shalbee att about the same," but also
not to interfere in any future plans "to bind him forth apprentice or the like." Even in the event that the boy's mother
died before disposing of him in an appropriate calling, Morey
was not allowed to influence the choice made by the boy's legal
guardians.[18]

It seems that choosing a calling for New English children
was regarded with some scrupulosity as the prerogative of the
child's natural parents. Accordingly, many parents made specific provisions in their wills for the disposition of their children after their death, knowing—or hoping—that their wishes
would not be discarded lightly. Because of the largely reflexive
nature of most choices, in which the son followed unconsciously in his father's footsteps, many of the parental preferences expressed in wills consciously named callings that might
otherwise have gone unchosen. Most numerous were the
fathers who tithed one son to the Lord's work by leaving him
special resources with which to be educated at the "School of
the Prophets" in Cambridge or New Haven. Henry Mountfort,
wealthy Boston shipowner, merchant, and man of learning,
gave to the overseers of his will in 1691 "the inspection of my
only child, Ebenezer Mountfort, that he be trayned up in
learning in the charge of my Estate, my desire being that he
should be a scholar." Young Mountfort was ranked second in
the Harvard class of 1702 and later took his master's degree,
but business and an inheritance of nearly £3,500 called louder
than scholarship. Unfortunately he died at thirty, unmarried
and unfulfilled. Joshua Gee, also the son of a prosperous
Boston shipbuilder, enjoyed more success. He was the second
Joshua of the family, the first dying in childhood, so his
father in thankfulness "lent him to the Lord," with the advice
of Cotton Mather. A chamber of the family mansion was fitted
up as a study and a choice library collected "in the most
learned Languages, as well as French & English" with which

18. Thomas Fuller, "The Good Widow," *The Holy State and The Profane State* (London, 1840), p. 21; *The Mayflower Descendant* 14 (1912) : 15–
16.

Joshua "made a large Progress in solid Literature." After graduating from Harvard in 1717, he eventually commanded the pulpit of Boston's prestigious Second Church.[19]

But perhaps the will of William Brinsmeade, dated 1647, expresses as well as any the practices and preferences of the exceptional fathers who wanted their children to follow callings in life different from their own. Brinsmeade left 40 percent of his estate to his eldest son, William Jr., and the remainder to his three other children. Young William was obviously intended for a learned career, for he was "to be kept at schoole" and to have all his father's books. Another son, Alexander, if he was "capable & willing," was to "have so much bestowed as may fit him to write well & cast accounts, fit for a Navigator." But the girl of the family, Mary, easily got the short end of the stick, as she was probably wont to do in that patriarchal society. She was "to be so imployed as that there may be so much saved for [the boys'] future portions as may conveniently bee for the good incouragement that I have of my sonne William concerning his learning." [20]

In spite of the ministers' preference, however, parental authority over the choice of calling eroded with the gradual recession of patriarchalism in the wake of, among other things, the economic conditions of the New World. For in New England, perhaps especially in the eighteenth century, "the generality" of men were "very near upon a level," and "although some amongst them had handsome fortunes, yet in general their estates were small, barely sufficient to provide them houses and necessary accommodations." It was this subdivision of estates, as Tocqueville saw, that contributed "more than anything else to change the relations existing between a father and his children." For "when the property of the father of a family is scanty, his son and himself constantly live in the same place and share the same occupation; habits and necessity bring them together and force them to hold constant communication. The inevitable consequence is a sort of familiar

19. *Sibley's Harvard Graduates* 5 : 166–68; 6 : 175–76.
20. *NEHGR* 3 (1849) : 266–67.

intimacy, which renders authority less absolute. . . . In a democratic family the father exercises no other power than that which is granted to the affection and the experience of age." [21]

This growing bond of affection and the consequent decline of parental domination over the choice of calling can be seen in the relations with their sons of Samuel Sewall and the Reverend Ebenezer Parkman, both ordinarily disposed to cleave to older Puritan precept. In February 1695 Samuel Sewall Jr., sixteen years old, was planning "to be disposed to such a Master and Calling, as wherein he may abide with God." By July his prominent father had secured, after a day of secret prayer for "Sam's being to be placed out," the willingness of Captain Samuel Checkly to take the boy "to be his Prentice." Yet less than seven months later, the boy's discontent with his new calling rose to the surface. On 7 February 1696 his father confided to his diary: "Last night Sam. could not sleep because of my Brother's speaking to him of removing to some other place, mentioning Mr. Usher's. I put him to get up a little wood, and he even fainted, at which Brother was much startled, and advis'd to remove him forthwith and place him somewhere else, or send him to Salem and he would doe the best he could for him. Since, I have express'd doubtfullness to Sam. as to his staying there."

But Sam did not need any prompting from the wings. "He mention'd to me Mr. Wadsworth's Sermon against Idleness, which was an Affliction to him. He said his was an idle Calling, and that he did more at home than there, take one day with another. And he mention'd Mr. Stoddard's words to me, that should place him with a good Master, and where had fullness of Imployment. It seems Sam. overheard him, and now alleged these words against his being where he was because of his idleness. Mention'd also the difficulty of the imployment

21. Thomas Hutchinson, *The History of the Colony and Province of Massachusetts-Bay,* ed. Lawrence Mayo (Cambridge, Mass., 1936), 1 : 370; Alexis De Tocqueville, *Democracy in America,* ed. Phillips Bradley (New York, 1945), 2 : 194–95.

by reason of the numerousness of Goods and hard to distinguish them, many not being marked; whereas Books, the price of them was set down, and so could sell them readily. I spake to Capt. Checkly again and again, and he gave me no encouragement that his being there would be to Sam's profit; and Mrs. Checkly always discouraging."

Sam had obviously learned one of the lessons of calling well, especially when it suited his purpose, but he had certainly neglected another, that "every man abide in that Calling, wherein he was called." Perhaps the rub was that Judge Sewall had not adequately consulted the boy's "Capacities and Inclinations"; on the other hand, it may have been a doting father's reluctance to impose his best judgment upon a favorite son. At any rate, a year later young Sam went to live with Richard Wilkins, a Boston bookseller. On the night of his departure the family read Galatians 6 : 9: "In due season we shall reap, if we faint not," to which the diarist could only pray, "Lord furnish father and Son with Faith." [22]

Ebenezer Parkman's experience with his two sons was even more frustrating, for some of the same reasons. On 17 April 1744 his second son, Thomas, aged fourteen, left the Westborough parsonage for Boston "to begin apprenticeship with Joshua Emms, Goldsmith." One month later Mrs. Parkman returned from a trip to Boston with the news that Tom was "much out of Health and Mr. Emms discourag'd about him and would have me send for him home." Several inquiries in the capital for another master brought no "direct Success," but finally, in February 1745, Joseph Batchellor, a weaver of Grafton, "agreed to take my Son Thomme a Prentice next April." So again, in the middle of April, Tom rode off to seek his calling, and again, one month later, "Thomme came home ill from Mr. Batchellors." After recovering at home for three weeks, young Tom returned to Grafton. A week later, "Thomme return'd home again from Grafton being in such Pain and under So great Discouragement that his master sends all his Things Home with him." His father could only exclaim,

22. *Colls. MHS*, 5th ser., vol. 5 (1878), pp. 398, 409, 421, 452.

"God grant the Grace and Wisdom needed under every Trial!" [23]

And pray he needed to, for four days before Tom came home from Grafton, the minister had discovered that his eldest son, Ebenezer, was disinclined to follow the clerical career that had been chosen for him. "I have discover'd," he wrote with a clearly heavy pen, "that though Ebenezer performs his Tasks of Lessons, yet he has an inward heavyness and drops now and then a word how glad he Shall be to be at Work upon the place, how much better the place Should Soon be if he Should labour etc. I therefore took the Opportunity this Morning to talk with him, and I once More still gave him Liberty to Choose what Method of Life Should Suit his Genius best." The seventeen-year-old boy did not respond with Adam Martindale's alacrity, but two days later "Ebenezer discovers by all his Conduct that he preferrs Labour to Studying—and tho it grievously wounds me, yet I yield the point finally." [24]

It was probably fortunate for New English children that the final choice of a calling fell by default to them, since there are few sources of unhappiness greater than the suppression of nascent talents and strong inclinations. One incident at least shows that it was equally fortunate for the parents. In 1698 the Reverend John Higginson of Salem wrote to his son Nathaniel, a prosperous merchant in the East Indies, "I intended you for the ministry & it was a Sore affliction to me that you was Diverted from it." Apparently the Puritan father did not see the irony in his lament, for his whole letter was a plea for financial help in the face of poverty brought on by heavy taxation, the Boston fire, inflation, and the "arbitrary Government" of Governor Andros. Josiah Cotton, too, clearly reaped many benefits from his chosen calling but could not see them in the glare of his Puritan upbringing. Lingering

23. After another fling with apprenticeship, this time to a saddler of Marlborough, Tom wound up on the family farm helping his brother. In 1759 he was killed fighting for King George (*PAAS*, n.s. 72 [1962] : 175, 185, 189, 354–55, 363, 367, 370; *PAAS*, n.s. 73 [1963] : 60; *Sibley's Harvard Graduates*, 6 : 525).

24. *PAAS*, n.s. 72 (1962) : 368, 370.

headaches and fatigue in study persuaded him to forsake his parents' plans of a ministerial career for him and to assume the schoolmaster's birch. But he entertained doubts about the wisdom of his decision long afterward. "Though after all it is possible," he mused in his memoirs, "that some of my disappointments since have been owing to my thus diverting from the business designed me by my parents, and would therefore caution others against diverting from the business as they are brought up to & in some measure fit for, which is too much practised in the Country to the damage of the commonwealth. For whilst too many endevour to live easy, the laborious part of life is too much neglected. The Husbandman, the Mechanick becomes Merchant and sometimes Minister & anything to shift off the labour that God has given as the portion of the children of men." [25]

When the young person found a calling that satisfied him and, if possible, his parents, he then entered a period of formal education to prepare for its full and competent exercise.[26] A select minority of boys entered Latin grammar schools to prepare for college and the liberal arts or enlisted in His Majesty's military forces to learn the arts of command. But a larger number of both boys and girls, choosing to enter the crafts and trades of England, "the sinewes, and life itselfe of Common-weale" according to one of their champions, similarly bound themselves apprentice to the masters of their callings, the practitioners of the mechanical arts. To contemporaries, though formal distinctions were necessary to an orderly world, there was small difference between the educational functions of apprenticeship and higher learning. Edward Gibbon pointed out that "the use of Academical degrees, as old as the thirteenth century, is visibly borrowed from

25. *EIHC* 53 (1917) : 182–86; Memoirs of Josiah Cotton, Mass. His. Soc., pp. 113–14.

26. We are speaking, of course, only of relatively small numbers because, as we have seen, the majority of children actually had little choice over their callings in the first place, which probably meant that their competence was shaped more by the force of habit and repetition at their fathers' sides than by formal instruction.

the mechanic corporations, in which an apprentice, after serving his time, obtains a testimonial of his skill, and a license to practise his trade and mystery." And Edmund Bolton argued, with the growing force of precedent behind him, that "though the Schooles, and Camp, are most proper for Honor and [heraldic] Armes, yet the ancient wisedome, and the like ancient bounty of our Sages, did ever leave the gates of Honor open to City-Arts, and to the mysteries of honest gaine. . . ." A master, he added, reducing the question to its simplest terms, is "a meer *Discipliner,* or Teacher." In its best days, apprenticeship was indeed not merely a system of technical instruction, but also a method of education, the only method available to the majority to young English men and women.[27]

To acquire this education in the mechanical arts, the young apprentice (from *apprehendere,* to learn) and his parents had first to make a civil contract in the form of an indenture with the master. In the sixteenth and seventeenth centuries the terms of their agreement were written twice on a paper or parchment, which was then cut apart along an indented (jagged) edge and one part given to each party; in the eighteenth century printed forms were frequently used, though it was advised that they too be duly indented to avoid fraud. The agreement was then supposed to be entered in the public record, at the courts of the Master and Wardens of the guilds in England, or in the registers of the town clerks of New England, but from the court records of Massachusetts it

27. *The Auto-biography of Edward Gibbon, Esq.,* ed. John, Lord Sheffield (New York, 1846), p. 48; Edmund Bolton, *The Cities Advocate* (London, 1629), sigs. A3v., A4r., p. 23; O. Jocelyn Dunlop, *English Apprenticeship and Child Labour* (London, 1912), p. 172; Lawrence Towner, "A Good Master Well Served: A Social History of Servitude in Massachusetts, 1620–1750," (Ph.D. diss., Northwestern University, 1955), p. 32; Edmund Morgan, *The Puritan Family* (New York, 1966), p. 132. In 1793 Charles Nisbet, the Scottish-born president of Dickinson College in Carlyle, Pennsylvania, lamented that "if ever Learning shall prevail in this Country, the people must be persuaded that as much time at least is necessary for acquiring it, as is required to serve an Apprenticeship to any Mechanical Profession, which is far from being the Case at present" (Richard Hofstadter and Wilson Smith, eds., *American Higher Education: A Documentary History* [Chicago, 1961], 1 : 255).

is apparent that compliance in the New World was irregular at best.[28]

The nature of the agreements followed time-honored lines, even to the rhythmic measures of the apprentice's rules of conduct designed for oral memory: [29]

> This Indenture Witnesseth, That *Swain Lawton of the District of Pepperill in the County of Middlesex, a minor* Hath put *him*self, and by these Presents doth voluntarily, and of *his* own free Will and Accord, and with the Consent of *his Father Thomas Lawton of Pepperill afors: Housewright* put and bind *him*self Apprentice to *Jonas Wright of Pepperill aforesaid, Cordwainer,* to learn *his* Art, Trade or Mystery, and with *him* after the Manner of an Apprentice, to serve from the *Date hereof untill he shall arrive to Twenty years of age,* to be compleat and ended: During all which Term, the said Apprentice *the* said *Master* faithfully shall Serve, *his* Secrets keep, and Lawful Command every where gladly obey. *He* shall do no Damage to *his* said *Master* nor suffer it to be done by others, without letting, or giving Notice thereof to *his* said Master, shall not waste the Goods of *his* said *Master* nor Lend them Unlawfully to any. *He* shall not commit Fornication, nor Matrimony contract within the said Term. At Cards, Dice, or any other unlawful Game *he* shall not play: *he* shall not absent *him*self by Day or by Night from the Service of *his* said *Master* without *his* Leave; nor haunt Ale-Houses, Taverns, or Play Houses; but in all Things behave *him*self as a faithful Apprentice

28. Bolton, *Cities Advocate,* pp. 9–10; Dunlop, *English Apprenticeship and Child Labour,* pp. 161–64; Walter Robinson, *Every Master and Servant His Own Lawyer* (London, 1780), pp. 4, 15; Towner, "A Good Master Well Served," p. 38. New England schoolboys were taught to copy indenture forms as a writing exercise, which at the same time familiarized them with the terms of apprenticeship (Exercise book of Ebenezer Belcher [1793], Harvard University Archives, Cambridge, Mass.).

29. Mass. His. Soc. This is obviously a trial copy because of the absence of the validating signatures of the town officials or justices of the peace at the end.

ought to do towards *his* said *Master* during the said Term.

And the said *Jonas Wright* for *him*self doth hereby Covenant and Promise to Teach and Instruct, or cause the said Apprentice to be taught and instructed in the Art, Trade or Calling of a *Cordwainer* by the best Way or Means *he* may or can (if the said Apprentice be capable to Learn) And to find and provide unto the said Apprentice good and sufficient *Meat, Drinke, Washing, Lodging, Physicke & Surgery in Case of Sickness or Lameness* during the said Term: And at the Expiration thereof to give unto the said Apprentice *Two good suits of apparril for all parts of his body, one suitable for Lords Days & other Publick Occations, the other for every Days & to write a Legiable hand & Cypher as far as the Rule of three & to Read the English Bible.*

In Testimony whereof the Parties to these Presents have hereunto Interchangeably set their Hand and seals the *31st* Day of *March* In the *Second* Year of the Reign of our Soverign Lord [*3 George*] of Great Britain, &c. Annoque Domini, One Thousand Seven Hundred and Sixty *Two.*

Signed, Sealed and Delivered in the Presence of us [blank]

There were two further agreements sometimes made between master and apprentice but seldom entered in the indenture. One was for a premium of money to be paid to the master for taking the apprentice. This was a custom more common in the wealthier restricted trades of England than in New England with its seller's market for labor, but even Benjamin Franklin was deterred by the practice on his home ground in Boston. When he was twelve and searching for a calling, his father "at last fix'd upon the Cutler's Trade, and my Uncle Benjamin's Son Samuel who was bred to that Business in London being about that time establish'd in Boston, I was sent to be with him some time on liking. But his Expectations of a Fee with me displeasing my Father, I was taken home again" before being apprenticed to his brother James in the printing business. Young Franklin's arrangement to serve his cousin "on liking" indicates the second custom, that of serving a short time with a chosen master on "trial." For example, in the court case of a New Haven farmer, Henry Bishop, accused of cruelly neglecting and ill-treating a young apprentice, a witness testified that "he thinkes the boy hath bine bad inough, but yet Goodman Bishop hath at first given commendation of him, and hee had bine three monethes upon tryall, yet after took him to be his servant for five yeares." Where both religious sanction and the practical difficulty of effecting a change after several years of preparation gave an undue burden of gravity to the young person's decision, the trial period helped—however little—to ease the irrevocability of his choice of calling.[30]

The stated terms of the indenture established the educational nature of apprenticeship as familial, as Englishmen, and especially Puritans, understood that word in its fullest sense. According to Puritan casuistry the duties of masters were synonymous with those of natural fathers, since "Domesticall Duties" were determined not so much by the actual persons who composed the family as by the impersonal relationships they bore to one another by virtue of the "several Ranks & Orders" to which they were "Providentially" born. An apprentice stood in the same relationship to his master as "a child under his father." Masters therefore were expected to "instruct their apprentices and servants in the knowledge of their occupations and trades, *even as parents would teach their owne children,* without all guile, fraud, delaying, or concealing" and "when correction is necessary, that then they give it them with such discretion, pitie, and desire of their amendment, *as loving parents use to deale with their deare children.*" This was the relationship William Hoskin had in

---

30. Richard Morris, *Government and Labor in Early America* (New York, 1965), p. 369; *The Autobiography of Benjamin Franklin,* ed. Leonard Labaree et al. (New Haven, 1964), p. 57; *New Haven Town Records,* March 1652, 1 : 167–68; Morgan, *Puritan Family,* pp. 68–69.

mind when he apprenticed his six-year-old daughter Sarah to Thomas and Winifred Whitney of Plymouth, bidding them to use her "as their child" and to be "unto her as father and mother," as well as to "instruct her in learneing and soweing [sewing] in reasonable manner." It was also the relationship assumed by the Massachusetts General Court in 1668 when they ordered the selectmen of the towns to "take a list of the names of those young persons . . . who do live from under Family Government, viz. do not serve their Parents or Masters, as Children, Apprentices, hired Servants, or Journey men ought to do, and usually did in our Native Country, being subject to their commands and discipline." In both old and New England, parents and masters were spoken of in the same breath.[31]

Within the limits of custom and law, the terms of indenture were subject to wide variation—and execution. The most variable item, perhaps, was the length of service. In England, where the Elizabethan Statute of Artificers (1563) officially governed economic relations until its repeal in 1814, apprentices to "any art, mystery or manual occupation" were bound "for 7 years at the least, so as the term of such apprentice do not expire afore such apprentice shall be of the age of 24 years at the least," and apprentices to husbandry, "until his age of 21 years at the least." The act of 1563 largely codified the existing practices of the guilds of London, whose Common Council in 1556 had established the twenty-four-year minimum age for completing an apprenticeship to avoid "over hastie marriages and over sone [soon] setting up of householdes of and by the youth and young folkes of the said citie." Because seven years of service was also a minimum, many indentures agreed to longer terms. Of the sixty-seven indentures recorded in 1561–62 by the Stationers Company, for example, twenty-three were for seven years, sixteen for eight years, seven for

31. Willard, *Compleat Body of Divinity*, pp. 598, 614; Bolton, *Cities Advocate*, p. 28; Dod and Cleaver, *A godly forme of housholde governement*, sig. Z5r.–v. (my emphasis); *Plymouth Records*, 12 January 1644, 2 : 67–68; *Mass. Records*, 14 October 1668, 4, pt. 2 : 395–96.

nine years, fourteen for ten years, and seven for over ten years, which meant that most children were at least fourteen years old when they were bound out.[32]

In New England, on the other hand, there was not a similar need to prevent young people from leaving agriculture or to regulate craft competition in the guilds—two of the animating motives for the English Statute of Artificers—so it was never reenacted by any of the colonial legislatures. Because custom alone dictated their relations, New English masters and apprentices agreed upon lengths of service virtually unknown at home. In Providence a two-month-old baby girl was apprenticed until eighteen to learn the "Trade and art of a Tailor in making Aparrill," while many children were taken for only three or four years. The "sad experience" of Boston tradesmen with these truncated terms resulted in a town ordinance passed in 1660 requiring apprenticeship until twenty-one, with a minimum term of seven years. Youths without such training, the law said, had shown themselves "uncapable of being artists in their trades, besides their unmeetness at the expiration of their Apprenticeship to take charge of others for government and manual instruction in their occupations." Furthermore, with a sidelong glance at London, such a practice was asserted to be "contrary to the customes of all well Governed places." But even under such legislation and changing economic conditions, the lengths of service did not appreciably change in Massachusetts; at least, if anything, they dropped slightly. Of some 107 indentures recorded from 1620 to 1750, almost as many stipulated terms of less than seven years (47) as did those of seven years or more (60). And no apprentice was required to serve later than his twenty-first birthday.[33]

32. Great Britain, 5 Eliz. Cap. IV, f. 18–19; Dunlop, *English Apprenticeship and Child Labour,* pp. 52–54. See also Margaret Davies, *The Enforcement of English Apprenticeship: A Study in Applied Mercantilism, 1563–1642* (Cambridge, Mass., 1956).

33. Dunlop, *English Apprenticeship and Child Labour,* pp. 37–40, 65–67; Morris, *Government and Labor in Early America,* pp. 370–76; Towner, "A Good Master Well Served," p. 36, Appendix A. From 1650 to 1750, 53 percent of the indentures specified terms of seven years or more; from 1680 to 1750, only 49 percent did so.

The reasons for the shorter terms of apprenticeship in New England are not hard to find. Labor in general, and skilled labor in particular, was scarce, and therefore, according to the laws of supply and demand, wages were high, from 30 to 100 percent higher than the wages of contemporary English workmen. During the first half century of settlement, poverty was rare. In 1680 Governor Leete of Connecticut could still report to the Parliamentary Committee for Trade and Plantations that "there is seldom any want releife; because labour is deare, viz. 2 *sh.* and sometimes 2 *sh.* 6 *d.* a day for a day labourer, and provision cheap." There proved to be an element of accuracy in John Winter's early prediction that, if the high rate of wages continued, "the servants wil be masters and the masters scrvants." Even as immigration filled the coastal towns, there was no glut on the labor market to reduce wages because, as soon as a workman had accumulated a small amount of money, he often bought a tract of land to the west and settled on it to farm. As a colonial report to the Board of Trade in 1767 described this quixotic attraction to the soil, "the genius of the People in a Country where every one can have Land to work upon leads them so naturally into Agriculture, that it prevails over every other occupation. There can be no stronger Instances of this, than in the servants Imported from Europe of different Trades; as soon as the Time stipulated in their Indentures is expired, they immediately quit their Masters, and get a small tract of Land, in settling which for the first three or four years they lead miserable lives, and in the most abject Poverty; but all this is patiently borne and submitted to with the greatest chearfulness, the Satisfaction of being Land holders smooths every difficulty, and makes them prefer this manner of living to that comfortable subsistence which they could procure for themselves and their families by working at the Trades in which they were brought up." [34]

High wages meant two things for apprenticeship. The first

34. *Conn. Records,* 3 : 300; Morris, *Government and Labor in Early America,* pp. 44–49.

was that few young people would voluntarily choose to lock themselves into long terms of unpaid apprenticeship when they could be exercising this new earning power quickly and easily. By the same token, if a youngster did wish to postpone his immediate earning potential to master a craft that would bring him a higher future reward, he did not—understandably—wish to postpone it to excessive lengths. Secondly, since very little capital was necessary to establish oneself in the handicraft trades when they merely served their local communities, as most of them did, young journeymen just released from their indentures did not take long to accumulate sufficient funds to open their own shops. And since in most communities there was a scarcity of goods and services rather than a fear of competition, masters were not averse to allowing shorter apprenticeships. It was this need for labor freedom and new crafts in an emerging market economy that accounted for the abbreviated terms of apprenticeship in colonial New England.

The second major aspect of an indenture where the articles were negotiable was the master's provisions for the apprentice's welfare. Since he was acting as a surrogate father, a master had to assume a father's responsibilities in providing the minimum of "Meat, Drinke, Washing, Lodging," and medical care. But if the nature of apprenticeship ever changed from that of familial education to a more purely economic relationship, the extent of the master's responsibility for his servant's personal welfare would obviously diminish. This is what occurred in England from about 1680, when certain crafts and trades began to outgrow their household origins. The parents of the apprentice began to provide certain necessities which formerly had been provided by the master, such as shoes, socks, mending, and medical costs. And then the small amounts of pocket money that the apprentice received grew into something like wages, out of which he had to pay for his master's domestic services. The final step was taken after 1700 when many apprentices, bound to large industrial establishments of as many as forty boys, were forced to live and board out in local lodgings rather than their master's house. As Daniel Defoe lamented in 1726, "fifty or sixty years ago, servants were infinitely more under subjection than they are now." [35]

New Englishmen could be every bit as pessimistic about their servants as their metropolitan cousins were. In 1657 the Reverend Ezekiel Rogers of Rowley complained to a colleague that it was "hard to get a *Servant* that is Glad of *Catechising,* or *Family-Duties:* I had a rare Blessing of Servants in *Yorkshire;* and those that I brought over were a Blessing; But the *Young Brood* doth much afflict me. Even the *Children* of the Godly here, and elsewhere, make a woful Proof." By the 1670s the lonely clerical voices crying in the wilderness had grown to a veritable chorus of jeremiads issuing from the colonial legislatures. Connecticut's was typical. Because of "the calamitious time of New England's distresse by the war with the Indians, in the yeares seventy-five and seventy-six," a host of evils had sprung up: "prophanation of the Sabboth; neglect of cattechiseing of children and servants, and famaly prayers; *young persons shakeing of[f] the government of parents and masters;* boarders and inmates neglecting the worship of God in the famalyes where they reside; tipleing and drincking; uncleaness; oppression, in workemen and traders." To prevent "young persons getting from under the government of parents and masters before they are able to govern themselves"—which was perhaps partly a result of short apprenticeships—the General Court "seriously and heartily" recommended to the selectmen of the several towns "to be carefull to prohibit and not to grant liberty to unmeet persons to entertaine boarders or sojourners," and ordered that "all such borders and sojourners as doe live in famalies as such, shall carefully attend the worship of God in those famalys where they so board or sojourn, and be subject to the domesticall government of the said famaly, and shall be ready to give an account of their actions upon

35. Dunlop, *English Apprenticeship and Child Labour,* pp. 195–98; Daniel Defoe, *The Complete English Tradesman,* 5th ed. (London, 1745), 1 : 143.

all demands, upon the penalty of forfeiting of five shillings for every breach of this order; and that no children shall be at liberty to dispose of themselves upon pretence of lawfull age without the parents' consent, and approbation of the authority of the place." [36]

And yet, as we shall see, the change in the nature of New English apprenticeship was only partially due to the forces operating upon the English system. Whereas the increasing size of the economic unit in England made it impossible for many masters to carry responsibilities for their apprentices that belonged to the conjugal family, most trades and crafts in New England remained on a family scale until the advent of industrialism in the early nineteenth century. For the population of New England was simply not very large. On the eve of revolution the colonies of Massachusetts, Rhode Island, Connecticut, and New Hampshire had a total population of less than three-quarters of a million persons, most of whom lived in widely scattered towns of less than a thousand inhabitants. In such communities, domestic economy and domestic government were still the rule.[37]

Much of the apprentice's personal welfare was explicitly provided for in his indenture, but another aspect of it was regulated by the unwritten law of custom, which said that he was entitled to reasonable working conditions suited to his age and capacities. Virtually only one item was not so regulated; the length of the working day was dictated more by the rhythm of the seasons than by any predetermined standard of child welfare. According to the Statute of Artificers, hired laborers in England were to work a fourteen- or fifteen-hour day in the months between March and September, with a total of 2½ hours off—an hour for dinner and a half hour each for

36. Cotton Mather, *Magnalia Christi Americana* (London, 1702), bk. 2, pp. 103–04; *Conn. Records,* 15 May 1676, 2 : 281–82 (my emphasis).

37. James Cassedy, *Demography in Early America* (Cambridge, Mass., 1969), p. 190; Michael Zuckerman, *Peaceable Kingdoms: New England Towns in the Eighteenth Century* (New York, 1970), p. 47; William Weeden, *Economic and Social History of New England, 1620–1789* (Boston, 1891), 1 : 387–98; 2 : 492, 588, 679–83, 779, 848–57; Allan Kulikoff, "The Progress of Inequality in Revolutionary Boston," *WMQ* 28 (July 1971) : 378.

breakfast, drinking, and naps (between May and August)—and "from the spring of the day in the morning until the night of same day" in the winter months. New English law was less precise but just as clear. In statutes concerning "Masters, Servants, Labourers," the General Courts of Massachusetts and Connecticut said only that "all Workmen, shall work the whole day, allowing convenient time for food and rest." [38]

But if the apprentice's work day could not be prescribed except by light, weather, and the demand for his master's goods or services, his physical safety at work could be to some extent. He was not immune from "moderate Correction" or "resonable Chastisement," which was often specified in his indentures as one of his master's parental obligations, but even here there were recognized limits beyond which no master could legitimately go. The Essex County quarterly court seemed to mark those limits in 1682 when it indicted Phillip Fowler for abusing his servant, Richard Parker. Although the court "justified any person in giving meet correction to his servant, which the boy deserved, yet they did not approve of the manner of punishment given in hanging him up by the heels as butchers do beasts for the slaughter." Nevertheless, Fowler got away with only a warning and court costs, as if his transgression had been venal. At the same session another deponent presented an example of what was obviously "meet correction" when she testified that, although her husband had equally ample justification for punishing their servant for disobedience, smoking in bed, neglecting family duties, profaning the Sabbath, and night walking, upon his coming home one night after his nine o'clock curfew, "her husband took him upon his knees as well as he could and whipped him with his hand *which broke no bones and brought no blood.*" If it left no "long red marks sixteen hours after the whipping," "waled and swollen" wrists, "great bunch[es] on his head," or other obvious abrasions or contusions, presumably the correction had been "meet." [39]

38. Great Britain, 5 Eliz. Cap. IV, f. 9; *Colonial Laws of Massachusetts,* 1672, p. 104; *Conn. Records,* 1650, 1 : 538–39; Dunlop, *English Apprentice-ship and Child Labour,* pp. 175–76.
39. *Essex Co. Court Records,* 8 : 302, 315–16 (my emphasis).

Presumably. And yet Thomas Bettis was returned to his master and forced to serve six months additional time for running away. His master was "advised moderation in the usage of his servant, and if he could agree with some other suitable person, to dispose of said servant." This is the boy's declaration before the Essex court: [40]

> my master haith this mani yeares beaten me upon small or frivelouse ocasion. I have indevored to please and give my master content but I seldom can: he brocke my hed twice, strucke me one the hed with a great stick: w[hi]ch stick was tow long to strike me in the house for the flore: he brocke it upon his knees and then he strok me one the hed and stounded me; I fell downe against the wall: the blood ran downe all my cloths to my feett. my master tooke me up and washed of the blood with a pigin of watter; he fetched sum suger and bound it up with a cloth. I was so disie all day that I cold nethr well se: or stand up right: my Arme wos so sore wth beating me att the same time that it was all black and blew: I cold not lift it up to my hed: yett my master wold have me goe to worke as sune as I cold and because he had so beat me that I cold not keepe up wth my cumpani as I used to doe: my master told me that I was a hipokritte: after this I was abused sevarall times by him: One time he tied me to a beds foott: another time to a table foott: and also to a cradell foott and every time beate me cruely: and I was almost starved for want of cloth in the winter season in spesall when I stood most need of cloths. . . .

Tom Bettis and other harshly treated servants at least had some chance of finding better treatment with new masters; fourteen-year-old John Walker, apprenticed to Robert and Susanna Latham of Marshfield, was not so fortunate. When the Plymouth authorities conducted an inquest into his death, they found that his body was "blackish and blew, and the

40. Ibid., pp. 91–92. For other masters exonerated by the courts, see ibid., pp. 222–26, and *New Haven Town Records*, 1 : 165–68.

skine broken in divers places from the middle to the haire of
his head, viz. all his backe with stripes given him by his
master." He had bruises on his arms, hips, and "one great
bruise of his brest"; his toes and heels were frozen and rotten;
"the dead corpse did bleed att the nose." Further investigation
found that "he did want sufficient food and cloathing and
lodging, and that the said John did constantly wett his bedd
and his cloathes, lying in them, and soe suffered by it, his
clothes being frozen about him; and that the said John was
put forth in the extremity of cold, though thuse unabled by
lamenes and sorenes to performe what was required." Some
few days before his death he had been "forced to carry a logg
which was beyond his strength, which hee indeavouring to
doe, the log fell upon him, and hee, being downe, had a
stripe or two" from his master. Although such cruelty was
the rare exception in colonial New England, it was sufficiently
well known to merit the eternal vigilance of parents and neighbors and occasionally specific prohibitions in apprenticeship
indentures. It was certainly known to Captain Rowland
Storey, who gave his young son to Ebenezer Parkman with the
admonition, "Impose not on him those heavy burthens that
will either Cripple him or Spoil his Growth." [41]

Part of the reason that the treatment of some servants was
harsh enough to land their masters in the civil courts was the
close company they kept in small New English homes. According to the time-honored formula of English indentures,
the apprentice "shall not absent himself by Day or by Night
from the Service of his said Master without his Leave." This
constant contact in crowded confines, coupled with the natural
but exasperating exuberance and inexperience of youth, must
have brought the tempers of many masters to the boiling
point. Yet at the same time that close family living hampered
youthful freedom, it also inadvertently provided an important
opportunity for the young apprentice to gain an education in
another essential part of adult life.

41. *Plymouth Records,* 6 February 1655, 3 : 71–73, 82; *PAAS,* 20 January 1726, n.s. 71 (1961) : 124.

The third age of man, wrote Shakespeare, is "the lover,
sighing like a furnace, with a woeful ballad made to his
mistress' eyebrow." It was no mere coincidence that this star-
struck age coincided with the years of apprenticeship. If hard
work, long hours, and adult killjoys were part of the apprentice's world, so too was love. Love cost William Reeves and
Susanna Durin public censure, a whipping, and £9 between
them, but it seems to have been worth every farthing, at least
to the boy. From jail Will begged charity from the court which
had him under indictment for fornication resulting in bastardy.
"Its not unknowne," he said, "that I & the young woman lived
servants in a house together unto whom my affections were &
still are so deare as to make her my wife & would have Asked
for her . . . but being in the condition that we were both
durst not attempt it though I well could perceive my mistress'
apprehension concerning such a Thing." Unfortunately, he
either had a short memory or was trying to protect Susanna
and "her poore babe," for other deponents presented a much
different picture of their involvement. Margery and Sarah
Williams testified that Susanna often came to their house and
asked Sarah to go over to sit with her when there was nobody
at home but Will, saying that she could not abide to be with
him alone. And Thomas Ives, aged about twenty, deposed that
Will had wondered aloud to him what "aileth our maide, for
as soone as I come in at the dore she either runeth into the
other roome or up into the Chamber." So unsmitten was
Susanna that Will also resorted to "a Certaine pouder called
Love powder a portion whereof he would give to Susanna
. . . in some maner of Drinke, to cause her to follow him."
He obviously needed an aphrodisiac to further his cause because Tom also heard Susanna say that she wished her mistress
would send her away until Will had left his master's service.
How love conquered Susanna's cold heart is not in the public
record, though it may be hazarded that, just as familiarity may
breed contempt, it may also simply breed.[42]

42. Shakespeare, *As You Like It,* act 2, sc. 7, lines 147–49; *Essex Co.
Court Records,* June 1668, 4 : 38–40.

The close quarters of the colonial home, in which men and women servants frequently slept in the same room, provided the setting for nocturnal dalliance on more than one occasion. In 1674 Elizabeth Fowler testified against Hannah Gray that Hannah "was a lying girl, and several times in the night when deponent waked, she missed her and heard her laughing and giggling at the boys' bed which was in the same room." On another occasion before the Middlesex Court someone informed on Joseph Graves, who, tarrying the night at the home of Thomas Goble of Concord, "after the said Thomas Goble was in bed, who lay in the same roome, and also two mayds in another bed viz: Ester Necholls and Mary Goble . . . went and set by the bedside and talked with them privately and after that sung some short songs to them" and after a while ended up "in bed with them—the [bed]cloathes were over him" but the maids were "in their naked beds." Ellis Mew did not have it so easy with his fellow servant Susan Clarke, whose father complained to the New Haven court that one day, when their master and mistress were away, Mew "came in the room where his daughter . . . was, and offered to abuse her in a filthy way, throwing her downe upon the bed, kissing her, pulled down his breeches, and would have forced her, but she cryed out and he left her." The culprit threw the court into a quandary by insisting that he had only thrown her upon the bed and kissed her, "but that was all and hee intended no hurt, and when she bid him let her alone, else she would tell her master and dame, then he let her alone." When Goody Jones testified that Susan "was verey merry and seemed not troubled at all" since the alleged crime, and indeed "had that day purled the sleve of Ellis his shirt, as he had it on," the judges conceded their uncertainty and let Mew off with a whipping for his abortive adventure. In 1655 John Pecke of Rehoboth was hauled before the Plymouth court "for laciviouse carriages and unchast in attempting the Chastitie of his fathers maide servant, to satisfy his fleshly, beastly lust, and that many times for some yeares space, without any intent to marry her, but was alwaies resisted by the mayde, as hee confesseth." Not all girls were as strong. Jane Powell, a servant on Cape Cod, succumbed one evening to the Irish charms of David Ogillior, another servant, when he came her way for water. She desperately wanted to marry him, "beeing shee was in a sadd and miserable condition by hard service, wanting clothes and living discontentedly," but the court knew that her indenture forbade her to "contract Matrimony" during her service and charitably sent her home without punishment.[43]

There was one final item in the apprenticeship indenture that was subject to the "minute variation of two persons in symbiotic relationship"—the freedom dues. English custom and New English law held that "all servants that have served diligently and faithfully, to the benefit of their Masters, Seven years, shall not be sent away empty." But all indentures, whether for seven years or less, agreed upon specific dues, primarily to ensure that the servants would not become public charges when dismissed. The usual reward was two suits of clothing, "one suitable for Lords Days & other Publick Occasions, the other for every Days," as Swain Lawton's indenture read. A variety of other things were often promised as well: land, produce, seed, livestock, money, or tools. And sometimes, as Swain Lawton's father insisted, one of the apprentice's dues was to be the ability to "write a Legiable hand & Cypher as far as the Rule of three & to Read the English Bible." Such provisions, however, with one class of exceptions, were rare: for example, less than 16 per cent of more than 180 Massachusetts indentures drawn between 1620 and 1750 contained references to any of the 3Rs. Francis Worden complained to the Suffolk court with justice that training, clothing, *and* education was "more than is Comonly practiced to be put in Indentures." [44]

43. *Essex Co. Court Records,* March 1674, 5 : 290; Morgan, *Puritan Family,* p. 129n.; *New Haven Town Records,* 5 July 1653, 1 : 182–83; *Plymouth Records,* 6 March and 4 October 1655, 3 : 75, 91.
44. Towner, "A Good Master Well Served," pp. 46–49, Appendix A; *Colonial Laws of Massachusetts,* 1672, p. 105; *Conn. Records,* 1650, 1 : 539; Morris, *Government and Labor in Early America,* pp. 393–98.

In one sense it was unnecessary before 1695 to include educational provisions because a long series of laws in nearly every colony required parents and masters "to teach, by themselves or others, their Children and Apprentices, so much learning, as may enable them perfectly to read the English tongue, and knowledge of the Capital Lawes" and to "once a week (at the least) Catechize [them] in the Grounds and Principles of Religion." After 1695, however, such provisions would have served a useful purpose, for in that year the Privy Council disallowed two acts of the newly united legislature of Massachusetts and Plymouth which continued all compulsory educational legislation enacted before the advent of Sir Edmund Andros, governor of the Dominion of New England from 1686 to 1689. Because no law was passed between 1692 and the Revolution enjoining the formal education of *all* children —the exceptions were poor children bound out by the town selectmen—apprentices in the principal colony of New England received an education in basic literary skills solely with the sufferance of their parents and masters. Connecticut was little better in preserving its high seventeenth century standards, for by an act of 1702 parents and masters unable to teach their children and servants "perfectly to read the English Tongue" had only to compel them to memorize "some shorte orthodox Catechisme." [45]

The conditions of freedom, of course, were the fulfillment on both sides of the indenture contract. Servants who ran away before their time was up were often forced to serve double or triple the time absent at the end of their contractural term. Likewise, masters who failed to fulfill their obligations were often required to pay their servants additional freedom dues, such as the £15 that William Hailstone paid to Jonathan

---

45. *Colonial Laws of Massachusetts*, 1672, reiterating laws of 1642 and 1648, p. 26; *Conn. Records*, 1650, 1 : 520–21; Marcus Jernegan, *Laboring and Dependent Classes in Colonial America, 1607–1783* (New York, 1931), chap. 6, pp. 103–04, 109. For poor apprentices, see Jernegan, *Laboring and Dependent Classes*, chaps. 6–8; Towner, "A Good Master Well Served," chap. 3; and "The Indentures of Boston's Poor Apprentices: 1734–1805," *PCSM* 43 (1966) : 417–68.

Briggs because "hee did not learn him the trad[e] of a tayler."
Occasionally the parents of an apprentice would try to secure
his freedom prematurely, resorting to chicanery, legal or illegal, as the case demanded. Charles Attwood of Ipswich had
been indentured with his father's approval to William Baker
to serve until 1699, a period of thirteen years, when he would
be twenty-one years old. But the final "nine" was inadvertently omitted from the date and Charles took advantage of
the error by quitting two years early. Whereupon his master
prosecuted him for running away. When the widow Attwood
was told, "You know in your Conscience that the nine was
forgetfully omitted and that Charles time is not out till the
year 1699," she replied that "whatever was the Intent, that
which it writ must stand, and she had discovered several
understanding men about it, that said what was written must
stand." A literal-minded court upheld her interpretation;
Charles went free.[46]

The family of Hope Tyler, the thirteen-year-old servant of
Thomas Chandler of Andover, was more unscrupulous in its
efforts to secure his release. In 1658 Nathan Parker was asked
by both parties to "make a writing to bind Hope" to the
blacksmith's trade for 9½ years and to "keep said writing
safely, which he did for about three years between the joists
and the boards of the chamber." Job Tyler, the boy's father,
often asked Parker to let him have it, but he refused "because
it was agreed by both parties that [Parker] should keep it."
Finally Moses Tyler, Hope's older brother, and their mother
went one day to Parker's house when he and his wife were
away, removed the indenture, and returned home with it.
There, according to an eyewitness, Moses boasted, "I have
got my Brothers indentuers and nowe lat Chandler dou what
he can wee will take away Hope frome him" and burned it
"in the sight of his father." And then he said, "Now father
you may take away Hope when you will from Chandler and
let him prove a righting if he can." Fortunately for colonial

46. *Plymouth Records,* 6 June 1654, 3 : 51; *EIHC* 11 (1872) : 74–80,
235–38.

justice, the court restored the boy to the blacksmith, much to the chagrin of the Tylers, who had "gratly Tryemped" over their escapade.[47]

The elaborate efforts of some parents to free their children were far surpassed in the colonial period by countless bold and headlong dashes for freedom by the apprentices themselves.[48] There was something heady in the air of New England that emboldened young people to seek their liberty, real or imagined, for it began very early. In 1633, for instance, when two servants drowned while oyster fishing, John Winthrop concluded that their watery end was "an evident judgment of God upon them, for they were wicked persons. One of them, a little before, being reproved for his lewdness, and put in mind of hell, answered, that if hell were ten times hotter, he had rather be there than he would serve his master, etc. The occasion was, because he had bound himself for divers years, and saw that, if he had been at liberty, he might have had greater wages, though otherwise his master used him very well." John Clarke's goals were less clear, but his fondness for freedom was no less pronounced. At his trial in 1662 for running away three times from a kind and patient master, he confessed in private to the New Haven judges that he fled mainly "that he might goe where he might have more liberty, for one from Connecticutt [colony] told him if he lived there he might live merrily & sing & daunce." [49]

Most apprentices, however, did not run *to* an alluring goal but *away from* an unhappy situation, most typically physical abuse or violations of their indentures. Those who stayed and took their grievances to court more often than not won their just desserts; 55 percent of 200 Massachusetts cases were settled in the servant's favor. Not surprisingly, it took some family backing and a familiarity with the practice of Anglo-

47. *Essex Co. Court Records*, June 1662, 2 : 403–05.

48. Lawrence Towner counted 676 cases of runaway servants in the Massachusetts court records between 1620 and 1750 ("'A Fondness for Freedom:' Servant Protest in Puritan Society," *WMQ* 19 [April 1962] : 213).

49. *Winthrop's Journal*, 1 : 103–04; *New Haven Town Records*, 6 January 1662, 2 : 23–25.

American law to attempt legal recourse, both of which most apprentices—being white—enjoyed in the seventeenth century. In the eighteenth century, however, the Negro and Indian servant population, many of whom were enslaved or involuntarily bound by the state, rapidly outnumbered the white, and predictably the number of runaways increased dramatically. More than anything else, it was this change in the membership of the servant class that was instrumental in altering the nature and character of New English apprenticeship. For although the domestic economy of the family remained the backbone of the New England economy well into the eighteenth century, the educational function of the family began to diminish in the second half of the seventeenth and was supplemented by other institutions, many of them new to American society.[50]

Although to contemporaries this process had the appearance of unhealthy decline, it was an inevitable and salubrious lifting of responsibilities that the English family, in its move to a virgin society, had had to assume from the parish, the borough, and the state. Once the social development of New England had proceeded to a certain point, the family could slough off its excessive social burden and concentrate on its strongest talent—the nurture of its own children. In the process, unfortunately, apprenticeship came to be regarded less as an educational institution than as a solely economic one. As the personal, familial obligations that bound master and servant were reduced, the general educational functions of the apprentice-family were transferred to external agencies.

We have seen how, as early as the 1660s, a major portion of the responsibility for catechising children and apprentices fell to the churches and the towns. A further step in this direction was taken in 1702, when Cotton Mather told the masters of New England that they should "even *Hire* [their servants] to learn their *Catechisms,* rather than that they should not." In 1720 Boston got its first private evening school where "they whose Business won't permit 'em to attend the usual School

50. *WMQ* 19 (1962) : 201–19.

Hours, shall be carefully attended and instructed" in grammar, writing, mathematics, navigation, surveying, geography, and bookkeeping. Founded for the purpose of relieving masters of the indentured burden of teaching their servants to read, write, and cipher, the evening school eventually assumed part of their vocational responsibility as well and helped to transform the "mystery" of the Puritan calling into an economic commodity on the open market of public education. Next to go was the "domesticall government" of society's misfits and deviants. In 1727 the Connecticut General Assembly approved the erection of a house of correction in Hartford for "rogues, vagabonds, common beggars, and other lewd, idle dissolute and disorderly persons," whose choice company included "runaways, stubborn servants and children [and] such as neglect their callings, mispend what they earn, and do not provide for themselves or the support of their families." It was symbolic of many of the changes in New England society that in the northwestern corner of the New Haven green in 1748 stood the grammar school, cheek by jowl with the jail, the poorhouse, and the court house, all within the ken of the imposing First Church.[51]

At the end of July 1728, "having got in [his] Hay, Rice, Barley, and Wheat," the Reverend Ebenezer Parkman of Westborough dismissed his hired servant. Three weeks earlier their last serving girl had been taken home by her mother, causing "much Trouble and Concern with us respecting our weak-handedness." "Now," he noted in his diary with some astonishment, "we are intirely alone, having no Servant nor any one in the House. Our Loneliness gives Scope for Thought." One of the thoughts he might well have had was for the future calling of his year-old-son, who would seventeen years

51. Cotton Mather, *Cares about the Nurserie* (Boston, 1702), p. 45; Robert Seybolt, *The Private Schools of Colonial Boston* (Cambridge, Mass., 1935), p. 15; Robert Seybolt, *The Evening School in Colonial America* (Urbana, 1925); *Conn. Records,* 12 October 1727, 7 : 127–30; Wadsworth map of New Haven (1748, New Haven, Yale University Library).

later reject his father's choice of a clerical calling to become
a farmer. Another might have been the memory of talking
with his maid servant two years earlier and finding that "she
had received but very barely in her Education," but never
stopping to consider that the blame may have belonged less
to her own family than to her new one. Nor could he have
foreseen that ten years later he would buy the time of a wild
Irish boy and have his house defiled when the lad tried to
rape his thirteen-year-old daughter. In the summer of 1728 he
simply could not see the changes that would transform the
educational role of apprenticeship in colonial New England.[52]

52. *PAAS*, n.s. 71 (1961) : 155, 219–21, 444; 72 (1962) : 54–58.

4

And Each in His Place

A miserable Thing to be a rebel.
John Brock

A child born in any land is a stranger to equality. From birth he knows only bigger and presumably better people. His parents and his brothers and sisters all loom above him in stature and skill, and despite all their efforts to pull him into maturity, he can never forget that they all have a headstart. Even as he grows into manhood on a physical par with his family, he cannot easily erase the hereditary boundaries that separate them or the subtle lines of authority and affection that bind them. And when he steps outside the home, the established order is still felt, perhaps even more openly. The child's world is a hierarchy from the day he enters it, and unless the idea of social equality is consciously learned, it will never intrude upon his intellectual horizons.

In colonial New England the child's world, like his parents', was a tightly ordered, highly reticulated organism. It was universally believed that "God Almightie in his most holy and wise providence hath soe disposed of the Condicion of man-kinde, as in all times some must be rich, some poore, some highe and eminent in power and dignitie; others meane and in subjeccion." [1] One of the chief goals in educating the New English child was, therefore, to show him his proper place in

1. John Winthrop, "A Modell of Christian Charity," in Edmund Morgan, ed., *The Founding of Massachusetts* (Indianapolis, 1964), p. 190.

his society, to help him understand the necessity of his place-ment there, and to give him appropriate manners and means of expressing his relationship with others.

All societies are arranged in some way that promotes their communal goals. There can be no coherent social life unless the social relationships that bind people together are at least to some extent orderly, institutionalized, and predictable. If they are not, chaos reigns and society dissolves. Therefore people must be subjected to a degree of compulsion to main-tain the normal expectations of social relations. Every society has rules, written or unwritten, and means of enforcing them which seek to constrain the behavior of its members. Though these rules and means differ greatly in each society, their pur-pose is the same: to ensure the degree of social order without which the purposes of the society would be defeated.

As children are born into a society, they are educated into its cultural patterns, the particular modes of thinking, acting, and feeling that its members share. Among these patterns are the social constraints they are expected to endure for the sake of social order. No single agency, but society as a whole, is responsible for helping the child to define his social iden-tity, a task which is tailored to the society's particular condi-tions, needs, and goals.[2]

When the English colonists came to educate their children in the social mores of their new society, they responded to the forces of their English heritage, as well as to the special conditions of the American wilderness. The dominant cos-mology of seventeenth century men was rooted in the concep-tion of a "great chain of being" that stretched in serried regu-larity from God's very throne to the meanest of inanimate objects. To disturb that hierarchy, or the internal hierarchies of each of the links, was to risk the unleashing of elemental forces beyond man's comprehension. "When degree is shak'd . . . the enterprise," whether cosmic, social or domestic, "is sick."

2. Alfred Kroeber, *Anthropology* (New York, 1948), chap. 1, sec. 6; John Beattie, *Other Cultures* (New York, 1964), chaps. 9–10.

How could communities,
Degrees in schools and brotherhoods in cities,
Peaceful commerce from dividable shores,
The primogenitive and due of birth,
Prerogative of age, crowns, sceptres, laurels,
But by degree stand in authentic place?
Take but degree away, untune that string,
And hark, what discord follows!

As the English church had known for nearly a century, a world view that yoked the cosmos with the social order would not be taken lightly by men responsible for giving their children a sense of social place. This was a certainty that lost no force when men quarrelled with the Church, or even moved to another continent. It was an implicit—and often explicit—assumption of the settlers of colonial New England.[3]

The second premise shared by Stuart Englishmen was the reprobative nature of the newborn child. Benjamin Wadsworth's grim description would have found few demurrers in the seventeenth, or even eighteenth, century:

Their Hearts naturally, are a meer nest, root, fountain of Sin, and wickedness; an *evil Treasure* from whence proceed *evil things*, viz. *Evil Thoughts, Murders, Adulteries* &c. Indeed, as sharers in the guilt of *Adam's* first Sin, they're *Children of Wrath by Nature*, liable to Eternal Vengeance, the Unquencheable Flames of Hell. But besides this, their Hearts (as hath been said) are unspeakable wicked, estrang'd from God, enmity against Him, eagerly set in pursuing Vanities, on provoking God by actual Personal transgressions, whereby they merit and deserve greater measures of Wrath.

Parents were not to be fooled by the child's size, for "though his bodie be but small, yet he hath a great heart, and is al-

---

3. William Shakespeare, *Troilus and Cressida*, act 1, sc. 3, lines 101–10; "An exhortation concerning good order, and obedience to Rulers and Magistrates," *Certaine Sermons appointed by the Queenes Majestie* (London, 1595), sigs. I2v–I3v.

together inclined to evill: and the more he wexeth in reason by yeares, the more he groweth proud, froward, wilfull, unrulie, and disobedient." Inevitably these "fruits of natural corruption and roots of actual rebellion both against God and man" had to be exorcised before the child could enjoy the society of men.[4]

Perhaps the strongest legacy of the past was one that is seldom felt yet holds inexorable sway over the thoughts and actions of most men. They are uneasy when persuaded by the force of reason alone; in their complexity, they need the assurance of something that transcends the rational. Custom is one such source of assurance. When the New English colonists began to educate their children for their new life, it was the simple custom of centuries of social stratification and deference that lent the greatest support to their designs. Like their parents before them, they remembered vividly their own education by adults who knew the exact dimensions of their social place and the proper ways of relating to persons beyond its perimeter. Since neither time nor distance could obliterate the colonist's memory of education as socialization for a highly structured society, that memory fittingly served as the emotional counterpoint to their educational efforts in the new world.

But equally decisive in delimiting the colonial task was the New England wilderness. The novelty of Indians, rattlesnakes, and wolves was much less challenging than the sheer loss of community that emigration entailed. The security and familiarity of ancient English towns and villages gave way to the imposing forests, broad waters, and mercurial climate of North America. The hostile "howling desarts" forced the settlers to gather in communal enclaves, but the trickle of emigration never supplied enough people for more than a handful of substantial towns. In 1710, for example, Massachu-

4. Benjamin Wadsworth, "The Nature of Early Piety," *A Course of Sermons on Early Piety* (*Boston*, 1721), p. 10; John Dod and Robert Cleaver, *A godly forme of housholde governement* (London, 1612), sig. S8r.–v.; *The Works of John Robinson,* ed. Robert Ashton (Boston, 1851), 1 : 246.

setts had barely sixty thousand inhabitants, less than a hundred adult males in the average town. Even as late as 1765, only fifteen towns among some two hundred had populations of twenty-five hundred. On the eve of the Revolution, Connecticut had fewer than two hundred thousand souls. The distances between communities, therefore, remained long, and isolation prevailed.[5]

But this was only isolation of the social whole. Within each town, the limits of physical space and the ubiquity of children, neighbors, and townsmen contributed to a dense collective experience. Living at such close quarters was a powerful incentive for men to abide by acknowledged rules of social conduct. For the frequent and naked encounters of a face-to-face society, if not regulated and guided by a larger concern for the group, can easily tear the fragile understanding that binds it together.[6]

The final circumstance to which the colonists responded was their remoteness from the source of executive power. The Atlantic Ocean stood between their commonwealth and Whitehall. Even the General Court at Boston, which from the founding of the colony had been the source of law and order, could be effectively ignored after the charter of 1691 imposed a royal governor and council, as it had been to some extent throughout the previous sixty years. With executive authority removed to England, only the towns could impose the constraints vital to social harmony. But there too, adequate agencies of enforcement were notoriously lacking, throwing the responsibility for social order back upon the community as a whole. Thus the crucial role for education was created, for without an inner acceptance by the townsmen of the canons of order, there could scarcely have been any order at all.

5. Michael Zuckerman, *Peaceable Kingdoms: New England Towns in the Eighteenth Century* (New York, 1970), p. 47; J. Potter, "The Growth of Population in America, 1700–1860," *Population in History*, ed. D. V. Glass and D. E. C. Eversley (London, 1965), p. 650.

6. Zuckerman, *Peaceable Kingdoms*, pp. 47–48; John Demos, *A Little Commonwealth: Family Life in Plymouth Colony* (New York, 1970), pp. 33, 47.

There was simply no external agency powerful enough to compel compliance.[7]

All these conditions defined the colonists' need for a serried society that sorted its children into proper stations and taught them respect for authority. New England's response to this need is revealed in its choice of educational goals, the ideal characteristics they held up for their children to emulate. Significantly, these qualities were most frequently and most forcefully expressed in the negative, a habit in character with the age's limited and negative view of childhood. Instead of giving positive encouragement to the child, New English parents tried to dissuade him from becoming "disobedient, wilful, stubborn, untractable, independent, contentious, insubordinate, rebellious, unwieldy, inflexible, obstinate, and proud." [8] The assumption, of course, was that the child's natural tendencies inevitably leaned toward these unsocial qualities. Consequently, New England primarily educated its children, not toward an ideal of human nature, but away from a postlapsarian Adamic character; instead of guiding and nurturing the natural child, it did its best to suppress and remake him.

Such a view of childhood must have made the educational process doubly difficult for the adult society, not to mention the children themselves. For motivationally, it is simply harder to work against something than for it; but, more important, the child himself could never be asked or trusted to advance his own education. Society expected to carry the burden of education alone, and it was not denied this role. This may help to explain why the full force of society—its individuals, groups, and institutions—was needed to ensure even minimal success in giving its children a sense of social place.

Long before New England was even conceived, the English

7. Zuckerman, *Peaceable Kingdoms*, chaps. 1, 3.
8. Most of these descriptive adjectives can be found in John Robinson's essay "Of Children and their Education" (*Works of John Robinson*, 1 : 242–51).

church had prepared its members for their own roles as sustainers of the social order. At least once a year, and especially in times of social unrest, the parish priest or his curate read from the official book of homilies "an exhortation concerning good order, and obedience to Rulers and Magistrates." After being reminded that "Almighty God hath created and appointed all thinges in heaven, earth and waters, in a most excellent and perfect order," the congregation was instructed in the implications of the correspondence of the natural order and human society.

> Every degree of people in their vocation, calling and office, hath appointed to them their duety and order: some are in high degree, some in low, some kings and Princes, some inferiors and subjects, Priests, and lay-men, Maisters and Servauntes, fathers and Children, husbandes and wives, riche and poore, and every one have neede of other, so that in all things is to be lauded and praised the goodly order of God, without the which, no house, no Citye, no commonwealth can continue and endure or last. For where there is no right order, there raigneth all abuse, carnal libertie, enormitie, sin, & Babilonicall confusion. Take away kings, Princes, Rulers, Magistrats, judges, & such estates of Gods order, no man shall ride or goe by the high way unrobbed, no man shal sleep in his own house or bed unkilled, no man shal keep his wife, children, and possessions in quietnes, all things shall be common, and there must needs follow all mischeife, and utter distruction both of soules, bodies, goods, commonweales.[9]

And as they were listening to the priest's message, many of them must have remembered from their own childhood their response to the catechist when he asked, "What is thy duty towards thy Neighbour?": ". . . . To honour and obey the King, and all that are put in authority under him. To submit

9. *Certaine Sermons appointed by the Queenes Majestie*, sigs. I2v.–I3v.

myself to all my governors, teachers, spiritual pastors and
masters. To order myself lowly and reverently to all my betters. . . ." [10]

When an Englishman finally left his parish to cast his lot
with New England, his new church offered additional help in
his preparation for social teaching. Indeed, the covenant by
which he bound himself to his new community contained the
central message. Its form was unanimous consent, and a pledge
of peace was an essential part of its substance. Because it was
voluntarily subscribed to and thus morally binding, the "mutual love and respect" sworn by the community "bound up
together in a bundle of life" received human as well as divine
sanction. To break it was to alienate oneself from the benefit
of law and the trust of men; to uphold it was to commit oneself to rigid conformity.[11]

As in England, on normal occasions and rare, sermons am-
plified the call for authority. "God hath suited Duties to the
several Orders, which He hath placed Men in," observed
Samuel Willard in 1703 from the pulpit of Boston's South
Church, "[but] these Duties cannot be mutually discharged, as
they ought, without a due respect born each to other, according to the Order wherein they stand so related." In one of
his earliest sermons in the new world, Thomas Shepard warned
the voters of Massachusetts that the "Sins of men are like [the]
raging Sea, which would overwhelm all if they have not
bankes; the bankes are wholesom lawes. These bankes will
breake down unles some keep them. Hence magistrates."
Thirty-five years later, he observed with sadness the mounting signs of withdrawal from God in New England: contempt
for the clergy and magistracy, fatigue from covenant obliga-

10. "A Catechism," *The Book of Common Prayer . . . According to the
Use of the Church of England* (London, 1620).

11. Zuckerman, *Peaceable Kingdoms*, pp. 54–56. The covenant in New
England soon outgrew its Puritan origins to serve traditionalism as "a
felt-need evoked by the very nature of the settlement process." Even an
eighteenth century Anglican church in Connecticut was formed by the
covenant of its members (Darrett Rutman, *American Puritanism* [Phila-
delphia, 1970], p. 125).

tions, pride and "a spirit of sovereign, *unsociable,* rigid *independency.*" Connecticut's William Burnham knew the consequences of religious declension. Without government and order, he said, the world would soon become "a heap of Confusion, a stage of mournful Tragedies, a Theater of woful Spectacles." Since it is God who disposes all people in their proper stations, "Persons of a Lower Rank should not Envy those of a more Exalted Station. It becometh us to submit to, and acquiesce in Gods Providence in this matter, because he hath done it. . . . He knows how to Rule the world better than we do." But Jeremiah Wise of Berwick, Maine, went to the heart of the matter for the parents in his audience in 1729. In civilizing children, he assured them, education

> takes down their Temper, tames the Fierceness of their Natures, forms their minds to vertue, learns'em to carry it with a just Deference to *Superiours;* makes them tractable or manageable; and by learning and knowing what it is to be *under Government,* they will know the better how to *govern others,* when it comes to their Turn.

Certainly the parents would not have been struck by the secondary place given to the positive encouragement of "forming their minds to vertue." In that regard, as in so many others, advice from the church and the social assumptions of New England were of a piece.[12]

The children, too, felt the weight of religious authority as they were being fitted for the social order. The one book that nearly every New English child knew, *The New England Primer,* let no opportunity slip to inculcate the habits of obedience and social duty. One of the many sentences to be memorized was "The Dutiful Child's Promise": "I will fear GOD, and honour the KING. I will honour my Father &

12. Samuel Willard, *A Compleat Body of Divinity* (Boston, 1726), p. 598; Thomas Shepard, 1638 election sermon, *NEHGR* 24 (1870) : 363; Thomas Shepard, *Eye-Salve* (Boston, 1673), p. 23 (my emphasis); William Burnham, *God's Providence in Placing Men in their Respective Stations* (New London, 1722), pp. 2, 17; Jeremiah Wise, *Rulers the Ministers of God* (Boston, 1729), p. 31.

Mother. I will obey my Superiours. I will submit to my Elders. . . . I will as much as in me lies keep all God's Holy Commandments. I will learn my Catechism. . . ." So as to leave no doubt, the Westminster *Shorter Catechism* or John Cotton's *Spiritual Milk for Boston Babes* was always appended to provide a concise explanation of the Fifth Commandment, which "requireth the preserving the Honour & performing the Duties belonging to every one in their several Places and Relations, as Superiours, Inferiours, or Equals." And lest the child misjudge the gravity of that commandment, an "Alphabet of Lessons for Youth" reminded him of the cause and consequence of failure: "Foolishness is bound up in the heart of a Child, but the rod of Correction shall drive it far from him." The child's life was obviously a hard one in such a land of self-fulfilling prophecy.[13]

Some lessons were overt; others were learned, not from words, but from actions or social situations, such as the way the congregation was seated in the meetinghouse each Sabbath. As the microcosm of the whole community, the seating arrangements in a new church were the equivalent of a "new edition of the social register." Boxford's experience was not untypical. In January, 1701, the town meeting selected a five-man committee to seat "our inhabitanc in our meting hous a Cording to thair Sivel wrights, having Regard Chefly to Esteats yet soe as to have Respacts to ould age." Over the next two years, certain members of the congregation, out of a sense of injustice, or plain orneriness, refused to sit in their assigned seats, and a town meeting was called to discuss their case. They could not have been pleased with the verdict, which warned that "thoes that wil not sit in thair seats . . . may Justly be coled *brackers of good order* and have a fien layed upon them that will sit forwerder then they shal be seted."

Little difficulty arose from age, for that was ascertainable, but the criterion of tangible estate and the more elusive touchstone of "Sivel wrights" were universal bones of con-

13. *The New-England Primer,* ed. Paul L. Ford (New York, 1897).

tention in New England. Boxford, for example, was a small town of small farmers nearly upon an economic level; the richest man in the tax list of 1687 owned but twenty acres, four oxen, and three horses and paid a modest 13s. 6d. As for the "Sivel wrights" and dignity thereof, only military rank or public office was readily known. The social conflict, therefore, that brewed almost constantly in the colonial meetinghouse offered a lesson that could not have been missed by children segregated to rickety galleries or drafty back benches.[14]

In a life full of lessons for the children of New England, even death possessed a certain eloquence. In a culture beset and preoccupied with man's mortality, the threat of death was frequently invoked to secure the obedience of the young. Early in the seventeenth century John Robinson presented the issue with chilling simplicity: "The Lord promises and affords long life to such a 'honour father and mother'. . . . On the other side, he cuts off from the earth stubborn and disobedient children suddenly and in sundry ways." By the eighteenth century the traumatic potential of such advice had not diminished. Cotton Mather could not disguise his meaning when he let the young people of New England know that "God will do dreadful things upon you, if you do not *hearken* to [your parents]." In addressing a young men's religious society, Daniel Lewes beat around no verbal bushes. "Undutiful rebellious Children," he assured them, "often dye in such manner, that what their Sin was may be read in the Punishment of it." No further word was needed to describe the lot of those "Children flagitious" who stood condemned at the left hand of Christ on Judgement Day.[15]

14. Ola Winslow, *Meetinghouse Hill, 1630–1783* (New York, 1952), chap. 9; *EIHC* 36 (1900): 78, 91 (my emphasis). See also Robert Dinkin, "Seating the Meeting House in Early Massachusetts," *New England Quarterly,* September 1970, pp. 450–64.

15. *Works of John Robinson,* 1 : 250; Cotton Mather, *Repeated Warnings* (Boston, 1712), p. 9; Daniel Lewes, *The Sins of Youth, Remembred with Bitterness* (Boston, 1725), p. 7; Michael Wigglesworth, *The Day of Doom* (Cambridge, Mass., 1662), stanza 33.

The church was an important school of order, but, on the clergy's own admission, the home was supreme. If the family could not instil a sense of place and the habit of obedience, the more impersonal institutions of society could hardly be expected to restore the loss. As Benjamin Wadsworth put it:

Without *Family care* the labour of Magistrates and Ministers for Reformation and Propagating Religion, is likely to be in a great measure unsuccessful. It's much to be fear'd, Young Persons wont much mind what's said by Ministers in Publick, if they are not Instructed at home: nor will they much regard good Laws made by Civil Authority, if they are not well counsel'd and govern'd at home.

The reason, an election preacher demonstrated, was uncomplicated. " 'Tis natural for Children to think their Parents to be the most wise and powerful of Mankind. . . . As they grow up, if they are not well governed, they are prone enough to improve their young Logic to this conclusion, viz. That their Superiours in Church or State, must yield to their Stubborn Wills." Discipline within the family was necessary to ensure harmony without, for the reigning assumption of the time was that families, not individuals, were "the Constituent Parts of Nations, and Kingdoms." Consequently, it was assumed that *"Well-ordered Families* naturally produce a *Good Order* in other *Societies."* [16]

The opportunities for social education within the family were, as they are today, numerous. The family—the primary matrix of the emotional development of the child—also bears primary responsibility for his sense of social place, his understanding of the various statuses he will occupy in the social order, and his ability to perform the roles expected of each. Through their guidance, responses, and love, the members of

16. Benjamin Wadsworth, *The Well-Ordered Family* (Boston, 1712), p. 84; John Swift, *A Sermon* (Boston, 1732), p. 24; Deodat Lawson, *The Duty & Property of a Religious Housholder* (Boston, 1693), p. 51; Cotton Mather, *A Family Well-Ordered* (Boston, 1699), p. 3.

a family give the child his first rewards and punishments, his first self-image, and his first models of social behavior.[17]

Obviously the task was a large one for families isolated in a strange wilderness, but they lacked for nothing in the way of advice from the Puritan clergy. A prodigious literature of "household government" existed to ensure that the Fifth Commandment was properly obeyed by every member of society in his several relations with others. Children, for their part, should be taught to be "Respectful to [their parents], to Civil Rulers, to Ecclesiastical Rulers, to all Superiors in age or Office. Yea, . . . to all persons whatsoever, according to their Rank and Station." Few contemporaries would have quarrelled with Hezekiah Woodward's opinion that "obedience is the best lesson that a parent can teach the childe," but most perhaps would have balked at his conclusion. Unlike the common stock of English pedagogues, this gentle Puritan schoolmaster argued that teachers and parents should "handle the child freely and liberally, in a sweet and milde way." Harshness, he knew from his own schooldays, "loseth the heart, and alienates the affections." [18]

Far more typical of the seventeenth century was the prescription of John Robinson, who, as the minister to the Plymouth colony, was impressed by the child's innate "stubbornness, and stoutness of mind arising from natural pride."

> For the beating, and keeping down of this stubbornness parents must provide carefully for two things: first that children's wills and wilfulness be restrained and repressed, and that, in time; lest sooner than they imagine, the tender sprigs grow to that stiffness, that they will rather break than bow. Children should not know, if it could be kept from them, that they have a will in their own,

17. Frederick Elkin, *The Child and Society: The Process of Socialization* (New York, 1960); Charles H. Cooley, *Human Nature and the Social Order* (New York, 1902).

18. Wadsworth, *Well-Ordered Family*, p. 53; *British Journal of Educational Studies*, 9 (May 1961) : 136. See also William Gouge, *Of Domesticall Duties* (London, 1634), p. 159: "The best duty that a parent can doe for his childe, *Admonition of the Lord*."

but in their parents' keeping. . . . The second help is an
inuring of them from the first, to such a meanness in all
things, as may rather pluck them down, than lift them
up: as by plain, and homely diet, and apparel; sending
them to school betimes; and bestowing them afterwards,
as they are fit, in some course of life, in which they may
be exercised diligently, and the same rather under than
above their estate; by not abetting them one against
another, nor against any, specially before their faces,
without great cause: nor by making them men and women, before they become good boys and girls.

Although he was aware of the danger of producing "base-
spirited and abject" creatures with the rod, he discounted it on
the strength of his religious assumptions: "for being Adam's
sons . . . they will not easily be found unfurnished of stomach
and stoutness of mind more than enough; wherein a little is
dangerous, specially for making them unmeet for Christ's
yoke, and to learn of him, who was lowly and meek." And
although the mindless ease of corporal punishment was
sufficient argument for some parents, William Gouge revealed
a worthier benefit to parents: "It freeth them from the guilt
of their childrens sinne, so as they are not accessory thereto."
To a people fraught with a sense of sin, that was a reason more
welcome than most.[19]

In teaching their children appropriate attitudes and behavior toward the rest of society, each family could naturally
resort to many different methods. But because of the imitative
and flexible nature of young children, Puritan writers recommended that parents provide a good personal example of any
values or actions they wished their children to learn. Dod and
Cleaver believed that

Verball instruction, without example of good deeds, is a
dead doctrine; and contrariwise, good examples are the
life of instruction, to make it profitable and effectuall.

19. *Works of John Robinson,* 1 : 246–48; Gouge, *Of Domesticall Duties,*
p. 562.

. . . Children profit more by good *example* in one month, than by instruction in a whole yeare. . . . Experience teacheth us that children like or mislike more by countenance, gesture and behaviour, than by any rule, doctrine, or precept whatsoever.[20]

Instruction and admonition were necessary to the educational process, but the persuasiveness of parents as models could drive those lessons home most effectually. And because of this influence, the social relations within the family could and did serve as the principal model for those without. The way children were taught to behave toward the members of their own families was a paradigm for their behavior toward every other member of society in their several relations because of the direct correspondence between the order of families, of societies, and of creation. The responses appropriate to one were universally appropriate to the others because they were all hierarchies. Wherever in any pyramid of order one was placed, be it family or universe, the attitudes and behavior expected of that position were the same as in any other order. Children, then, had essentially to learn only behavior appropriate to their family, especially their parents, to be prepared for social intercourse with society at large. Although Puritan casuists frequently addressed themselves to the duties of children to the larger society, their efforts were unnecessary, though not lost, for the lessons of the one order were equally germane to the other.

The duty of children to their parents was generally understood to consist of due subjection of their authority, and relief and maintenance of them in their old age and necessity. Under the first and foremost responsibility it was expected that "they obey their parents, and doe serve them, and also do feare, love, honour, and reverence them; not onely in word and deed, but in their hearts and mindes also, that they follow their good precepts and examples of life, [and] that

20. Dod and Cleaver, *A godly forme of housholde governement,* sigs. Q8v., T5v.

they patiently take correction at their hands," or, as Samuel
Willard expressed it, "with great Submission" and "an Obe-
diential Frame and Carriage." Beyond that the formal advice
seldom went, giving to each family the freedom of detail and
nuance.[21]

Yet in their discussions of the importance of good manners,
which always offered "many precepts of reverencing our superiours, and carying our selves with respect one to another,"
the ministers indicated in some detail how they expected
children to behave toward their parents. According to one of
the most popular Puritan treatises, children should be taught
to "rise up to their betters, to uncover the head, to make
obeisance, to be curteous towards their equals, to be gentle and
loving to their inferiours, and loving and kind to all." They
must always allow their betters to speak first and to "keepe
silence while their betters are in place, untill they be spoken
unto, and then they must make answer in few words, without
unnecessary circumstances, and directly to the matter."

The "gesture of their bodies," as the outward expression of
their inner feelings, was equally important. Children were
admonished to

1. meet those that are comming towards them.
2. rise up to elders and betters, when they passe by them.
3. stand while their betters are sitting in place.
4. bend the knee, in token of humilitie and subjection.
5. give the cheife place to their betters, and to offer the
   same to others in courtesie.
6. uncover their head.

The specificity of Dod and Cleaver's advice was untypical of
the literature of "household government," for they were writing
for Englishmen whose assumptions of social behavior were
widely shared and largely unquestioned. Theirs was a society
untouched by social revolution and still bound by the example

21. Ibid., sig. Y1r.; Willard, *Compleat Body of Divinity*, p. 607; Wadsworth, *Well-Ordered Family*, pp. 90–99.

of a mannerly court and the habits of deference. As the major part of Puritan casuists realized, there was little reason in such a setting to articulate the details of good manners; general principles were sufficient.[22]

But the physical and emotional landscape of New England was dramatically different, as the *Mayflower*'s passengers discovered when they stepped ashore at Plymouth in 1620.

> Being thus passed the vast ocean, and a sea of troubles before in their preparation . . . they had now no friends to welcome them nor inns to entertain or refresh their weatherbeaten bodies; no houses or much less towns to repair to, to seek for succour. . . . If they looked behind them, there was the mighty ocean which they had passed and was now as a main bar and gulf to separate them from *all the civil parts of the world.*

Throughout the colonial period, and indeed until the frontiers of the west were finally closed in the late nineteenth century, Americans worried about the dangers of "barbarism," "rudeness," "Criolian degeneracy," and "heathenish ignorance" because they felt separated from "all the civil parts of the world" and surrounded by the satanic wiles of the Indian. Under such anxiety they understandably attached great importance to the forms of civilized behavior which their English contemporaries could take for granted.[23]

Josiah Cotton, responding to the social conditions of eighteenth century Plymouth, spoke for many colonists who were forced to adjust their advice and their actions to the new world. In 1723 this Harvard-bred schoolmaster and public servant moved his family from the center of Plymouth to his wife's estate two miles in the country. He was pleased that his nine children were now "at further distance from the evils incident to a populous place," yet at the same time he re-

22. Gouge, *Of Domesticall Duties*, p. 538; Dod and Cleaver, *A godly forme of housholde governement*, sigs. R7v.–S2r.
23. William Bradford, *Of Plymouth Plantation, 1620–1647*, ed. Samuel Eliot Morison (New York, 1952), pp. 61–62 (my emphasis).

minded himself to "regulate [his] Children & Servants better," obviously because they were equally removed from the civilizing potential of the town. Thus, torn between the city and the country, he was compelled to specify the "rules for [his children's] observation" that would effectively make the home the center of civilization in the New England wilderness. According to his list, the Cotton children were expected

1. To pray as soon as they awake in the morning & going to bed at night.
2. To make a bow or Curtesy when they see their Superiours first in a Morning, & when going to bed at night, & when they give or take anything from them, & when prayers are done in the family &c.
3. Not to speak when others are speaking, nor talk too much or all at once, nor speak before they think.
4. Not to behave themselves aukwardly or untowardly by Gaping, Staring &c.
5. Not to repeat what others say, or stand listening when they have other business to mind.
6. Not to Contend or fight with one another.
7. To keep themselves neat & clean, & to be so in everything.
8. Not to seat themselves first at the Table nor to stand between others & the fire, or put things out of their places.
9. Not to stay too long when sent on an Errand or desert the business & Duty required of them.
10. To use proper Titles & terms to men & Women.
11. To stand up at Craving a Blessing & returning thanks, & to behave themselves decently in all other parts of divine Worship & at all other times.[24]

They cannot have disappointed him much since he considered that a man's children are "himself multiplied; and

24. Memoirs of Josiah Cotton, Mass. His. Soc., pp. 160, 167–68. *The School of Good Manners*, a detailed compilation by Eleazar Moody from earlier English manuals of the same title, was reprinted several times in the colonies between 1715 and the Revolution.

the greater the sum the better, provided they take good courses and are faithful in their generation. Happy is the man," said this father of fourteen, "that hath his quiver full of them." [25]

The final effectiveness of the New English father in giving his children a sense of social place, however, did not spring from his ability to enumerate the points of civilized behavior, or brandish a ready birch, or even to set an emulous example. Children obeyed their parents for all these reasons—and many more, as we shall see—but perhaps the simplest reason of all was that their fathers often controlled the pursestrings of their futures.

In any farming community, the distribution and use of land are of central importance in shaping both the community itself and the character of the family life of its residents. Because of the value and indispensability of land, the patterns of inheritance decide ultimately the measure of a father's authority over his children. In rural New England, as in all farming communities, young men waited to marry until they could support a wife and household, which normally meant until they possessed enough productive farm land of their own to do so. In some communities, however, their fathers held a virtual monopoly of the existing land. This left the sons with three alternatives: they could sever the bonds of kinship by moving to an undeveloped area of the colony to establish a new town (if a grant of land could be obtained from the provincial government); they could try to earn enough money to buy any land available in the town or a bond of apprenticeship to a craftsman; or they could stay at home and work their father's fields until his death brought them final independence through inheritance. The first alternative was never popular, the second difficult, so most sons probably endured the strains of patriarchalism in anticipation of its future rewards.[26]

25. *Sibley's Harvard Graduates*, 4 : 402. Five of his children died in infancy.

26. Philip Greven, Jr., *Four Generations: Population, Land, and Family in Colonial Andover, Massachusetts* (Ithaca, 1970), chaps. 3–4; Kenneth Lockridge, *A New England Town, The First Hundred Years: Dedham, Massachusetts, 1636–1736* (New York, 1970), pp. 74–75; Sumner C. Powell,

Some suffered more than others, for the more authoritarian the father, the longer the son had to wait to become his own master. In Andover, Massachusetts, for example, the degree of patriarchalism was—untypically perhaps—very strong. The first generation of settlers, though they accumulated very large estates by English standards, an average of almost two hundred acres, were reluctant to part with any appreciable part of them during their lifetimes. Only two founding fathers divided their land before their deaths among all of their sons and gave the sons deeds of gift for their portions. Nine others gave outright deeds of gift to only one or two sons, keeping the rest in economic dependence. Fourteen, on the other hand, carried the title of all their land to their deathbeds, passing control to their children only through their last wills and testaments. Consequently, though direct evidence is scarce, there was probably an important transfer of deference from the economic to the wider social sphere. "Sons who were dutiful, obedient, and in some measure dependent were probably the rule among the extended, patriarchal families of seventeenth-century Andover." In New England towns of a similar nature, similarly desirable behavior must have obtained.[27]

In spite of the best intentions, the New England home was incapable of being an educational law unto itself. The centrifugal forces of a growing economy and the congenital imperfection of human parents made the supervision of the state necessary. In its very conception, New England was expected to be a holier place than England, so the details of personal and social conduct had to be overseen with greater

---

Puritan Village: The Formation of a New England Town (Middletown, Conn., 1963), chaps. 8–9; Charles Grant, *Democracy in the Connecticut Frontier Town of Kent* (New York, 1961).

27. Greven, *Four Generations*, pp. 59, 82–83, 99n.; Kenneth Lockridge, "Land, Population, and the Evolution of New England Society, 1630–1790," *Past and Present* 39 (April 1968) : 64–66. John Demos has noted a similar economic basis of moral control in Plymouth Colony in the seventeenth century ("Notes on Life in Plymouth Colony," *WMQ* 22 [1965] : 282).

zeal. But since "the generality of the colony [was] very near upon a level, more than common provision was necessary to enforce a due obedience to the laws, and to establish and preserve the authority of the government."

> For, although some amongst them had handsome fortunes, yet in general their estates were small, barely sufficient to provide them houses and necessary accommodations; a contempt of authority was therefore next to a capital offence. The country being new and uncultivated, the utmost industry, oeconomy, and frugality were necessary to their subsistance, and laws, with heavy penalties, to enforce the observance of them. They were in the midst of savages, whose numbers were much greater than their own, and were under continual alarms and apprehensions of danger, and a strict discipline could not be dispensed with. [Also] they were at their full liberty, the troubles in England taking off from the colonies, the attention of the several successions of supreme power there, for near thirty years together.[28]

Growing sensitivity to these conditions in the early years of settlement prompted the Massachusetts General Court to exercise special care for the right ordering of children and servants in the revised edition of their *Lawes and Libertyes,* first published in 1641. Two articles were added to the 1649 version which strengthened the family's authority over its young members. The first ruled that, if any child above sixteen years of age and "of sufficient understanding, shall CURSE, or SMITE their natural FATHER, or MOTHER," he shall be put to death, unless it could be testified that the parents had been "very unchristianly negligent" in his education or had so provoked him by "extream & cruel correction" that he was forced to protect himself from "death or maim-

28. George Haskins, *Law and Authority in Early Massachusetts* (New York, 1960), pp. 78, 81–82; Edmund Morgan, *The Puritan Family* (New York, 1966), pp. 142–43; Thomas Hutchinson, *The History of the Colony and Province of Massachusetts-Bay,* ed. Lawrence Mayo (Cambridge, Mass., 1936), 1 : 370.

ing." Death was also the sentence for any "STUBBORNE or REBELLIOUS SON of sufficient yeares and understanding" who would not obey his parents or hearken to their chastisements. Theoretically, no children could plead ignorance of the laws because the school law of 1642 ordered the selectmen of every town to see that no family neglected to teach their children "so much learning, as may enable them perfectly to read the english tongue, & knowledg of the Capital laws." But in reality the situation must have been very different, to judge from the absence of court presentments on the children's behalf. Colonial magistrates must have entertained similar suspicions of parental performance because they never pronounced the maximum sentence to send a child to the gallows.[29]

But they were never hesitant to order the "severe whipping" of any boy—girls were somehow too delicate or more virtuous —convicted of "stubborness and disobedience to his parents." The case of the junior John Porter of Salem, although unusual in its duration and consequences, vividly illustrates the normal expectations of filial obedience and the limits of social deviance in colonial New England.[30]

The record begins on 10 December 1661, when the Essex County quarterly court jailed John Porter for "his prophane, unnatural and abusive carriages to his natural parents, and for abusing authority." Morgan Jones, the key witness, revealed the nature of the offences in a deposition to the court.

> In the month of September, he abused [his father] in these words, saying "thou Robin Hood; thou Hipocrite; thou

29. *The Colonial Laws of Massachusetts*, ed. William Whitmore (Boston, 1889), pp. 136–37; Haskins, *Law and Authority*, p. 78. Connecticut passed identical laws in 1650 (*Conn. Records*, 1 : 515, 520–21). Besides John Porter (see below) there was one other near victim. On 4 July 1679 in Plymouth, "Edward Bumpas, for stricking and abusing his parents, was whipt att the post; his punishment was alleviated in regard hee was crasey brained, otherwise hee had bine put to death or otherwise sharply punished" (*Plymouth Records*, 6 : 20).

30. See Kai Erikson, *Wayward Puritans* (New York, 1966), chap. 1, on the sociology of deviance.

art a good member thou art a Fit grand juryman," etc. He also said to his mother, "your tongue goes like a perriemonger," etc., and on Oct. 4, he called her a hypocrite. His father, delivering him a warrant that morning, said John Porter took it, broke it to pieces, uttering words in contempt of authority, saying that he cared not for Hathorne and his commissioners. Joseph Porter [his brother] deposed the same and that said John called Hathorne and Batter vile names, saying that they had sent a warrant for him but "I will not goe beffore them: I will goe before Better men then they be."

It was not long before John was writing from jail contrite letters of apology to the court and to his father. To the court he acknowledged his grievous behavior, contrary to the light of nature and the word of God, which he had had bestowed upon him "for so many yeares both in the publick ministry and in my fathers family also." To his father he presented his "humble and childe like duty" and his unfeigned sorrow for the "Strange Distance" that separated them. At the time he was twenty-six years old, with an ample history of misfortune already to his discredit.[31]

A few years earlier, his father, John senior, a prosperous tanner and civil official of Salem, had lent him £400 in goods and money to improve in two voyages to Barbadoes and England. Not only did John "prodigally wast & riotously" spend the whole investment, but "by his evill courses he ran himself further into debt" in England and was imprisoned until "the charritable assistance of some friends of his father" obtained his release. Nevertheless, "his parents enterteined him wth love & tenderness as their eldest sonne" upon his return to New England, apparently hopeful that he had seen the light of God that they and the Church had so faithfully tried to reveal.[32]

Even the worst New England rebel would normally have

31. *Essex Co. Court Records*, 2 : 336–38; Joseph Porter, *A Genealogy of the Descendants of Richard Porter* (Bangor, 1878), p. 229.
32. *Mass. Records*, 4, pt. 2 : 216–18.

dropped from the records after such an expression of repentance, but, unfortunately, John Porter was cut from uncommon cloth. In November 1663 the Salem authorities remanded him to the Boston jail to await trial by the Court of Assistants, the supreme court of the colony. The offences were, as usual, colorful and multiple:

> He called his father theife, lyar, & simple ape, shittabed. Frequently he threatned to burne his fathers house, to cutt doune his house & barne, to kill his catle & horses, & did wth an axe cutt doune his fence severall times, & did set fire of a pyle of wood neere the dwelling house, greatly endangering it, being neere thirty rods.
>
> He called his mother Rambeggur, Gaṁar [Grandma] Shithouse, Gaṁar Pissehouse, Gaṁar Two Shooes, & told hir her tongue went like a peare monger, & sayd she was the rankest sow in the toune; & these abusive names he used frequently. . .
>
> He reviled, & abused, & beate his fathers servants, to the endangering of the life of one of them.
>
> He was prooved to be a vile, prophane, & comon swearer & drunkard; he attempted to stab one of his naturall brethren.

So heinous were his crimes that even "his oune naturall father openly complained of the stubbornes & rebellion of this his sonne, & craved justice & releife against him."

Since John showed no "signe of true repentance," the court proceeded on 4 March 1664 to pronounce his sentence: "to stand upon the ladder at the gallowes, wth a roape about his neck, for one hower, & afterwards to be severely whipt, & so comitted to the house of correction, to be kept closely to worke, wth the diet of that house, & not thence to be releast wthout speciall order from the Court of Asistants or the Generail Court, & to pay to the country as a fine two hundred pounds." The awesome charade of standing on the gibbet in a noose must have impressed the unrepentant sinner (though he left no evidence of it), for he knew that just one word stood between his life and death—his mother's. "If the mother of the said Porter had not beene overmooved by hir tender & motherly affections to forbeare, but had joyned wth his father in complaining & craving justice, the Court must necessarily have proceeded wth him as a capitall offendor, according to our law, being grounded upon & expressed in the word of God, in Deut 22 : 20, 21." Thus John Porter, aged 29, came within a breath of becoming New England's sole statistic of the capital laws against disobedient and rebellious children.[33]

Direct legal sanctions against unsocial behavior were only one way in which New England sought to give its children a sense of social place. Another was the sumptuary laws which prohibited men, women, and children from dressing above their means and station. From the earliest years of settlement, the colonial authorities worried about the influx of "costly apparel and immodest fashions" from England. On 3 September 1634 the Massachusetts General Court forbade "greate, supfluous, & unnecessary expences occaconed by reason of some newe & imodest fashions, as also the ordinary weareing of silver, golde, & silke laces, girdles, hatbands, &c. under the penalty of forfecture of such cloathes." Except for a mysterious lapse from 1644 to 1651, the Court maintained a vigilant proscription of any sartorial signs of pride and extravagance throughout the seventeenth century. The order of 14 October 1651 was the most explicit in expressing the Court's concern that

men or women of meane condition, educations, & callinges should take uppon them the garbe of gentlemen, by the wearinge of gold or silver lace, or buttons, or poynts at

33. *Essex Co. Court Records*, 3 : 117; *Mass. Records*, 4, pt. 2 : 216–18; *Records of the Court of Assistants of the Colony of the Massachusetts Bay, 1630–1692*, 4 March 1664 (Boston, 1928), 3 : 138–39. John's case later became the focus of a power struggle between the Massachusetts government and the four royal commissioners appointed by Charles II to inspect the legal structure of the colonies. Massachusetts successfully asserted its right to "full & absolute power & authority for the government of his subjects of this colony, & for the making of lawes suiteable to that end, (not repugnant to the lawes of England)" (*Mass. Records*, 4, pt. 2 : 146, 177, 195–96, 210–13).

theire knees, to walke in greate bootes; or women of the same ranke to weare silke or tiffany hoodes or scarfes, which though allowable to persons of greater estates, or more liberall education, yet, we cannot but judge it intollerable in persons of such like condition.[34]

Children and servants were as closely watched, and their parents liable to substantial fines (twenty shillings for the second offence) if they allowed them to wear "any apparrell exceeding the quality & conditions of their persons or estate." When the offence against the good order of society was compounded with a crime against God, the sentence was even heavier, as a hapless servant discovered in 1676. On 31 October Alice Wright's master charged her with "stealing from him severall parcells of mony & goods" valued at £14 4s. 3d. In the flush of sin, she had "laid out a considerable Summe of mony & bought herselfe costly apparrell unbeseeming her ranke, which were found upon her, and forgeing many pernitious lyes & Letters," perhaps to suit her newly assumed status. Unhappily, her unsocial dreams of glory were paid for with triple damages, costs of court, and thirty stripes on her bare back.[35]

Until its economic success shifted the whole character of New England society in the late seventeenth century, civil regulations of dress were reasonably effective. But there was one part of the body that could not be tamed by fiat, despite repeated and anguished efforts by the family, the ministry, and the civil government. When the power of custom admitted and then fostered the English innovation of long hair, the New England leadership raised a hue and cry that was not equalled until the mid twentieth century. Like many seemingly trivial events, the New England imbroglio over long hair magnified some of the colonists' deepest anxieties and disturbed their habits of thought at a time when very real challenges to their survival were being felt.

34. *Winthrop's Journal*, 1 : 132, 134; *PAAS*, n.s. 53 (1943) : 100; *Mass. Records*, 1 : 126, 274; 2 : 84; 3 : 243; 4, pt. 2 : 41. An estate of £200 allowed its owner to dress as he pleased.

35. *Suffolk Co. Court Records*, pp. 751–52.

The General Court first hinted at the gathering storm in their 1634 order against immodest fashions, but they were not moved to act as a body until 1675, when King Philip's War assumed in their eyes the form of a scourge from God for New England's "provoking evills." In a jeremiad that would have made any minister proud, the Court enumerated several "backslidings from God," two concerning the dress and appearance of godly Christians. The first condemned the "vaine, new, strainge fashions, both in poore & rich, wth naked breasts and armes" and "superstitious ribbons both on haire & apparrell." But equally offensive was the open manifestation of pride in that "long haire, like weomens haire, is worne by some men, either their oune or others haire made into perewiggs, and by some weomen wearing borders of haire, and theire cutting, curling, & imodest laying out of theire haire, which practise doeth prevayle & increase, especially amongst the younger sort." In both instances the Court strongly urged moderation because they were "offencive to them, and divers sober christians amongst us," and empowered the county courts to prosecute offenders.[36]

Yet earlier, in 1649, nine of the leading magistrates, led by the governor and deputy governor, had urged the elders of the churches to "manifest their zeal" against long hair in their respective congregations.

Forasmuch as the wearing of long haire after the manner of Ruffians and barbarous Indians, hath begun to invade new England contrary to the rule of Gods word w[hi]ch sayth it is a shame for a man to wear long hair, as also the Commendable Custome generally of all the Godly of our nation until wthin this few yeares Wee the Magistrates who have subscribed this paper (for the clearing of o[u]r owne innocency in this behalfe) doe declare & manifest o[u]r dislike & detestation against the wearing of such long haire, as against a thing uncivil and unmanly whereby men doe deforme themselves, and offend sober & modest men, & doe corrupt good manners.

36. *Mass. Records,* 1 : 126; 5 : 59–60.

The audience to which the court particularly spoke was Harvard College, where, it was said, the "lust" of long hair "first took head!" In 1655 Harvard's president, Charles Chauncy, published a defence of liberal education in which, since the issue was claiming public attention, he felt obliged to speak out on long hair. In his best academic manner, replete with numerous citations, he weighed the practice on the scale of Scripture and found it wanting. The Nazarites, he replied to his students (who had obviously ferretted out this scriptural precedent for their new fashion) grew long hair to differentiate themselves from the common sort, "but now the nourishing of the hair, is to hold correspondency with ruffians & Swaggerers & cavileers, yea the vilest persons in the country, yea Indians & pagans whose abominable customs the Lord hath forbidden his people to follow." And to add moment to his words, Harvard issued a new regulation on apparel in the same year: "neither shall it bee lawful for any to weare Long haire, Locks or foretopps, nor to use Curling, Crisping, parting or powdering their haire." It need hardly be said that in seventeenth century New England, as in twentieth century America, neither legislature nor college president could cure the young men who had been bitten by the bug of fashion.[37]

But another group tried valiantly, though with equal lack of success. Several prominent clergymen led a reasoned assault on hair from their pulpits and, in one instance at least, their homes. Their leader was John Eliot of Roxbury, "Apostle to the Indians" and staunch conservative of the congregational way. His "Exemplary Mortification" in his wilderness ministry led Cotton Mather to describe him as, "in all regards, *A Nazarite indeed;* unless in this one, that long Hair was always very loathsome to him."

> The Apostle tells us, *Nature teaches us, that if a Man have long Hair, 'tis a shame to him; . . .* Thus Mr. *Eliot*

37. *PCSM*, 10 May 1649, 15 (1925) : 37–38; *PMHS*, 2d ser., 29 (1895) : 99; Charles Chauncy, *Gods Mercy, Shewed to His People* (Cambridge, Mass., 1655), pp. 24–27; Samuel Eliot Morison, *Harvard College in the Seventeenth Century* (Cambridge, Mass., 1936), 1 : 86.

thought, that for Men to wear their Hair with a luxurious, delicate, foeminine Prolixity; or for them to preserve no plain Distinction of their Sex, by the Hair of their Head and Face; and much more, for Men thus to disfigure themselves with Hair that is none of their own; and most of all, for Ministers of the Gospel to ruffle it in Excesses of this kind, many prove more than we are well aware displeasing to the *Holy Spirit* of God.

His implacable hatred of long hair also found its way into the Roxbury church records, where he wrote: "Locks and Longe haire . . . is an offence to many a godly Christian, & therefore be it known to such they walk offensively." If a petition to the magistrates in 1672 is any indication, the minister held sway over his congregation for many years. In response to a plea for contributions toward a new building at Harvard, which also invited criticism of the college, Eliot and twenty-three townsmen expressed their wish for "the removal of an evyl (as it appeareth to us) in the educasion of youth in the colledg, and that is, that they are brought up in such pride as doth no wayes become such as are brought up for the holy services of the lord, either in the magistracy, or ministry especialy, and in perticular in their long haire, which lust first took head, and brake out at the Colledg so far as we understand and remember, and now it is got into our pulpets, to the great greife and offence of many godly hearts in the Country." It was probably in response to such pressure that the General Court frowned upon long hair three years later.[38]

Ezekiel Rogers of Rowley, the minister who found "greatest trouble and grief about the rising generation" of New England, also carried the fight against shaggy heads to the seat of government, but never abandoned the fray in his own family.

38. Cotton Mather, *The Life and Death of the Reverend Mr. John Eliot* 3d ed. (London, 1694), pp. 36–37; *NEHGR* 13 (1859) : 314; *PMHS*, 2d ser., 29 (1895) : 99. Eliot's strong disposition against the "heathenish" habit of long hair also found its way into the regulations of his Natick Indians: "All those men that weare long locks shall pay five shillings" (*Colls. MHS*, 3d ser., vol. 4 [1834], pp. 20, 22).

When he died in 1660, he left his brother's son only £160. The boy resented this and sued his uncle's widow for more. In the trial that followed, the reasons for the minister's parsimony were opened. It appeared that he reduced his nephew's share "1. Because he refused to dwell with him. 2. Because he would not keep at the College though he would have maintayned him. 3. Because he spoke to his mother to have his haire cutt but could not get it done." The boy's mother had championed him all the way: "When Mr. Ezekiel Rogers would have her son bound to let his haire be no longer than to the lower tip of his eares, she told him she would never yield to such a snare for her child, tho' he never had a penny of his while he lived." Against such collusion the clergy was helpless.[39]

However, that the New England leadership did not achieve their short-haired goals is not as important as the arguments they employed, for these reveal with great clarity some of New England's most compelling instruments of social constraint. In a sermon on Isaiah 3:16–26, the Reverend Michael Wigglesworth of Malden argued five propositions for his audience, which appears from the text to have been the students of Harvard College:

1. That length of hair, which either the special appointment of God, or nature allows, is not unlawfull.
2. That length of hair which is womanish and savors of effeminacy, is unlawfull.
3. That length of hair which is an effort or a badge of *pride* and vanity, though in it self it be nothing, yet it is unlawfull for thee, although it might be lawfull for another man.
4. That length of Hair which exceeds the ordinary length worn by persons that are most godly and gracious in the country where you live, & the Relation wherein you stand, that length is unlawful; *you are bound to imitate the generality of the best.*
5. That length of Hair which is offensive unto the weak is unlawfull.

39. *NEHGR* 13 (1859) : 313–14; *Essex Co. Court Records*, 3 : 233–35.

In answering rhetorical objections to the last point, Wigglesworth laid bare the ultimate grounds for conformity in New England, the final reasons why men—and especially children —were expected to bow to authority in matters of indifference as well as importance.

> If a Broth[er] be offended and he gives his reason, though it be a weak reason, yet I am to abstain from that which may offend him, so as it be indifferent . . . If you could wear it wthout offence and pride, [he asked,] why wil you do it in this country, where most of the people of God wear short hair? . . . Why should we wear it at such a time as this when every one useth it, the very basest sort of persons, every Ruffian, every wild-Irish, every hangman, every varlet and vagabond shall affect long hair, shall men of place and honour esteem it an honour unto them?

In conclusion, he said, "take 3 considerations with you":

1. God calls every christian to walk not onely sincerely but exactly. Is this exactness to go neer the brink of the pit?
2. Walk safely. If there be a sin in long hair it is certain it is no sin to wear short hair; chuse that which is most safe.
3. Consid[er] what an evil it wil be when God awakens thy conscience. You may wallow in all sins now, but the least sin when God casts it into the eye of conscience wil trouble you.

In the end, then, the children of New England shrank from "unsociable independency" because God and their fathers demanded conformity in the interest of an orderly world. And only pride—the original sin—threatened that world.[40]

40. *NEHGR* 1 (1847) : 368–71 (my emphasis).

5

Whipt Eminence

Almost all the great men of that period, and for many years back, had been whipt into eminence by Master Cheever.

Nathaniel Hawthorne

Seventeenth century Englishmen believed that a little learning was a dangerous thing, but there agreement ended. Some, particularly aristocrats, thought the antidote lay in less or no learning. During the Interregnum, for instance, William Cavendish, an ardent royalist in European exile, addressed a long memorandum to his former pupil, the future Charles II, on the form of government the exiled prince ought to establish upon the restoration of Crown and Church to prevent any future civil wars. "Thatt which hath dun moste hurte," he wrote, in a hand that subverted his argument, "is the Abundance off Gramer Scooles & Ins off Courtes. The [Lord] Tresorer [William] Burleygh sayde ther was to manye Gramer Scooles, because Itt made the plowe & the Carte bee neglected, which was to feede us, & defende us; for ther are fewe thatt Can reade thatt will putt their handes to the plowe or the Carte, & Armeyes are made off Comon Soldiers, & ther are verye fewe thatt Can reade that will Carye a muskett; & ther are so manye Scooles nowe as moste reade, so Indeed ther shoulde bee butt such a proportion, as to serve the Church & moderatlye the Lawe, & the merchantes, & the rest for the Labor, for Else theye run oute to idle & unesesarye People, thatt becoumes a factius burthen to the Comon wealth; for when most was unletterde," he concluded, "Itt was much a better worlde both for peace & warr." In the paraphrase of one of its opponents, this was the view that "Ignorance is the Mother of Devotion, and Obedience." [1]

But other Englishmen, especially Puritans, felt that the only cure for a little learning was more learning. "The *Devotion* of *Ignorance*," argued the Mathers, "is but a *Bastard* sort of *Devotion*." They held that "Ignorance is the Mother (not of Devotion but) of HERESY" for the simple reason that salvation—man's ultimate goal—was impossible without Christian knowledge and understanding. To those who believed that "the Word Written and Preacht is the ordinary Medium of Conversion and Sanctification," it followed naturally that there should be "Schools of Learning; those of a Lower Character, for the instructing of Youth in Reading, and those of an Higher, for the more Liberal Education of such, as may be devoted to the Work of the Ministry." And lest they forfeit to their aristocratic opponents the point that an emphasis on personal salvation would undermine social order, they argued that widespread schooling would also prevent the "many divisions of opinion which are sprung up amongst us," reduce idleness among the volatile poorer classes, and inculcate the habits of submission and obedience in all.[2]

In 1642, when Samuel Harmar published his *Vox Populi, or Glostershires Desire*, it was said that children roamed the streets of English towns, cursing and swearing, offering verbal and physical abuse to every creature that walked, and withal "drawing the vengeance of God upon the Land." The remedy, as Harmar saw it, was not fewer schools but more. "If there were a Schoole-master [in every parish throughout the land generally], Children would live in fear to hurt the least Childe

1. *A Catalogue of Letters and Other Historical Documents Exhibited in the Library at Welbeck*, ed. S. Arthur Strong (London, 1903), pp. 188–89; Christopher Wase, *Considerations concerning Free Schools* (Oxford, 1678), p. 7.

2. Cotton Mather, *Cares about the Nurserie* (Boston, 1702), p. 34; Increase Mather, *A Call from Heaven* (Boston, 1685), p. 127; Thomas Foxcroft, *Cleansing our Way in Youth* (Boston, 1719), p. 176.

that should come by them; for a Schoole-master would be a
terror to the malitious ones, because he would be alwaies resident like a Magistrate, to heare the complaints of any that
should complain against them, and so the Offender shall receive correction for his offence." Furthermore, "good Lawes
sowne among Children dayly in the Schoole, will be a speciall
meanes to keep them in *Subjection*, both for the glory of God;
the good of themselves, and the joy and comfort of their
Master, that have the tuition of them," and to give them an
early experience of adult life. A list of commandments read
twice weekly before the school—including the duty to honor
the Sabbath and to obey parents, elders, and superiors—
would go far to establish "Godliness and Manners, . . . the
very Diademe and Glory of all Learning," since "the Law being onely read, is a *Terror*." [3]

In a land that "growes weary of her Inhabitants," where
"children, servantes, and Neighboures especially if they be
poore are compted the greatest burthens," the use of education
for social control could be expected to appeal to the ruling
elite. For a government riddled with instability, social institutions—lay or religious—that were able to teach unquestion-
ing obedience to the powers that be, understandably commanded greater attention than institutions that sought to
liberate individual men from ignorance, sin, and damnation.
So strong indeed was the need felt for social stability in
Caroline England that even Puritans, who in other circumstances would have rehearsed education's key role in the
drama of salvation, often felt obliged to argue for schools in
terms that their opponents had set.[4]

But in the beginning New England was different. There,
no swarms of the idle poor pestered local government, no un-
employment or lack of supervision cast large numbers of unruly
children into the streets, and no civil or ecclesiastical leadership thwarted the search for salvation. Instead the community

3. Samuel Harmar, *Vox Populi, or, Glostershires Desire* (London,
1642), sigs. A3r., A4r., A5r., B1r., B2v. (my emphasis).
4. *Winthrop Papers*, 2 : 138–39.

bent together "as one man" in the common task of building a holy "Citty upon a Hill," where the settlers could "improve our lives to doe more service to the Lord . . . and worke out our Salvacion under the power and purity of his holy Ordinances." In New England the school renewed its original purpose of ministering to its pupils' souls, without forgetting, however, the English lesson that "Order is the Soul of Common Wealths and Societyes." [5]

James Garfield once said that "the ideal college is Mark Hopkins on one end of a log and a student on the other." With only a small assumption of literary license, his aphorism might equally apply to education in general, for every educational situation consists in some sense of a teacher, a learner, and a locus of interaction, which could be called a school. For colonial New England even "log" is not an inapt metaphor for its public schools since they were often as rough-hewn and narrow as the communities that built them. This quality in turn conditioned the nature and extent of education that took place there, not only what was learned but—perhaps more importantly—the way it was learned. If the medium was not the whole message, it certainly comprised an indispensable part.[6]

In 1647, after five years of trying to place the sole responsibility for education on the family's already stooping shoulders, the General Court of Massachusetts passed its famous "Old Deluder Satan" law, which required every town of fifty "families or householders" to "appoint one within their own town to teach all such children as shall resort to him to write and read," and every town of one hundred families to "set up a grammar school, the master thereof being able to instruct youth, so far as they may be fitted, for the university." But the law did not require that children be sent to the

5. Ibid., pp. 282–95; John Richardson, *The Necessity of a Well-Experienced Souldiery* (Cambridge, Mass., 1679), p. 13.

6. Frederick Rudolph, *Mark Hopkins and the Log* (New Haven, 1956), p. vii; Walter Ong, *The Presence of the Word* (New Haven, 1967); Walter Ong, *Rhetoric, Romance, and Technology* (Ithaca, 1971).

schoolmaster maintained by the town (as long as they were
educated at home), and it did not require the towns to build
proper schoolhouses. "School" was a generic term used to designate a permanent institution in which the absence of a
teacher was merely regarded as a temporary vacancy. If a
colonial town did build a schoolhouse, therefore, it did so for
the sake of convenience, tradition, or civic pride, and not
for fear of the colonial government.⁷

The law of 1647 further stipulated that the teachers of these
schools "shall be paid either by the parents or masters of such
children, or by the inhabitants in general, by way of supply
[taxation], as the major part of those that order the pruden-
tials of the town shall appoint." This represented a departure
from the English tradition of endowing schools and colleges
with money or income-producing land. Land was plentiful
and therefore cheap in New England, and few fortunes that
might permit large-scale philanthropy had yet been made in
commerce, so colonial schools were forced upon the purposes
and pocketbooks of the tax-paying public. If their lack of en-
dowments denied them a measure of security and independence, their dependence upon taxes made them intellectually
responsive to the society for which they acted.⁸

Consequently, in most towns, since funds were usually in
short supply, economy got the better of civic pride when it
came time to move the schools from rented rooms, barns,
shops, and meetinghouses to proper schoolhouses.⁹ As befitted
small communities of mean accomplishments in primitive settings, colonial schools were small, mean, and primitive. A typical edifice was perhaps twenty feet long, eighteen feet wide,
and only six or seven feet high at the ceiling. The construction
was frame and clapboard—log schools, like log cabins, were
largely the product of nineteenth century imaginations—with

7. *Mass. Records*, 11 November 1647, 2 : 203.
8. Ibid., W. K. Jordan, *Philanthropy in England, 1480–1660* (London,
1959).
9. Schools were also held in almshouses, blockhouses, and even, in one
case, a former pesthouse! (Walter Small, *Early New England Schools*
[Boston, 1914], p. 251).

perhaps a small loft above the main room, "a place to hang the bell in," and an entrance foyer with a closet. The interior walls were rough-boarded from floor to windows and plastered with lime from windows to ceiling; the plaster probably did as much to brighten the room as the windows themselves. Most schools were fortunate if they had two or three stationary windows eighteen inches square, so that much of the light for reading came from the flickering flames of a large fireplace. Three sides of the room were lined with long plank desks attached to the walls, in front of which the pupils sat— with what acute discomfort we can readily imagine—on backless plank seats, sawed side upwards, supported on legs driven into auger holes and often projecting above the planks. And at the end of the room, opposite the entrance stood the schoolmaster's large table, the symbol and locus of authority.[10]

The learning environment of the colonial school was dominated by the large fireplace, and later the Franklin stove, at the schoolmaster's end of the room. In spring and summer a fire was unnecessary and the door could be thrown open for fresh air. But during the cold winter months, when many children were freed from farm work to attend school, the crackerbox schoolroom without ventilation presented a stifling atmosphere for education. The blazing fire simply consumed the room's oxygen, producing drowsiness and inattention in the half-frozen, half-roasted children who lined the walls. Warren Burton, who attended a small district school in the late eighteenth century, recalled how "every cold afternoon, the old fire-place, wide and deep, was kept a roaring furnace of flame, for the benefit of blue noses, chattering jaws, and aching toes, in the more distant regions [of the room.] The end of my seat, just opposite the chimney, was oozy with melted pitch, and sometimes almost smoked with combustion. Judge, then, of what living flesh had to bear. It was a toil," he lamented, "to exist"—much less to learn. From the poor souls

10. Small, *Early New England Schools,* chap. 9; *EIHC* 68 (1932) : 239–40. Boston, of course, was a minor exception to the New England rule in education as in most things, largely because of its location and size.

in the "more distant regions," on the other hand, came the
continual and hardly deniable plea, "Measter m'I go to the
Fire." If any learning occurred in such settings, the local com-
mittees who built the schools could take no credit.[11]

The school fireplace, with its insatiable appetite for com-
bustibles, fed upon wood supplied by the parents of the children who attended. When the parents could not pay this separate school tax in either wood or money, their children were
penalized by suspension from school. But no matter how diligent the parents were to provide their fair share of wood, the
school always seemed to run out at least once during the cold-
est winter months, forcing the master to close its door or, on
some occasions, to find other quarters. In 1670 Richard Norcross, the master of the Watertown grammar school, entered
a complaint in the town records that "the schooling of children is like to be hindered for want of wood to keep a fire," to
which the selectmen responded, "the school being the town's,"
by setting a school wood assessment on all "inhabitants that
send their children to the school." Other masters were plagued
by less responsive communities. After enjoying his services for
eleven and a half years, Newbury was woefully unappreciative
of schoolmaster Richard Brown, in spite of the fact—among
many to his credit—that he took "the scholars to my own fire
when there was no wood at school as frequently." Master
Brown was perhaps unusual in having a decent fire to retreat
to, and certainly in his devotion to his students' progress.
More customary was the response of Thomas Robbins, the
young master of Sheffield, Connecticut, who recorded in his
diary on 7 March 1797: "No school on account of wood."[12]

When the physical setting of education is poor, the normally favorable chances of learning are stunted. In 1681 Rox-

11. Small, *Early New England Schools*, chap. 10, p. 262; Simeon Breed
to Simeon Baldwin, 2 April 1782, Baldwin Family Papers, box 3, Yale
University Library, New Haven, Conn.

12. The school wood tax usually amounted to a quarter of a cord or
"one load" of wood, or two to three shillings in money (Small, *Early New
England Schools*, chap. 10, p. 266); *Sibley's Harvard Graduates*, 4 : 338–39;
Diary of Thomas Robbins, DD., 1796–1854, ed. Increase Tarbox (Boston,
1886), 1 : 29.

bury's grammar school was poor indeed. Master Thomas Barnard complained to the feoffees of "the confused and shattered and nastie posture it is in, not fitting for to reside in; the glass broken, and thereupon very raw and cold, the floor very much broken and torn up to kindle fires, the hearth spoiled, the seats, some burnt and others out of kilter, so that one had as well nigh as goods keep school in a hog stie as in it." Yet even in normal circumstances, the learning experience of colonial children was disadvantaged, for the environment of New English schooling consisted of smoky rooms, unevenly heated and poorly ventilated, backless seats, full of unsuspected splinters and agonizing projections, inadequate lighting, and ceilings that were oppressively low, even for small children. It is a tribute to the tenacity and stern stuff of New England's children that they crowded such schools in increasing numbers before the Revolution, and moreover that they learned as much as contemporaries and visitors boasted they did.[13]

Although the children of New England enjoyed no easy existence when they arrived at school, getting there was often almost as troublesome. With the outbreak of King Philip's War in 1675 and almost continuously after 1689, when the French and Indian wars began, many children had to run the danger of Indian attacks or kidnapping on their way to school. Understandably, many outlying towns were loath to endanger their children for a little learning and pleaded with the General Court to exempt them temporarily from the school law of 1647—so many indeed that the Massachusetts House of Representatives passed a bill on 21 March 1703 exempting all towns from court penalties for two years, citing as its main reason that "Diverse of the frontier Towns which are by Law Obliged to Maintain a Grammar School, are in such Hazard of the Enemy, that it is unsafe for the children to Passe to and from the Schools." [14]

But the wars dragged on, and the towns continued to ask

13. *PCSM* 35 (1951): 262. For the educational accomplishments of colonial New Englishmen, see Lawrence Cremin, *American Education: The Colonial Experience, 1607–1783* (New York, 1970), chap. 18.

14. Mass. Archives, vol. 58, fol. 240. The bill was renewed in 1705 for three years (fol. 243).

for leniency. In 1710 Chelmsford claimed that it could not support a school because "our habitations are very scattering & distant one from another, so that althô a school were placed in the Centre it would be very remote from the greater part of our Inhabitants, & our Children in passing too & from the same would be so greatly exposed to the snares of our Lurking Enemy, that very few would Venture to send them to School in such danger." Twelve years later Dover asked for a similar exemption, pleading that "the houses being so scattered over the whole township that in no one place six houses are within call, by which inconvenience the inhabitants of said town can have no benefit of such grammar school, for at the times fit for children to go and come from school, is generally the chief time of the Indians doing mischief, so the inhabitants are afraid to send their children to school, and the children dare not venture, so that the salary to said schoolmaster is wholly lost to said town." In most cases the representatives were receptive to such pleas, but the Governor's Council was not, willing instead to let the certainty of high standards outweigh uncertain harm.[15]

When new children arrived, they entered the school sharing two characteristics. They were usually the same age—seven or eight years old—and they had had about the same amount of preparation. The standard requirement for admission to the town grammar school was the ability to read a passage from the Bible or Psalter containing two- or three-syllable words. Probably most children were taught to read at home by their mothers from simple catechisms, hornbooks, or stick drawn sketches on sand floors, much as Richard Brown was taught in seventeenth century Newbury. This young Goodman Brown was born 12 September 1675, he tells us in his diary, and "educated under the wing of my parence, especially my mother, who was a pious and prudent woman, and endeavored to instill into [me] the principals of Religion and holiness; . . . she was unwearied in her watchings, instructions, admonitions, warnings, reproofs & exhortations, that she might bring

15. Ibid., fols. 276–77; Small, *Early New England Schools*, p. 51.

[me] up in the nurture and admonition of the Lord, and continued she to train me up betimes, and when she had caused me to read well at home, she sent me to school. . . ." [16]

Many children, in big towns and small, were also sent to dame schools to begin their formal education. In Elizabethan England children "almost everie where are first taught either in private by men and women altogeather rude, and utterly ignoraunt of the due composing and just spelling of wordes: or else in common schooles most commonlie by boyes, verie seeldome or never by anie of sufficient skill." But many grammar masters were not sanguine about the results, "for how fewe be there under the age of seaven or eight yeares," one of them asked rhetorically, "that are towardly abled, and praysablie furnished for reading? And as manie there be above those yeares, that can neither readilie spell nor rightly write even the common wordes of our Englishe." So they wrote books addressed to "such Men and Women of Trade, as Taylors, Weavers, Shopkeepers, Sempsters, and such others as have undertaken the Charge of Teaching others," promising that "thou may'st sit on thy Shop-board, at thy Loom, or at thy Needle, and never hinder thy Work to hear thy Scholars, after once thou hast made this little Book familiar to thee." [17]

In the literate Puritan culture of New England, however, where the educational role of the family was accentuated, the dame school was initially and largely the domestic enterprise of a woman with children of her own, who charged a small fee to care for the neighborhood children—as young as two years old—and prepare them to receive the Word. In later

16. Small, *Early New England Schools*, pp. 290–94; Lilley Eaton, *Genealogical History of the Town of Reading* (Boston, 1874), pp. 52–54. Josiah Cotton, Benjamin Franklin, and John Trumbull also learned to read at home (*PCSM* 26 [1927] : 278; *The Autobiography of Benjamin Franklin*, ed. Leonard Labaree et al. [New Haven, 1964], pp. 52–53; *The Autobiography of Colonel John Trumbull*, ed. Theodore Sizer [New Haven, 1958], p. 5).

17. Francis Clement, *The Petie Schole* (London, 1587), pp. 4, 9; Edmund Coote, "Preface to the Reader," *The English School-Master*, 54th ed. (London, 1737), (1st ed., 1596). See T. W. Baldwin, *William Shakspere's Petty School* (Urbana, Ill., 1943).

years, the town hired a school dame to teach the youngest children either during the summer or in one of the district schools during the winter, but her domestic precursor continued to flourish in most New English towns and villages until the Revolution and after.[18]

Although at entrance New English schoolchildren had age and preparation in common, they differed from town to town in sex ratio, social status, and ambition, especially over the course of a century and a half. In the decades following the enactment of the Massachusetts school law in 1647—which by 1677 was reproduced almost verbatim by the Connecticut, New Haven, and Plymouth colonies—most town grammar schools, like New Haven's, existed "principally for the Instruction of hopeful youths in the Latin tongue, and other learned Languages Soe far as to prepare such youths for the Colledge and Publique service of the Country in Church and Commonwealth." And by "youths" the trustees meant "boys": "All Girles be excluded as Improper and inconsistent with such in Grammar Schoole as the law injoines and is the Designe of this Settlement." [19]

But by the final quarter of the seventeenth century, many towns began to alter the character, and some the composition, of their grammar schools. Even in staunch New Haven, for example, the town meeting had many a "loving debate" about the grammar school before expressing its corporate desire in 1677 that "parents, or such as have children, would be carfull to send theyer children to the schoole, and to continue them

18. Small, *Early New England Schools*, chap. 6. Two-year-olds were not uncommon "pupils" of New English school dames. On 7 August 1664 the Plymouth Colony court held an inquest into the death of Elizabeth Walker, age two and a half, who accidentally drowned in a river near Rehoboth, "shee being sent to scoole." Joseph Sewall, the son of the judge, was sent off before he was three "to School to Capt. Townsend's Mother's, his Cousin Jane accompanying him, carried his Horn-book" (*Plymouth Records*, 4 : 83–84; *Colls. MHS*, 5th ser., vol. 5 [1878], p. 344. See also *The America of 1750: Peter Kalm's Travels in North America*, ed. Adolph B. Benson [New York, 1937], 1 : 204).

19. School laws of 1684, in Thomas Davis, Jr., *Chronicles of Hopkins Grammar School, 1660–1935* (New Haven, 1938), p. 157.

at it." Yet they appropriated only £20 for the school, £10 less than usual, and then only upon condition. For "one of the Townsmen & then many others desyred that the Master that should bee procured for the schoole might teach English allsoe and to write, especially at present being but few Lattin schollars." [20]

New Haven was simply experiencing the weariness common to most smaller New England towns in the years after the wars with the Indians. Sapped of money, energy, and often population, these country towns had very few boys who wanted or needed a facility in Latin to make their way in the world, but a great many children—boys and girls—who needed to read and write good English and to "cypher," if not for heavenly at least for earthly salvation. The New English still clung to "the custom of our predecessors and that common practice of the English nation to bring up theyer chilldren in Learninge" so that the next generation "may attaine to some proficiency, wherby they may com to bee fitt for service to god in church and common wealth." But they were beginning to define "Learninge" in a new way, just as their English contemporaries were doing, leaning toward the practical and that which was useful immediately. Most towns were simply too depressed, too anxious about the future, to honor the impossibly high ideals of the founders.[21]

The Middlesex county court sensed the malaise of New England in 1679, when it asked its towns to report on the state of their populations, schools, and ministry. Three towns— Charlestown, Cambridge, and Concord—reported populations of over one hundred families, which made them responsible by law for the maintenance of a grammar school; only two maintained such a school. Both, by their proximity to the relative safety of the Massachusetts Bay settlements, had escaped the ravages of King Philip's War. Inheriting the popular legacy of Ezekiel Cheever, New England's legendary schoolmaster who had taught there until 1671, Samuel Phipps drew 53

20. *New Haven Town Records,* 31 July 1677, 2 : 365.
21. Ibid.

Latin grammar students from Charlestown's 200 families. From the 121 families of neighboring Cambridge, however, Elijah Corlet could only garner 9 Latin scholars, a depressing decline from the 70 or 80 he had enjoyed in the 1640s, and his competition, two English teachers, had to share a mere dozen students. Concord, one of the exposed victims of the Indian war, could report no Latin grammar students "except some of honored Mr. Peter Bulkley's and some of reverend Mr. Estbrookes', whom he himself educates." It was the accommodation of the ideal with the realities of New English life and the gradual transformation of exclusively classical schools to all-purpose grammar schools for both Latin and English that prompted ministers such as Thomas Shepard of Cambridge to lament the "great decay in *Inferiour Schools*." [22]

One of the signs of "decay" the clergy may have regretted was the admission of girls into the hitherto male dominion of the grammar school. Although never a widespread phenomenon, a number of towns began to open the doors of their secondary schools to "all sexes for reading and writing English, and for cyphering." Typically such towns were frontier settlements—Deerfield, Hatfield, Northampton, Farmington, Meriden—where Latin learning was held superfluous to the struggle for existence, and the girls were in a distinct minority in the school. But by the middle of the eighteenth century, when the new, largely English grammar schools became the rule, and brightened social conditions sent swarms of children to them in every town, large and small, the proportion of girls rose considerably. In coastal Stonington, Connecticut, for instance, a total of 132 children attended the school kept by Ephraim Fellows "at my house" between 1746 and 1762; half were girls. Stonington was probably unusual in the extent of its commitment to female learning, but it was not unreliable as a barometer of the general trend of education in New English society. For the influx of girls into such schools was simply the rural equivalent of a change in urban education that

22. *NEHGR* 5 (1851) : 172–73; Mass. Archives, 17 October 1668, vol. 58, fol. 61; Thomas Shepard, *Eye-Salve* (Boston, 1672), p. 44.

saw private schools for the "female arts" established in Boston, Providence, and other large towns as prosperity spread over the commercial classes.[23]

Perhaps the crucial difference among New English school-children was social status, which in that day, as in ours, was largely based upon wealth. In the seventeenth century the cost of grammar shcools and their preparatory latinity tended to restrict them to the moderately prosperous who planned and could afford to go on to college. Besides tuition that averaged threepence a week for instruction in reading and cyphering, fourpence for writing, and sixpence for Latin—about twenty to twenty-five shillings a year—most schools levied fees for entrance, candles, books, ink, quills, paper, and, perhaps most expensive of all, firewood, which ranged from two to six shillings a year. All this was in addition to the taxes paid by all members of the community for at least partial support of the schoolmaster and perhaps the construction and maintenance of a proper schoolhouse.[24]

The major exception to the pattern of schooling for the prosperous was the widespread provision for the very poor in the great majority of towns in which the schools were not free from tuition charges. Salem was characteristic of larger New English towns in the seventeenth century. On 30 September 1644 the town meeting voted "that if any poore body hath children or a childe to be put to schoole & not able to pay for their schooling That the Towne will pay it by a rate." The Salem vote was an extension of the Massachusetts education law of 1642, which was in turn an extension of English practice embodied in the Elizabethan Poor Law of 1601. Both gave authority to the elected officials of the town or parish to raise by taxation sufficient funds to "put fourth apprentice the children of such as shall not be able and fitt to employ and bring them up, nor shall take course to dispose of them" and

23. Small, *Early New England Schools,* chaps. 11 and 13; school accounts of Ephraim Fellows, MS. 73524, Conn. His. Soc.; Robert Middlekauff, *Ancients and Axioms: Secondary Education in Eighteenth-Century New England* (New Haven, 1963), chap. 7.

24. Small, *Early New England Schools,* chap. 7.

to "provide that a sufficient quantity of materialls, as hempe, flaxe, etc. may bee raised in their severall townes, and tooles and implements provided for working out the same." Puritan Massachusetts simply and characteristically added the requirement that all children be given by their parents or masters the "ability to read and understand the principles of religion and the capital lawes of the country," a duty that many townsmen found easier to discharge by supporting public schools "free for the Poorest without Expence." [25]

Before they were generally altered in the eighteenth century, however, these arrangements for the prosperous and the "poorest" had the effect of squeezing the children of lower middle income families out of the grammar schools and the upward mobility they promised. It was these families, probably the majority in most New England towns, who, from the time of King Philip's War, began to drag their feet when the town meetings made their annual requests for school appropriations. Presentments by the county courts for violations of the school law increased as economic and emotional depression set in, as settlements spread to the remote corners of the towns, away from the centralized church and school, and as a general lack of interest in Latin learning became widespread.[26]

Naturally the classically trained ministry was sensitive to this "declension," especially in their annual election sermons. Before the Massachusetts legislators, in 1701, Joseph Belcher of Dedham urged a concerted improvement in the quality and quantity of secondary schools, "which too many of our unlearned seem to be possessed with prejudice against. . . . The coldness, indisposition, not to say opposition, that is in so many to things of this nature, gives too much ground to fear, that they will in a great measure sink and fall." Although the

25. George Jackson, *The Development of School Support in Colonial Massachusetts* (New York, 1909), chaps. 1, 3; *EIHC* 9 (1867) : 132; *Mass. Records*, 14 June 1642, 2 : 6–7; Thomas Prince, *The People of New-England* (Boston, 1730), p. 34. See also Marcus Jernegan, *Laboring and Dependent Classes in Colonial America, 1607–1783* (New York, 1931), chap. 5.
26. Jackson, *Development of School Support*, pp. 77–78.

invocation to cherish education attained a threnodic quality by being "so frequently mentioned, & inculcated upon, from this *Desk,* on these *Publick Occasions,"* the speakers in the decades from King Philip's War (1675–76) to the Peace of Utrecht (1713) detected real opposition to the standards of the founders. In 1712 a *symptom* of opposition was noticed by the Reverend John Woodward of Norwich when he told the Connecticut legislature that the school laws were being evaded "by many, who are more Subtil than Solidly Thinking, who seem to have a Superior Affection to their Money, than to the Good Education of their Children." The *source* of discontent was penetrated by Windsor's Jonathan Marsh some nine years later. "There needs something more to be done in *scattered places,"* he counselled, "to make the benefit of our Schools more extensive. . . . It grates the spirits of men to see the Privilege of their Neighbours and they not able to share in it, to be sure without extraordinary charge, which don't come within the compass of many poor Families." The support of, and access to, the public schools were the issues that troubled New England at the close of the seventeenth century, not mere greed or apostasy from the Puritan faith in education.[27]

The first effort of the townsmen to solve the school problem sought to abolish that part of the 1647 school law that required every town of one hundred families to maintain a grammar school. In its place they proposed that only the county town of each shire maintain such a school, supported by a county-wide rate and to which "all persons within the said Count[y] shall be Admitted freely." In 1690 the Connecticut legislature was the first to accede to the demands of its constituents by effectively discarding the one-hundred-family law for one that required only its four county towns—New Haven, New London, Hartford, and Fairfield—to support "Grammar Learning."[28]

27. Joseph Belcher, *The Singular Happiness of such Heads or Rulers* (Boston, 1701), p. 42; John Woodward, *Civil Rulers are God's Ministers* (Boston, 1712), pp. 43–44; Jonathan Marsh, *An Essay* (New London, 1721), pp. 44–45.
28. Middlekauff, *Ancients and Axioms,* pp. 40–45.

But Connecticut was not the last, for within the same decade even Massachusetts voters attempted to establish county grammar schools. For the first time, in June 1699 a bill was introduced in the House of Representatives which was finally accepted on 14 March 1701. But it was ultimately defeated by the implacable opposition of the Governor's Council and by a bill of opposition that picked several holes in the proposal. To the proponents of the county system, who undoubtedly represented towns of more than one hundred families, the opposition, probably representing smaller towns, pointed out that "every towne must [still] have an Inglish schole" and ought not have to also pay toward a grammar school, from which they would have no benefit. Financial considerations, however, were only a minor part of the opposition to the bill; in 1700, as in the past, social status was more important, and the next three arguments drove the point home.

It is well knowne that the genarallyty of the Pulpits are suplyed by scholers desending from the middle sort of men which will be genarally much disinabled if all advantages be removed farr from them: for the middle sort of men have borded thare children at home, and with the help of thare Minnister and scholes adjoyning have trained up meany as are now famous amongst us. . . .

It is apprehended that County scholls will be chiefly beanyfisiall for the richest mens sons as have no need of helpe and seldum improve thare learneing for the publick good so much as thay that take to the minnistry. . . .

If all advantages of gramer learning be restrained from remote Country townes thare will be few or none fit for publick busness in the Townes, much less for the provence, and the Country people will be estemed acordingly.[29]

When the opponents of the 1647 school law saw they were losing the county school fight, they switched their objective to a one-hundred-fifty-family law. But again the Council was adamant, refusing to concur with any House proposal for edu-

29. Mass. Archives, vol. 58, fols. 184–86, 222.

cation until 27 June 1701, when the original "Deluder Satan" law was renewed, with even a stiffer fine for delinquent towns, £20, to appease the high standards of the Council. Clearly some other way around the school problem had to be found.[30]

In the final decade of the seventeenth and the opening decades of the eighteenth century, the majority of New England towns discovered a threefold solution. Their first act was to establish "free schools," by placing the support of public education squarely on the shoulders of the taxpayers through the imposition of an equitable town rate. Their reasoning was that free schools, unlike schools supported by tuition and fees, existed "for the Benefit of the Poor and the Rich; that the Children of all, partaking of equal Advantages and being placed upon an equal Footing, no Distinction might be made among them in the Schools on account of the different Circumstances of their Parents, but that the Capacity & natural Genius of each might be cultivated & improved for the future Benefit of the whole Community." But in the expanding country communities, where many families lived far from the social center, equal access to a central grammar school was difficult if not impossible. So the towns hit upon the ingenious and perfectly legal plan of holding school for three months in each of their four quarters, on a rotating basis. Further modified by a gradual transition of emphasis from Latin to English, these publicly supported "moving schools" enjoyed a tremendous success in the middle decades of the eighteenth century, until and even after some old opposition to Latin learning reemerged, albeit somewhat anachronously, in the years following the Stamp Act.[31]

On 29 January 1769 the Reverend Andrew Eliot of Boston wrote to the great English Whig patron of learning, Thomas Hollis, that "Some sordid, niggardly souls, enemies to all learning, of which there are always enough in our General As-

30. Ibid., fols. 217–18, 224–25.
31. Jackson, *Development of School Support*, pp. 73–92; Robert Seybolt, *The Public Schools of Colonial Boston* (Cambridge, Mass., 1935), p. viii; Harlan Updegraff, *The Origin of the Moving School in Massachusetts* (New York, 1908).

sembly, have ever looked upon this [1647 grammar school]
Law with envy, and have desired to get it repealed. We were
alarmed when a considerable Town instructed their representative to move for a repeal." The town was Worcester, which
instructed its representative in 1766 "that the law for keeping
of Latin grammar schools be repealed and that we be not
obliged to keep more than one in a county and that to be
kept at the county charge," and in 1767 "that you use your
endeavors to relieve the people of the Province from the great
burden of supporting so many Latin grammar schools, whereby
they are prevented from attaining such a degree of English
learning as is necessary to retain the freedom of any state."
Although "the ministers openly appeared in defence of it"
and succeeded in quashing Worcester's motion before it was
even made, an old rent had been widened in the fabric of
Massachusetts' educational history, a tear that would gape in
1789, when the new state passed a *two*-hundred-family school
law.[32]

Unaware of the political machinations over education in
the provincial capitols, the children who tumbled into New
England's tiny schools in the eighteenth century were affected
only by their daily routine in the classroom and their relations with the man who oversaw it. And if one aspect of that
routine stands out from contemporary accounts, it is the
premium that was placed on rote memorization. Whether the
child was learning Latin grammar from Cheever's *Accidence,*
the rule of three from Cocker's *Arithmetic,* or the pantheon
of Greek gods from Homer, sheer memory was called upon
time and again to overcome the limitations of poor teaching
or premature age, to parrot and to squirrel away random nug-
gets of information in the hope that someday they would make
coherent sense. As if Gutenberg and Caxton had never lived,
colonial schools forced their pupils to use the diminishing
power of a smaller, more personal, oral culture—verbal mem-

32. *Colls. MHS,* 4th ser., vol. 4 (1858), pp. 436–37; Small, *Early New
England Schools,* pp. 42–43; Middlekauff, *Ancients and Axioms,* p. 129.

ory—to control and order the proliferating, impersonal products of a print culture. So anachronous was the method of school learning that memory, as in the medieval university, where books were at a premium, was still considered the primary qualification of a scholar.[33]

"My parents were very carefull to instruct me in the principles of religion when I was young," Joseph Green recalled, "and altho I was a very untoward corrupt child, yet God blessed me with a good memory, and so my parents were urged to make me a scholar &c." According to his own Puritan sensibilities, his memory was strong enough to excuse his other misqualifications. "When I came to be big enough to go to school I went to the Dames School, where I was bad enough, but I at length went to mr Corlets school and he gave my parents encouragement to make me a scholar and they kept me to school: but I was Idle and lazy. . . ." Fortunately he was rescued from his unscholarly foibles by religious conversion just in time to accept the rod of the Roxbury Grammar School, where he presumably taxed the memories of his pupils as much as he did their posterior dignity.[34]

Josiah Cotton was also fortunate. "My school exercises were not attended with that difficulty that some meet with," he confessed, "by reason of a memory which God had favored me with." But he and Joseph Green must have been in a small minority, for even some of the most outstanding men of their generation had no very high opinion of their schooldays. John Trumbull, artist and patriot of the American Revolution, attended Nathan Tisdale's famous school in his native Lebanon, Connecticut, at an early age and "could read Greek at six years old." But this precocious victory was a hollow one, he confessed in his autobiography. "I do not mean to say that, at this time, I possessed much more knowledge of the Greek language, than might be taught to a parrot; but I knew the forms of the letters, the words, and their sounds, and could

33. Ong, *Presence of the Word;* Ong, *Rhetoric, Romance, and Technology.*
34. *PCSM* 34 (1943) : 236.

read them accurately, although my knowledge of their meaning was very imperfect." [35]

The widely shared experiences of the future president of
Harvard, Josiah Quincy, at Phillips Academy stand as a serious indictment of the quality of education fostered in both
the public and private schools of colonial New England. When
he entered at the age of six,

> the discipline of the Academy was severe, and to a child,
> as I was, disheartening. The Preceptor was distant and
> haughty in his manners. I have no recollection of his ever
> having shown any consideration for my childhood. *Fear
> was the only impression I received* from his treatment of
> myself and others. I was put at once into the first book of
> Cheever's Accidence, and obliged, with the rest of my
> classmates, to *get by heart* passages of a book which I
> could not, from my years, possibly understand. *My mem-
> ory was good,* and I had been early initiated, by being
> drilled in the Assembly's Catechism, into the practice of
> repeating readily words the meaning of which I could not
> by any possibility conceive. *I cannot imagine a more dis-
> couraging course of education than that to which I was
> subjected.*
>
> The truth was, I was an incorrigible lover of sports of
> every kind. My heart was in ball and marbles. *I needed
> and loved perpetual activity of body,* and with these dis-
> positions I was compelled to sit with four other boys on
> the same hard bench, daily, four hours in the morning and
> four in the afternoon, and study lessons which I could not
> understand. . . .
>
> The chief variety in my studies was that afforded by
> reading lessons in the Bible, and in getting by heart Dr.
> Watt's Hymns for Children. *My memory, though ready,
> was not tenacious,* and the rule being that there should be
> no advance until the first book was conquered, I was kept

35. *PCSM* 26 (1927): 278; *Autobiography of Colonel John Trumbull,*
p. 5.

in Cheever's Accidence I know not how long. All I know
is, I must have gone over it twenty times before mastering
it. *I had been about four years tormented with studies not
suited to my years* before my interest in them commenced;
but when I began upon Nepos, Caesar, and Virgil, my re-
pugnance to my classics ceased, and the Preceptor gradually relaxed in the severity of his discipline, and, I have
no doubt, congratulated himself on its success as seen in
the improvement he was compelled to acknowledge. During the latter part of my life in the Academy he was as indulgent as a temperament naturally intolerant and au-
thoritative would permit.[36]

As young Quincy testifies, the normal colonial school day
consisted of long periods of crowded monotony, punctuated by
apprehensive trips to the master's desk to recite lessons dubi-
ously comprehended. Consequently, in most schools, the success or failure of the educational experience, the quality of the
lessons, explicit and implicit, depended to a large degree on
the teacher. In New England, unfortunately, he was seldom
qualified for the task he had assumed.

The great majority of schoolmasters were, significantly, future ministers. Confronted with the virtual necessity of earning
an M.A. to qualify for ordination, the young Harvard or Yale
graduate usually chose one of three options for passing his
statutory three years. The first belonged to the well-to-do or
the exceptionally talented, that of staying at college as a paying, full-time student, a college tutor, or a librarian. Given the
sparse economic resources of the parents of most students, this
was an option seldom taken by the ministerial hopeful. More
frequently enjoyed was the old custom of living and reading
theology with an established minister, perhaps a father, an
uncle, or a father's classmate or friend. But by far the most
common practice for the would-be minister after graduation
from college was to teach in a public school. About 40 percent

36. Edmund Quincy, *Life of Josiah Quincy* (Boston, 1869), pp. 24–25
(my emphasis throughout); Small, *Early New England Schools,* chap. 18.

of Harvard's colonial graduates and 20 percent of Yale's taught
school for some period, usually only a year or two, after graduation, and nearly all of them were ministerial candidates.[37]

Although it was surely better than nothing, the short tenure
of these mobile teachers created difficulties for many of their
students. Richard Brown was one. After he was taught to read
at home by his mother, he was sent to school "under an ingenious and learned master, Mr Edward Tompson, under
whom I profited much and went on with delight in Gramer,
Sententiae and Cato. But then I was deprived of my master
who, being called to the ministry, Left the schoole to his pupils
great damage. After came Mr Shove, to whom I went yet
profited Little; then came another who tarried not Long;
then came Mr John Clark of Exeter, a worthy man under
whom I studied one year, by whome I was sent to, tho not
well fitted for, the Colledge; for by this change of masters I
suffered great damage." Perhaps his own unhappy experience
explains why he stayed eleven and a half years when he returned to Newbury from Harvard to be schoolmaster at the
grammar school he had attended as a boy.[38]

Another shortcoming of the recent graduate was his age and
lack of experience. At nineteen or twenty, possessed of little
beyond "small latine & lesse greeke," unacquainted with the
art of teaching or with children, except perhaps through his
own family, the new teacher was "exceeding raw and unin-
structed." In 1769 Andrew Eliot, speaking rather as a minister
than as the secretary of Harvard, claimed that the 1647 school
law was "a happy provision for our young gentlemen, when
they leave college, and prevents their hurrying into the learned
professions, as they might otherwise do for a subsistence." But
he had clearly forgotten that in 1700 the president and faculty
of Harvard had complained to the House of Representatives
of the lack of a steady supply of qualified freshmen. "As the
Case is at present," they lamented, "the most that are Offered
for admission are . . . utterly Unfit to apply themselves to
academical Studys or Exercises; possibly of fourteen or fifteen

37. See below, chap. 6, n. 18.
38. Eaton, *Genealogical History of Reading*, pp. 52–54.

persons that are Offered we may find one or two fit for Admission. And thus it hath been for several Years past." They were compelled to take the chaff with the wheat, they said, "or none in the Revolution of a few Years become Schoolmasters in the Country." But this perpetuated a vicious circle: poor masters turned out poor freshmen, who in turn became poor masters. The only way to break the circle was for the government to provide an "honorable maintenance" to "some Ingenious & Qualified persons to settle to the work of Schoolkeeping and make it the business of their Lives. . . . Unsettled School masters who come one Year and go the next we are sure will doe Little good." [39]

One other solution, had it been possible in the congregational independency of New England, might have been a more rigorous examination of the pedagogical capabilities of the prospective teacher. In 1654 Massachusetts had placed an ordinance on its books "commending it to the serious consideration and special care of . . . the selectmen in the several towns not to admit or suffer any such to be continued in office or place of teaching, educating, or instructing of youth, or child . . . that have manifested themselves unsound in the faith or scandalous in their lives, and not giving due satisfaction according to the rule of Christ." But understandably New England had never had a formal licensing system for schoolmasters like that of the mother country, where in the seventeenth and eighteenth centuries the established church passed on the qualifications of all teaching candidates.[40]

At least one minister, however, worried about the pedagogical, if not religious, quality of New England's teachers. In 1767

39. *Colls. MHS,* 29 January 1769, 4th ser., vol. 4 (1858), pp. 436–37; Mass. Archives, 14 February 1701, vol. 58, fols. 211–12.

40. *Mass. Records,* 3 May 1654, 3 : 343–44; W. E. Tate, "The Episcopal Licensing of Schoolmasters in England," *Church Quarterly Review* 157 (1956) : 426–32. On 20 February 1701 the Massachusetts Council, in response to the Harvard faculty's complaint of poorly qualified matriculants, initiated a bill that required all schoolmasters to secure the testimonial of the Harvard faculty. The House of Representatives voted it down on 7 March and substituted the approval of the town's minister and two neighboring ministers, perhaps to preserve local religious orthodoxy from Harvard's "liberalism" (Mass. Archives, vol. 58, fols. 213–18).

John Devotion heard the election sermon preached at Hartford by the Reverend Edward Eells of Middletown who "told his Honr. that there was much Heresie in the Land, & by way of Improvement exhorted their Honours to execute their Lawes, and recommended it as a good Guard against Heresie to have all School Masters examined & licensed. . . ." Actually, his printed sermon gives another impression, resembling the annual exhortations of its kind to foster New England's whole educational system more than it represented the tense ecclesiastical tractate that Devotion made it seem. Having reiterated the Puritan ideal of education for virtue and useful knowledge, Eells simply urged that "Teachers should be qualified Persons, of good Characters; who will instil the best Principles into [their students], by Instruction, and a good Example, of Virtue and Religion; and instruct them, by Rule, in those Parts of Learning, which are needful, to furnish them for Usefulness in their Day. For that End, perhaps it might be well, if none be suffered to Teach in our Schools, but those who have been examined and licensed by proper Judges, of their good Qualifications, to be wise and profitable Instructors. The Want of special Provision in this Case, has proved such a destructive Evil already, that Multitudes grow up in Ignorance and Vice, which will naturally occasion a sad Decay in Religion and Virtue, and make them unprofitable Members of the common Wealth." There was no hysteria and no heresy hunt, as far as the printed text reveals. There was simply the Puritan concern for the quality of formal education being offered to New England's children voiced by a minister selected to jar the sensibilities and jimmy the pocketbooks of the colony's chosen leaders once a year. If he went farther in suggesting the licensing of teachers than his colleagues tended to do, his concern might better be explained by rank teaching than by rank heresy.[41]

Even when the candidates were qualified, not enough of

41. *Extracts from the Itineraries of Ezra Stiles,* ed. F. B. Dexter, 6 June 1767 (New Haven, 1916), p. 465; Edward Eells, *The Foundation of the Salvation of Sinners* (Hartford, 1767), pp. 25–26.

them could be found. The New England school laws saw to it that the demand from the country for teachers exceeded the supply of graduates. Some towns of a hundred families swallowed the court's fine for not maintaining a grammar school rather than go to the trouble and expense of obtaining a proper schoolmaster. The more conscientious of them simply doubled their efforts to hire worthy graduates, sending paid representatives to Cambridge or New Haven to consult with the college president about the availability of suitable candidates. Sometimes, when the college classes were small, even these efforts were fruitless, and the threat of court presentation had to be met in other ways.

In 1713 the selectmen of the frontier town of Andover confessed that after numerous teachers had come and gone "we fourthwith aplyed our selves to the collidge [Harvard] to The president for advise and he could Tell us of none," referring them to the faculty, who were equally unhelpful. They begged the court's indulgence for their "great extremity" because "we cannot compell gentell men to come to us and we doe supose thay are somthing afraid of the Reason we doe Ly so exposed to our Indgon enemys." Two years earlier the delinquent fishing town of Gloucester had been defended at court by their minister, John White, who testified that "the Reason why we are now destitute [of a schoolmaster] is not for want of caring for & seeking after one, but rather because at this juncture there is none to be had." Four separate trips to Cambridge by the minister and one by the selectmen yielded nothing from the source of pedagogical supply.[42]

Although the scarcity of qualified teachers might have made for a seller's market, the basic laws of economics seem to have done little to change a stable and undesirable wage level for those who were virtually forced to teach for a preordination living. In the years before the currency depreciated enormously, the typical salary for a year's teaching was between £25 and £40, including salary in "country pay" (goods and

42. *EIHC* 58 (1922): 290–91; John Babson, *Notes and Additions to the History of Gloucester*, 2d ser. (Salem, 1891), p. 5.

produce), livery and boarding allowances, and students' fees. With their patrimonies dwindling, however, young graduates could often do little else but accept it if they seriously intended to enter the ministry in three years' time.[43]

As might be expected, many young teachers were unhappy and unappreciated. One of these, Richard Brown, taught for eleven and a half years, as we have seen, all of them, he thought, unappreciated by his townsmen. Although "I have sent nigh as many to College as all the masters before me since the reverend and learned Parker, . . . those I have bred think themselves better than their master (God make them better still) and yet they may remember the foundation of all their growing greatness was laid in the sweat of my brows. If to find a house for the school two years, when the town had none, gratis, if to take the scholars to my own fire when there was no wood at school as frequently . . . then it is my due, but hard to come by." Yet even this hard usage could not extinguish the "delight" he felt in training up youth in "learning and the knowledge and fear of God and teaching to reverence their superiors." [44]

He was not alone. In the later years of his life, Boston's minister of the New North Church, John Webb, "sometimes said, that the Year in which he kept School afforded him more Satisfaction than almost any Year of his Life." Before he began to rise in the world, John Adams had had similar thoughts. "I sometimes, in my sprightly moments," he wrote, "consider my self, in my great Chair at School, as some Dictator at the head of a commonwealth. In this little State I can discover all the great Genius's, all the surprizing actions and revolutions of the great World in miniature. . . . Let others waste the bloom of Life, at the Card or biliard Table, among rakes and fools, and when their minds are sufficiently fretted with losses, and inflamed by Wine, ramble through the Streets, assaulting innocent People, breaking Windows or debauching young Girls. I envy not their exalted happiness. I had rather sit in school

43. Small, *Early New England School*, chap. 5.
44. Eaton, *Genealogical History of Reading*, p. 54.

and consider which of my pupils will turn out in his future Life, a Hero, and which a rake, which a phylosopher, and which a parasite, than change breasts with them, tho possest of 20 lac'd wast coats and £1000 a year." And though "fortune [had] overturned, & overturned, & reoverturned" all the immediate postgraduation plans of Yale's Timothy Langdon (1781), he "engaged a school in [Farmington, Connecticut, and found] it to be a very agreeable one." "This Pedagoguing business," he wrote to a classmate who had also taken a school, "does very well—It is by no means dishonorable—You & I are both Presidents—Ay & more than that we are Kings (if not Tyrants) we issue laws & govern our little societies as we please & no one has a right to say, why do you! In short we are Judge, Jury & executioner." If this Moloch fed largely upon his imagination, another classmate probably spoke more accurately for the majority of colonial teachers when he bemoaned his position, "neither in the World, nor out of the World—confined to a little obscure Place, where I can neither do anything nor be idle." Sacrificing comparative wealth and status for service and subsistence, most colonial teachers merely perdured until they were called to the pulpit.[45]

Their heady catapult from collegiate abasement to scholastic dominance, coupled with their total unpreparedness for coping with perhaps thirty young children wildly mixed in age, needs, temperament, and knowledge, must have been unsettling for many new teachers. Caught between fluctuating moments of elation and fear, between impossible demands and implausible power, some of them must have felt "in danger of being of a tyrannical disposition." Joseph Green certainly did and was saved only by religious conversion. When he was appointed master of the Roxbury Latin School, he found it "very

45. *Sibley's Harvard Graduates,* 5 : 464; *Diary and Autobiography of John Adams,* ed. L. H. Butterfield, 15 March 1756 (New York, 1964), 1 : 13–14; Timothy Langdon to Simeon Baldwin, 4 December 1781, Baldwin Family Papers; box 3; Simeon Breed to Simeon Baldwin, 2 April 1782, Baldwin Family Papers, box 3. See John Adams' remark: "I have no Books, no Time, no Friends. I must therefore be contented to live and die an ignorant, obscure fellow" (*Diary and Autobiography,* 23 May 1756, 1 : 22).

much out of order by reason of the Sloathfullness and unfaith-
fulness of my predecessor" and was "forced to be severe and
angry sometimes" with his pupils. Fortunately, conversion
"melted my heart," for "I feared least my discourse should
harden my boys." Obviously Josiah Cotton's temperament ran
to the same extreme. "When I kept School (which was above
Thirteen years in the whole)," he reminisced, "as I had a great
deal of occasion, so I gave too much Liberty & vent to a passionate hasty disposition, which thereby is become too much a
habit." [46]

Frustration often gives way to anger and anger to physical
force. It was an old human formula that English schoolboys
had witnessed for centuries. The apotheosis of a long line of
English "Brain-breakers" was Dr. Richard Busby, master of
London's famous Westminster School, called none too affec-
tionately by his pupils "Richard Birch-hard." The necessity of
the rod "to inspire fear" and to compel obedience was acknowledged by every schoolmaster "where numbers have to be
taught together. . . . Beating, however, must only be for ill-
behaviour," argued Richard Mulcaster of Merchant Taylors',
one of the best, "not for failure in learning. . . . Surely to
beat for not learning a child that is willing enough to learn,
but whose intelligence is defective, is worse than madness."
According to some, Dr. Busby had crossed the threshold. "Dr.
Busby hath made a number of good Scholars," admitted John
Aubrey, who generally denounced "the turning up of bare
buttocks for pedants to exercise their cruel lusts," "but I have
heard several of his Scholars affirme, that he hath marred by
his severity more than he hath made." One alumnus, John
Dryden, once said that he had left a packet of poems lying
around so long they had lost their spirit, "just as our Master
Busby used to whip a boy so long, till he made him a confirmed blockhead." [47]

46. *Diary of Thomas Robbins*, 7 May 1796, 1 : 9; *PCSM* 34 (1943) : 198,
239; Memoirs of Josiah Cotton, Mass. His. Soc., p. 157.

47. *The Educational Writings of Richard Mulcaster*, ed. James Oliphant
(Glasgow, 1903), pp. 32, 113–14; John Aubrey, *Brief Lives*, ed. Oliver Dick
(London, 1958), p. xc; John Dryden, *Works* (London, 1818), 18 : 160.

The tradition of the English schoolmaster flailing with a sturdy birch at the slightest provocation did not grow out of barren soil. John Aubrey denounced the *"ordinary* Schoolmaster's tyrannical beating and dispiriting of children [from] which many tender ingeniose children doe never recover again." James Tyrrell, a gentle-born product of the Camberwell free school, wrote to his like-minded friend, John Locke: "I doe not know one boy in 10 that learnes the better for much beating & I abhore that mechanic method in free schools where they administer the rod (as Mountebanks doe their pills) to all tempers & constitutions alike, without distinction." In Thomas Fuller's *Holy State,* the "Good Schoolmaster" is "moderate in inflicting deserved correction," but on the other hand, "is and will be known to be an absolute monarch in his school. If cockering mothers proffer him money to purchase their sons an exemption from his rod (to live as it were in a peculiar, out of their master's jurisdiction), with disdain he refuseth it, and scorns the late custom, in some places, of commuting whipping into money, and ransoming some boys from the rod at a set price." But he shuns like the plague the ignominious practice of "mauling them about their heads," a custom whose existence Henry Peachem confirmed when he said he abhorred "free and generous spirits" being "pulled by the ears, lashed over the face, beaten about the head with the great end of the rod, [and] smitten upon the lips for every slight offense with the *ferula.*" [48]

If physical punishment was an integral part of the English schoolboy's rite of passage, it was no less so for the New English schoolboy. Plymouth's John Robinson spoke for his Puritan brethren when he affirmed that "there is in all children, though not alike, a stubbornness, and stoutness of mind arising from natural pride, which must, in the first place, be broken and beaten down." One good way to inure them to

48. Aubrey, *Brief Lives,* ed. Dick, p. xc (my emphasis); Locke Manuscripts, 20 February 1688, c. 22, fol. 66, Bodleian Library, Oxford; Thomas Fuller, *The Holy State and The Profane State* (London, 1840), pp. 86–87; Henry Peachem, *The Complete Gentleman,* ed. Virgil Heltzel (Ithaca, 1962), pp. 33–35.

"meanness in all things, as may rather pluck them down, than lift them up," he thought, was by "sending them to school betimes." Certainly New England's quintessential schoolmaster, Ezekiel Cheever, wasted few words on prideful children. When the white-bearded pedagogue died in harness in 1708, after seventy years of teaching, Cotton Mather eulogized *Corderius Americanus* and paraphrased his parting advice to his successors: "Tutors, Be *Strict;* But yet be *Gentle* too: Don't by fierce Cruelties fair *Hopes* undo. . . . The Lads with *Honour* first, and *Reason* Rule; *Blowes* are but for the *Refractory Fool.*" [49]

But at least one of his pupils thought that the aged master neglected to follow his own sound advice. John Barnard, who entered the Boston Latin School at the age of eight, recalled that "though I was often beaten for my play, and my little roguish tricks, yet I don't remember that I was ever beaten for my book more than once or twice. One of these was upon this occasion. Master put our class upon turning Aesop's Fables into Latin verse. Some dull fellows made a shift to perform this to acceptance; but I was so much duller at this exercise, that I could make nothing of it; for which *master corrected me, and this he did two or three days going.* I had honestly tried my possibles to perform the task; but having no poetical fancy, nor then a capacity opened of expressing the same idea by a variation of phrases, though I was perfectly acquainted with prosody, I found I could do nothing; and therefore plainly told my master, that I had diligently labored all I could to perform what he required, and perceiving I had no genius for it, I thought it was in vain to strive against nature any longer; and he never more required it of me." Master Cheever, born and bred in the home country, was clearly in the English tradition, for as Queen Elizabeth's tutor, Roger As-

49. Walter Ong, "Latin Language Study as a Renaissance Puberty Rite," *Studies in Philology* 56 (April 1959): 103–24; John Robinson, *Works,* ed. Robert Ashton (Boston, 1851), 1: 246–48; Cotton Mather, *Corderius Americanus* (Boston, 1708).

cham, wrote, "even the wisest of your great beaters, do as oft punishe nature, as they do correcte faultes." It was a rare New English teacher who could say, as Thomas Robbins did upon leaving the Torringford school, "I was never irritated or spoke a cross word to one of them. Their affection and esteem for me appeared to be no less than I had for them." [50]

History has a way of coming full circle. In the decades of the seventeenth century before the Civil Wars, English education had been preoccupied with exercising physical and moral control over the mounting numbers of children who were going to school. The rush to formal education was propelled by the Puritans who, from the time of Elizabeth, solicited the philanthropy of the newly prosperous for the endowment of schools, colleges, and scholarships. They believed that salvation—as well as moral probity and social order—was impossible without literacy, knowledge of the Bible, and the inspired preaching of an educated ministry. While they still adhered to a society of hierarchy and rank, they felt that universal literacy would not breed social levelling but would actually render subordinates content with their God-given condition, while preparing their hearts for Christ's saving grace.[51]

When the Civil Wars erupted in 1642, the major sects emerged with grandiose blueprints for a full-fledged national educational system at all levels from the dame school to the university; the proponents were convinced from years of Puritan teaching that an educated public was "the main foundation of a reformed Commonwealth." Unfortunately, the emotional and financial drain of prolonged war dashed most of the bright hopes of the reformers, and the Restoration killed the rest. A severe reaction set in to what the restored aristocracy

50. *Colls. MHS*, 3d ser., vol. 5 (1836), p. 180 (my emphasis); Roger Ascham, *English Works*, ed. W. A. Wright (Cambridge, 1904), p. 188; *Diary of Thomas Robbins*, 2 April 1798, 1 : 54.

51. Lawrence Stone, "The Educational Revolution in England, 1560–1640," *Past and Present* 28 (July 1964) : 41–80; Stone, "Literacy and Education in England, 1640–1900," *Past and Present* 42 (February 1969) : 76–92.

viewed as one of the leading causes of the wars—insubordination and disorder encouraged by excessive education of excessive numbers. While the Clarendon Code sought to throttle the Puritans' zeal, their visionary plans for universal literacy were scuttled in favor of the reactionary scheme of William Cavendish. And only New England remained to carry the torch.[52]

But in 1792, an even century and a half after Samuel Harmar had written of the school's efficacy as an instrument of social control, Caleb Bingham, an usher at the North Writing School in Boston, wrote of the school as if the intervening years had never passed. "I know you will participate in my joy," he wrote a friend,

> when I inform you that I have gained a complete victory over my schoolboys. They are now nearly as still in the school as the girls. I was obliged to relinquish my method of detaining them after school, on account of Mr. C's conduct. I resolved then to bring the matter to a crisis, and know whether I was master or not. I laid aside all books for the day and spent it in preaching. The next day I undertook to find what virtue there was in the old *maple whig of seventy-six* [a large ferule]. I belabored them from day to day, till they finally gave me the victory. Now and then an old Woman, and a few who are not worthy the name of *men,* and who oppose the doctrines of our *forefathers,* have murmured, and complained to the [school] committee. But the boys are *silent* in school, and that is the main object with us; and I hope we shall be able to *silence* their parents. A certain Mr. Adams, whom we used to hear from last winter, came into the school this day with a complaint against the usher, and told us that he would not allow of his boys' receiving corporal punish-

52. Stone, "Literacy and Education"; W. A. L. Vincent, *The State and School Education, 1640–1660, in England and Wales* (London, 1950); Richard Greaves, *The Puritan Revolution and Educational Thought* (New Brunswick, 1969).

ment on any occasion whatever. We shall, therefore, expel them for the next offence.[53]

In spite of the resort to the rod of "our forefathers," New English education had clearly changed. One aspect was sheer size. In 1742 Boston's schools had enrolled 535 pupils; twenty-three years later the number had leaped to 908. But New English parents had changed too. Many of them no longer condoned the traditional heavy-handed subjection of their children. In 1780, "three children of one Mr. Clark at Mr. Hunt's school, having behaved improperly, were corrected by the usher" and "the father of the children . . . so resented it as to strike the said usher in the school." The Boston selectmen hailed Mr. Clark before them, suspended his children until he should apologize to the usher "in the presence of the scholars," and warned that "Mr. Clark's behavior had a direct tendency to destroy the influence of his usher and the *good order and government of the schools.*" Five years later, another father, Joseph Eaton, complained that his son "had received unsuitable correction from Mr. Carter of the writing school in Queen Street." Once again the selectmen found insufficient grounds for complaint. "Mr. Eaton was then reminded of the mischief which might follow from any weakening of the *government* of the public schools, and Mr. Carter was directed to continue his best endeavors to maintain *that* order *which has so much contributed to the present reputation of his school.*" [54]

New England had changed significantly from its primitive beginnings, and not the least affected were its public schools. The dilution of the founding religious ideal, the growth of towns and population, especially children, the vigorous expansion of education outward to women and downward to the unprosperous, the proliferation of social dependents—all these defined the school's role in revolutionary New England. The New English had not forgotten, as an election sermon had

53. *John Tileston's School,* ed. D. C. Colesworth (Boston, 1887), pp. 38–39.

54. Small, *Early New England Schools,* pp. 387–88 (my emphasis).

told them many years before, that "good Education tends to promote Religion and Reformation." Their altered circumstances, their *New* England, had simply forced them to emphasize the second part of the minister's message: "Peace and Order." The irony is that, in education at least, the American Revolution was the New English equivalent of the Restoration of 1660, not the Puritan Revolution of 1642.[55]

55. Seybolt, *Public Schools of Colonial Boston*, p. 63 and notes 33 and 34; Jeremiah Wise, *Rulers the Ministers of God* (Boston, 1729), p. 31.

6

The Collegiate Way

Freshmen have attained almost the happiness of negroes.

Yale freshman, 1765

Colleges "can only highly serve us," Emerson told Harvard's Phi Beta Kappas in 1837, "when they . . . gather from far every ray of various genius to their hospitable halls, and, by the concentrated fires, set the hearts of their youth on flame." [1] This is and always has been their strength. A college harbors constellations of time and talent, resources and models of adult integrity, apart from the demands of society so that its young may explore themselves and their past to prepare for the future. For its students, however, college represents a social hiatus, a "four-year moratorium on the irreparable," as Margaret Mead has called it, in which the freedoms of childhood are denied and the responsibilities of adulthood withheld. And in some cultural settings, it can be a time of "storm and stress," a social experience that coincides with or resembles the emotional turmoil of adolescence.

Colonial New England was such a culture. As we have seen, childhood was barely recognized as a distinct stage of life with its own emotional and physical needs and rhythm, and adolescence was yet to be born of industrial society. Adulthood was considered the norm for all behavior to such an extent that, after the age of six or seven, young people were simply re-

1. Ralph Waldo Emerson, *An Oration, Delivered Before the Phi Beta Kappa Society, at Cambridge, August 31, 1837* (Boston, 1838), p. 14.

garded as the subjects of imperceptible, evolutionary changes
toward full maturity. There was remarkable continuity in the
educational transition from child to father; the large majority
of young people felt no marked disjunction in their initiation
to New England culture. The major exception, however, was
the numerically small, but socially powerful, class of college
students. In effect, they were the only adolescents in a culture
that did not know adolescence, and the anomaly of their condition created socially disruptive tensions, which were not re-
lieved until they had contributed to the outbreak of revolution
and shared in its success.[2]

In 1620 New England was yet to be. There were no towns,
no schools or colleges—in short, no community founded on
love, or loyalty, or shared endeavor. So the colonists' principal
task was to carve a life from the American wilderness that
would withstand its threats and temptations and fulfill the
partial sense of community they had shared in England. "Wee
must delight in eache other," counseled John Winthrop,
"make others Condicions our owne, rejoyce together, mourne
together, labour, and suffer together, allwayes haveing before
our eyes our Commission and Community in the worke, our
Community as members of the same body."[3] Since many social institutions they had known in England had served them
well in the past, these institutions were brought to their
search for community, but many were irrevocably transformed
by the American experience.

When the need felt for higher education reached a peak in
1636, for instance, a peculiarly English institution was bent
to American purposes. Oxford and Cambridge were universities in a European sense—degree-granting faculties of higher
learning to which an international body of students resorted—

2. John and Virginia Demos, "Adolescence in Historical Perspective,"
Journal of Marriage and the Family 31 (November 1969) : 632–38; Kenneth
Keniston, "Youth: A 'New' Stage of Life," *The American Scholar* 39 (Au-
tumn 1970) : 631–54.

3. John Winthrop, "A Modell of Christian Charity," in Edmund Morgan, ed., *The Founding of Massachusetts* (Indianapolis, 1964), p. 203.

but they were also distinctly English in being collections of semiautonomous residential colleges, which shared their religious and academic duties with university-wide faculties and governors. But when Harvard was founded by the General Court of Massachusetts, the larger university was replaced by the single college, the locus of student society. As Cotton Mather, the son of a Harvard president, wrote in his history of the college in 1702, " 'Tis true, the University of *Upsal* in *Sueden,* hath ordinarily about seven or eight hundred students belonging to it, which do none of them live *collegiately,* but board all of them here and there at private houses; nevertheless, the government of *New-England,* was for having their students brought up in a more *collegiate* way of living." [4]

The reasons for their preference were quintessentially Puritan. For several years prior to the Great Migration, English Puritans had felt that the English universities had fallen to alarming moral depths, rendering them unsafe for Puritan sons. John Winthrop articulated these feelings in 1629 when he listed as one of the reasons for emigration that

> the Fountaines of Learning and Religion are soe corrupted as (besides the unsupportable charge of there education) most children (even the best witts and of faierest hopes) are perverted, corrupted, and utterlie overthrowne by the multitude of evill examples and the licentious government of those Seminaries, where men straine at knatts, and swallow camclls, use all severity for mainetaynance of cappes, and other accomplymentes, but suffer all ruffian-like fashions, and disorder in manners to passe uncontrolled.

As we shall see, the founders of New England preferred the "collegiate way of living" because it facilitated close moral supervision of the students and, at a time when old social

4. Mark Curtis, *Oxford and Cambridge in Transition, 1558–1642* (Oxford, 1959), chap. 4; Cotton Mather, *Magnalia Christi Americana* (London, 1702), bk. 4, p. 126.

assumptions and new social conditions demanded, promoted a deep sense of community among the members of at least one pivotal group of New Englishmen.[5]

The beneficiaries of New England's collegiate way were a mixed group, not unlike the contemporary student population. When the college faculty examined and admitted them annually in the late spring, they were anywhere from ten to thirty years old. Most were fifteen, but the leaven of significantly younger and obviously older classmates created an unusual social situation. The younger boys, who tended to come from upper-class homes where their natural precocity had been nurtured by private tutelage and parental solicitation, were too small to share fully in the rough-and-tumble camaraderie of the majority, while the older students—men in fact— usually burned their candles out trying to make up for lost time in preparing for the ministry.

Another difference was reflected in the college laws of 1650.

> If any Scholar shall transgresse any of the Lawes of God or the House out of perversnesse or apparent negligence, after twice admonition hee shall be liable if not adultus to correction, if Adultus his name shall bee given up to the Overseers of the Colledge that he may be publickely dealt with after the desert of his fault but in grosser offences such graduall proceeding shall not bee expected.[6]

Young scholars could be whipped openly in the hall before their peers or have their ears boxed by the President or Fel-

5. *Winthrop Papers,* 2 : 139. Lucy and Emmanuel Downing wrote to Winthrop in March 1637: "Its true the colledges here are much corrupted. . . . The name of a Colledge in your plantation would much advantage it considering the present distast against our universityes" (Samuel Eliot Morison, *The Founding of Harvard College* [Cambridge, Mass., 1935], p. 170).

6. Samuel Eliot Morison, *Harvard College in the Seventeenth Century* (Cambridge, Mass., 1936), 1 : 75–76, 2 : 450; Samuel Eliot Morison, *Three Centuries of Harvard* (Cambridge, Mass., 1936), p. 102; *Sibley's Harvard Graduates,* vols. 4–15, passim; *PCSM* 15 (1925) : 27.

lows, but their adult (eighteen-year-old) classmates were subject merely to fines and public admonition. The fatuity of trying to impose corporal punishment on strapping young men must have been obvious, yet a better reason to avoid such action was that these older students usually identified closely with the college hierarchy. Coming late to college from generally poor backgrounds, they naturally saw in their teachers models of the religious and social success they so earnestly aspired to for themselves. To those who had long ago put away childish things for the work of men, the petty pranks and studied frivolity of teenage boys only drove them closer to the viewpoint of college.

John Brock, for instance, was twenty-three when he entered Harvard in 1643. He had been discouraged from a higher education in England by the "wickedness" of some Cambridge students he had known, even though "I was not only very apt in my Book but did so love my Book that I would for the most Part choose to be studying while others were at Play." So he came to New England in search of religious purity and an unsullied education in the new School of the Prophets. Unable to farm because of "a weak Body," he turned to the Harvard faculty for a new model of adult success. Henry Dunster, later president of the college, was his tutor and "would come & visit me & encourage me, & I was to go & stay with him."

In turn, John "was an Informer, to further the Reformation in the College." He revealed his complete identification with the college faculty in a diary entry for 1644: "The Students suffer me to pray with them in the Tutors Absence." Neither an ordinary student, nor yet the possessor of authority commensurate with his age, the older student normally eluded the horns of his academic dilemma by squarely choosing the faculty side.[7]

7. "The Autobiographical Memoranda of John Brock, 1636–1659," ed. Clifford Shipton, *PAAS*, n.s. 53 (1943) : 96–105. This is an impression gained from *Sibley's Harvard Graduates*, vols. 1–15. Though I do not have the figures in hand, it would seem likely that the availability of a sufficient number of ministerial posts was a necessary precondition for the normal profaculty leanings of these older students. Otherwise New

The younger student, on the other hand, had problems of his own. Intellectually he was expected to feed on adult fare —Hebrew, logic, metaphysics, natural philosophy—but physically and emotionally he was still a child in the throes of puberty. The diaries of many colonial college students read like a strange mixture of John Calvin and Huckleberry Finn. Robert Treat Paine's is typical. In his first month at college this fourteen-year-old scion of a prominent Boston family began to attend the lectures in divinity and natural philosophy normally reserved for upperclassmen. A few months later he was initiated into the arcana of Hebrew and logic, sophomore subjects clearly capable of taxing the capacities of any man. Yet this lad measured only five feet, two inches tall, twenty-six inches around the waist and ten and a half inches at the neck. And he tipped the scales at all of eighty-nine and a half pounds. But, like all teenage boys, his body grew as fast as his curiosity. During one summer month he gained four pounds, only to add another thirteen by the following spring. This was the boy who skipped prayers with guiltless abandon to plant seedlings, make pets of robins and squirrels, draw landscapes, and go bird shooting and "turtling" on Fresh Pond—the same boy who "went home boozy" after a "Sumptuous treat" given by a college chum. But this was also the boy who, before he turned eighteen, served as a pallbearer for a classmate, saw his mother die, watched at the bedside of a dying professor, taught grammar school, and prepared for full membership in the Old South Church of Boston. The tension of being a child in fact while an adult in deed must have made the college experience for many a time of considerable stress.[8]

Although colonial students were mixed in age, they were socially less heterogeneous. Despite its early national pretensions, seventeenth century Harvard drew most of its students from

---

England would have been in danger of producing a body of "alienated intellectuals," without employment, and hostile to the elite whom they would hold responsible for their plight. See Mark Curtis, "The Alienated Intellectuals of Early Stuart England," *Past and Present* 23 (1962): 25–49.

8. Diary of Robert Treat Paine, 1745–55, vol. 1, Mass. His. Soc.

New England. The great expense of living away from home, the hazards of long travel, and perhaps the uncongeniality of the Puritan religious ideology served to keep the flow of applicants from other colonies to a trickle. Even before Yale was founded and drew off the students from Connecticut and its river valley, Harvard had become an almost local institution of the Massachusetts eastern shore.[9] Even this provincial locus, of course, encompassed a full spectrum of social ranks and classes, but the colonial college did not draw from them equally. The college, and the university of which it was a part, had grown from the aristocratic soil of feudal Europe, where privilege and a sense of caste had characterized education. So naturally, when the college was transplanted to New England, it carried roots that had long fed on inequality.

During Harvard's first century, the majority of students came from families that enjoyed high social status and the benefits of material wealth. They were the sons of ministers, magistrates, physicians, merchants, and prosperous farmers, many of whom had attended Harvard before their sons. By virtue of heredity, they were halfway members of a self-perpetuating elite. A Harvard degree secured them full admission and confirmed their birthright of social leadership. For New England had inherited a system of "sponsored mobility" from the mother country, in which recruits for the elite were chosen by the established elite, and elite status was irrevocably given—not earned—on the basis of some criterion of supposed merit established by the elite itself. For the New English, the

9. From 1690 to 1702 about one-fifth of each Harvard class—or three students—came from the Connecticut colony and valley. But after 1706, when Yale could be considered a going concern, less than 6 percent of each class—or less than one Connecticut student a year—made the trip to Cambridge. By the 1750s 87 percent of Harvard's classes came from Massachusetts, the great majority from the coast. This was merely the continuation of a trend in which 241 of 324 students with traceable origins entered from the Massachusetts Bay area between 1673 and 1707. More accessible to the middle colonies, from which it drew 49 students, Yale still accepted 78 percent of its classes from Connecticut during its first 45 years (*Sibley's Harvard Graduates,* vols. 4–15; *Dexter's Yale Graduates,* 1 : 773; Morison, *Harvard in the Seventeenth Century,* p. 449).

qualities marking a man for public trust were "good par-
intage, abilitye, integrity and fulness of estate." In other
words, social eminence and political authority corresponded
rather exactly. The function of education was less to make
these young men eligible for membership in the elite than to
complete and confirm their qualification, right, and obligation
to govern that already existed.[10]

The social goal of a system of sponsored mobility is to make
the best use of the talents available as a whole by sorting
persons into their proper niches. But, like all human inven-
tions, it is subject to human frailty. It is easy to slip from a conscientious employment of individuals according to their true
abilities to a callous deployment of social ciphers according to
the self-interest of the elite. Higher education then becomes
a closed corporation for what is in fact a caste. This was a sin
to which the Puritan leadership was sometimes prone, but one
of the few for which they failed to flagellate themselves in
sermon or diary. Only the brave charges of an occasional critic
or the implications of an elitist statement reveal the abuse.[11]

In the English Revolutionary skirmish over the learned
clergy, one of the sectaries, John Webster, accused the orthodox ministry of protecting the educational establishment, not
because of a disinterested love of learning, but because their
arcane sermons sought to "deterr the *common people* from
the *study* and *enquiry* after it, and to cause them *still* to expect all *Divinity* from the *Clergy,* who by their *education* have
attained to that Humane Learning which the *plain people*
are destitute of." There was much truth in his accusation,
as a prominent New England minister and Harvard spokesman unwittingly confessed on the eve of another revolu-

10. Ralph Turner, "Sponsored and Contest Mobility and the School
System," *American Sociological Review* 25 (1960) : 855–67; Richard Bush-
man, *From Puritan to Yankee: Character and the Social Order in Con-
necticut, 1690–1765* (Cambridge, Mass., 1967), pp. 11–13; Timothy Breen,
*The Character of the Good Ruler: A Study of Puritan Political Ideas in
New England, 1630–1730* (New Haven, 1970), chap. 1.

11. Edmund Morgan, *The Puritan Family* (New York, 1966), chap. 7,
documents a similar propensity toward tribalism in the Puritan regard of
full church membership as the prerogative of children of the elect.

tion. In 1769 Andrew Eliot informed an English correspondent that, when "some sordid, niggardly souls, enemies to all learning" tried to repeal the Massachusetts grammar school law a few years earlier, "the ministers openly appeared in defence of it." One largely unconscious motive may have been not entirely altruistic. In addition to promoting nearly universal literacy in New England, "even in the obscurest parts," boasted Eliot, the schools the law required were a "happy provision for our young gentlemen, when they leave college, and prevents their hurrying into the learned professions, as they must otherwise do for a subsistence." Of course there were sound and sufficient reasons for encouraging young ministerial candidates to ripen on the educational vine by teaching school before tackling a job of delicate personal and intellectual demands. But few ministers could have been ignorant of the elementary fact that a supply greater than the annual demand spurred the competition for the choicest pulpits. And being at once beneficiaries and benefactors of sponsored mobility, a contest was the last thing they wanted.[12]

Puritan spokesmen seldom revealed their social biases with the bluntness employed by a Harvard commencement speaker in the seventeenth century. If the fathers of New England had not had the wisdom to found Harvard, he told his select audience, "the ruling class would have been subjected to mechanics, cobblers, and tailors; the gentry would have been overwhelmed by lewd fellows of the baser sort, the sewage of Rome, the dregs of an illiterate plebs which judgeth much from emotion, little from truth."[13] The correspondence of social prominence and political authority could hardly have been made clearer, and a college education was the crown of the whole process.

In the eighteenth century Massachusetts Assembly, for ex-

12. For the controversy over the relation of temporal learning and religious insight, see Perry Miller, *The New England Mind: The Seventeenth Century* (Cambridge, Mass., 1939), chap. 3, and Richard Greaves, *The Puritan Revolution and Educational Thought* (New Brunswick, 1969), chap. 6; *Colls. MHS*, 29 January 1769, 4th ser., vol. 4, pp. 436–37.

13. Morison, *Founding of Harvard College*, p. 250.

ample, the political value of a Harvard degree was nearly palpable. Seventy representatives (or 13 percent of the total body) during the years 1740–55 were graduates of Harvard or Yale; 60 percent of these men became House leaders. By contrast only 13 percent of those without college experience belonged to the leadership. Furthermore, forty-four of the sixty-two Harvard graduates had ranked in the top half of their college classes. Of these men, thirty-two, or 73 percent, became House leaders. Since class ranking, as we shall see, was primarily based on "the supposed Dignity of Families," we have an index of the political value of social inheritance, especially when we consider that only 28 percent of the non-gentry Harvard men ever exercised political leadership in the House. A man who possessed a college education, judicial experience, and a Bay area constituency had a 73 percent chance of becoming a legislative leader. If he had but a Harvard degree his chances were still almost twice as good as a man who came recommended only by his experience on the judicial bench or in the affairs of the Bay shore, simply because the Harvard degree, more than anything else, measured inherited—or sponsored—social prestige.[14]

As we might expect, the New England elite replenished itself largely from its own stock, but not to the exclusion of others. Young men of promise from humble families were frequently recognized by the elite—by a frontier minister, perhaps, or by some well-to-do merchants, or even by the college itself—and encouraged to take a college degree. Often this encouragement was expressed as financial assistance. When Joseph Green, the eighth son of a Cambridge tailor, ran out of funds at Harvard, a number of gentlemen, including three college tutors, each agreed to contribute between ten and thirty shillings a year to see him through. Nathaniel Gookin's townsmen were equally generous. Over his four years at Har-

14. Robert Zemsky, "Power, Influence, and Status: Leadership Patterns in the Massachusetts Assembly, 1740–1755," *WMQ* 26 (October 1969) : 502–20.

vard they freely contributed £115 to help his father, their
pastor, cover his son's expenses. When Nathaniel graduated
in 1731, the family expressed its gratitude in an open letter to
The Boston News-Letter, with the hope that "other Congregations may be stirred up by this good Example to do the like
for their Ministers." [15]

Increasingly, the colleges themselves offered scholarships
and work opportunities to needy boys, though Yale seems to
have been less able to assist its students than the older, richer
Harvard. Between 1650 and 1660, when the majority of Harvard students came from gentle, propertied families, only ten
boys received financial aid. A century later, by contrast, almost
half of each class received some assistance, a third of them
from two or more scholarship funds. The change had occurred
at the turn of the century under President John Leverett and
Treasurer Thomas Brattle, who had won unprecedented popularity as tutors by making their students' concerns their highest priority. From 1693 to 1713 Brattle disbursed £679 19s. 6d.
to between a third and a half of the students. Compared to the
£400 that the college was founded on by the Massachusetts
legislature, the sum assumes respectable proportions.[16]

Another form of support for students that was countenanced by the colleges came from school teaching. Josiah Cotton (Harvard 1698) tells us that it was "customary for many
scholars to draw off in the winter," though his own experience
led him to speculate that "perhaps in the general [it was] not
advantageous." Three of his winters were spent away from
Cambridge, two under the tuition of ministers, one, of his
father. "The second winter I kept school for three months for
the Town of Plymouth in my fathers house & under his inspection." Like many of his classmates, he was trying to add

15. *Sibley's Harvard Graduates*, 4 : 229, 5 : 208.
16. Morison, *Harvard in the Seventeenth Century*, p. 107; **Joan Wall-
stein**, "The Social Origins of Harvard Students in the 17th and 18th
Centuries" (Seminar paper, Yale University, 1968); Margery Foster, *"Out
of Smalle Beginnings": An Economic History of Harvard College in the
Puritan Period (1636–1712)* (Cambridge, Mass., 1962), pp. 138–41, 206.

to his father's slender salary, even though his sixteen years might not have fully qualified him to handle both Cicero's *Orations* and obstreperous physical peers at the same time.[17]

Youthful exigencies being what they are, some students inconveniently emptied their pockets in the middle of term and had to look to a school to replenish them. The Harvard faculty was often asked to permit indigent seniors to conduct the Cambridge or Charlestown schools in the early spring, sometimes hard upon a long winter absence as well. Since a poor student was better than no student at all, they usually gave their blessing, "considering his straitned Circumstances," provided that he attended all college exercises and dined in Commons when not actually teaching. On other occasions, the president's study doubled as an employment agency. On 13 July 1784 Ezra Stiles of Yale jotted in his memorandum book that "Dow wants a school." Unfortunately Connecticut supported fewer schools than Massachusetts, and not every needy Yale man could be helped. In his years as president, Stiles more than once had to write that a student was "dismissed for Indigence." If the New England elite regretted the loss to their ranks, they could take comfort that such a boy probably placed in the bottom half of the collegiate social scale and that his superiors—their sons—would graduate in due course.[18]

Although their generosity was increasingly ample, the colo-

17. *PCSM* 26 (1924–26) : 278–80. After a three-week vacation in February, Samuel Gardner of Salem (Harvard 1759) wrote in his diary: "I seem to be out of my Element having lived from Coll[ege] so long" (*EIHC* 49 [1913] : 4).

18. Harvard Faculty Records, 16 February 1767; 6 December 1767; 8 April 1779, Harvard University Archives, vol. 3 (1766–74), vol. 4 (1775–81), Cambridge, Mass.; Ezra Stiles, Memoranda, Yale College, 10 November 1783, 10 December 1783, 12 February 1784, 4 June 1784, 13 July 1784, Yale University Library, New Haven, Conn. The widespread practice of teaching in the winter prompted the Harvard faculty to establish in 1749 a regular five-week vacation beginning on the first Wednesday of January (Morison, *Three Centuries of Harvard*, p. 110). Only 19 percent of Yale's graduates between 1701 and 1740 taught school at some time after college, while about 40 percent of Harvard's graduates did so; and Harvard's classes were normally larger than Yale's (Richard Warch, *School of the*

nial elite still effectively and decisively controlled the conduits of social success in New England, for the simple reason that their generosity was the factor that allowed talented but poor men to rise. One turn of the economic screws and the substantial minority of nongentle scholars who were granted places at Harvard and Yale would have shrunk to a handful. The cost of a college education was simply too great for all but well-to-do families. Without some kind of financial assistance, the children of the lower and even middle class could not hope to enjoy the collegiate way of living.

About three thousand men graduated from American colleges in the thirty years prior to the Revolution, more than twice the number of the previous hundred years. This basic statistic has prompted the wishful conclusion that "no American who could afford the fee of ten pounds a year for four years could fail to secure, if he wanted it, the hallmark of a 'higher' education." But £10 did not begin to cover his expenses, and three thousand was perhaps one out of two hundred eligible men (or one-half of 1 percent). The proportion was higher in New England, with its numerous and sometimes free grammar schools and its several colleges, including two of the country's largest, but still there was no numerical cause for celebration. However, neither did the number of graduates cause much remorse. The question of egalitarianism seldom arose until the Revolution, and by then the social ethos of selective colleges was firmly rooted in New England soil.[19]

Prophets. Yale College, 1701–1740 (New Haven, 1973), p. 270; Wilson Smith, "The Teacher in Puritan Culture," *Harvard Educational Review* 36 (Fall 1966) : 407.

19. Jackson T. Main, *The Social Structure of Revolutionary America* (Princeton, 1965), p. 247; Daniel Boorstin, *The Americans: The Colonial Experience* (New York, 1958), p. 183. In a comparative prerevolutionary period in England (1610–40), Oxford and Cambridge entered a *minimum* of one thousand men each year. Lawrence Stone estimates that this represents something over 2 percent of the annual male age-group, more than four times the American figure. If England's social mobility was sponsored, colonial America's was even more so (Lawrence Stone, "The Educational Revolution in England, 1560–1640," *Past and Present* 28

It was small consolation to men of Benjamin Franklin's ilk that Harvard and Yale were known to be cheaper than Oxford and Cambridge. All he could see in his famous dream—through the eyes of Silence Dogood—was that the passage to Harvard was kept by "two sturdy Porters named *Riches* and *Poverty*, and the latter obstinately refused to give Entrance to any who had not first gained the Favour of the former; so that I observed, many who came even to the very Gate, were obliged to travel back again as Ignorant as they came, for want of this necessary Qualification." Franklin found this doubly sad since "every Peasant, who had wherewithal, was preparing to send one of his Children at least to this famous Place," even though "most of them consulted their own Purses instead of the Childrens Capacities." [20]

The shafts of Franklin's satire were well aimed. Harvard in fact was restrictively expensive. In the seventeenth century, four years of college consumed an average of £40 to £55. For the same amount a man could purchase a small, clapboard house with three chimneys or hire an ordinary laborer for two full years. In other words, it required the full pay of a laborer for two years, or half to a third of the annual salary of a college president, to put a boy through college. By the

[July 1964] : 57). Peter Harris has estimated that colonial America experienced a cyclical (about every 22½ years) increase (20 to 30 percent) of opportunity, related not to political events but to long-range demographical changes. In the trough of the cycle, opportunity was largely restricted to the established elite ("The Social Origins of American Leaders: The Demographical Foundations," *Perspectives in American History* 3 [1969] : 186–90).

20. Cotton Mather, *Magnalia Christi Americana*, bk. 3, p. 158; Foster, *"Out of Smalle Beginings,"* p. 75n.; *New England Courant,* 14 May 1722. For this ambition, characteristically English, see James Howell's remarks in 1646: "Every Man strains his Fortunes to keep his Children at School; the Cobler will clout it till Midnight, the Porter will carry Burdens till his Bones crack again, the Plough-man will pinch both Back and Belly to give his Son *Learning;* and I find that this Ambition reigns nowhere so much as in this Island" (*Familiar Letters,* ed. Joseph Jacobs [London, 1892], 2, 523–24). One New England poet found such sacrifice misguided: "These are grave sophisters, that are in schools/ So wise they think their aged fathers, fools/ That plough and cart; and such they are indeed/ Or else they would not work so hard, to breed/ Their boys to flout them" (*NEHGR* 9 [1855] : 356).

next century, inflation and rising costs had increased the bill. Fathers left anywhere from £50 to £300 in their wills for their sons' "Liberal education." Two members of the Harvard class of 1697 spent £81 and £140 for their degrees. Colonel Joseph Parsons of Northampton reported in his will that he had spent £140 on his son Joseph's Harvard education (1693–7) and £100 for his son David's three years at Yale (1702–5). In 1720 a dunning letter to a wealthy grandmother said that £100 sterling would see her grandson through Harvard, a figure that probably stands for the century; on the eve of Revolution, George Morey estimated that he had spent £114 3s. 1d. for preparatory schooling and three years at Cambridge, "in clothes, in College affairs, Books, Jurneying, having the Small-Pox, [and] other Expenses of what name or nature soever." [21]

But £100 was a price that few could afford, even those members of the educated elite who were expected to furnish their own successors. When the Reverend Thomas Symmes (Harvard 1698) died in 1725, as poor as he had lived, his congregation had to contribute £50 to bury him. Successor to three generations of New England ministers and the head of his Harvard class (over the likes of a Bradstreet, a Mather, a Cotton and a Willard), Symmes was unable to send even one of his sons to college, a fact well broadcast in the Boston press. "A principal Reason was a want of Estate sufficient," his memorialist wrote, "for though He had as good a Maintenance as most Other Ministers in the *Country*; yet he could not (and no other Minister in the Country can, whatever some may think) bring up a Son at the College, besides suitable maintaining his Family, with 100£ per Annum, (paid in our Province-Bills, as they now run)." Only by speculation or farming—both adventitious to the curing of souls—could even a minister afford the means to ensure his son his own social status.[22]

21. Foster, *"Out of Smalle Beginnings,"* p. 83; Morison, *Harvard in the Seventeenth Century,* 1 : 106–07; *Sibley's Harvard Graduates,* 4 : 233, 294, 341, 366, 378, 526; *NEHGR* 27 (1870) : 294; *PCSM* 28 (1930–33) : 302–05.

22. *Sibley's Harvard Graduates,* 4 : 415.

Franklin was also right on the other count. Men of every station aspired to a college degree because higher education was in fact a guarantee of social success and many of its perquisites as well, just as it was in England. The colonial legislatures saw to that soon after the colony was settled. In the General Court of Massachusetts held on 14 October 1651, higher education was equated with gentle status in a colorful way. Regretting the "intollerable excesse & bravery" in apparel, "especially amongst people of meane condition," they felt compelled to

> declare our utter detestation & dislike that men or women of meane condition, educations, & callinges should take uppon them the garbe of gentlemen, by the wearinge of gold or silver lace, or buttons, or poynts at theire knees, to walke in greate bootes; or women of the same ranke to weare silke or tiffany hoodes or scarfes, which though allowable to persons of great estates, or more liberall education, yet we cannot but judge it intollerable in persons of such like condition.

Persons possessing estates of less than £200 were forbidden to wear these items of luxury, upon a ten shilling penalty for each offence and presentment to the grand jury, and a number of court cases testify that the regulation was enforced. As in so many instances, the New England leadership was simply reiterating an old English principle. In William Harrison's words, "Whoever studieth the lawes of the realme, who so studieth in the Universitie, or professeth Phisicke and the liberall Sciences, or beside his service in the rowme of a capitaine in the warres, can live idlely and without manuell labour, and therto is able and wil beare the port, charge and countenaunce of a gentleman," he shall be entitled to a coat of arms and the reputation "for a gentleman ever after." [23]

23. Hugh Kearney, *Scholars & Gentlemen: Universities and Society in Pre-Industrial Britain, 1500–1700* (Ithaca, 1970), pp. 26–27; *Mass. Records,* 3 : 243–44; William Harrison, *Description of Britain,* in Raphael Holinshed, *Chronicles of England* (London, 1577), 1 : 105.

The New English upper class enjoyed several privileges and exemptions that were denied to their social inferiors. The Massachusetts Body of Liberties, for example, provided that no "true gentleman, nor any man equall to a gentleman be punished with whipping, unles his crime be very shamefull, and his course of life vitious and profligate." Of more importance to the colleges themselves was the exemption granted to Harvard men in the first charter of 1650, and given in practice to Yale's graduates in the eighteenth century, namely, that all college officers, teachers and students were "exempted from all personall, civill offices, militarie exercises or services, watchings and wardings," and their estates not exceeding £100 from "all Country taxes or rates whatsoever and none others." In the statutes of medieval universities and English colleges, such martial activities were forbidden as being unsuitable for students of Christ and a waste of valuable time. But New England's scholars soon added a more beguiling argument: that common military duty was beneath the dignity of young gentlemen.[24]

This was the tack taken with gratifying success by Nathaniel Clark (Yale 1714) in a petition to the Connecticut Assembly in 1725:

At great Expence your Supplicant has been Educated in your Colledge then at Saybrook in the learning therein to be acquired, wherein your Supplicant made such proficiency as to be approv'd by your . . . Trustees of whom I obtained the honor of a Diploma, a Testimonial of my admission to the first degree for the liberal Arts; which may be supposed to Elivate the Gentlemen adorned with such a laurel something above the vulgar order; Yet by the laws of this Government are not priviledged from the most Comon Services (as in honor to their dignity upon the first Intimation the honorable Assembly will be of

24. *The Colonial Laws of Massachusetts,* ed. William Whitmore (Boston, 1889), no. 43, pp. 29–64; *PCSM* 31 (1935) : 5–6; Morison. *Founding of Harvard College,* p. 335 and 335n. 4.

opinion they ought), But are Constrained to a Compliance with the prescriptions that oblidge all Except a few orders of men to attend Military exercises, reparing the Comon highways and other Inferior offices. Accordingly your Honors Supplicant has been listed in the Comon muster Role of your Train Band in s[ai]d Coventry and Called forth to millitary and other Comon imployments, which I cant but suppose a disparaging imposition on the order above s[ai]d and indeed is an unpresidented Instance. Your honors will I humbly presume, therefore, for your Great wisdom and honor take effectual Care to free your Supplicant from the Burthen. . .

Master Clark (as he would have insisted on being called) wore neither his learning nor his status lightly in expressing the strenuous class consciousness of the colonial graduate. "Exemption from military duty," warned a recent Yale graduate in 1780, "is of great importance to such an institution; and ought to be carefully preserved and strenuously defended. As soon would I tamely suffer my Country to be deprived of its rights by the Tyrant of Britain, as Yale of this by a Militia Officer." So binding had the correspondence of liberal education and gentle status become by the Revolution that even the patriot cause could not shake them loose from each other.[25]

These, then, were the college students of colonial New England. They were young, growing, and unmistakably male. Their preparation had been classical, with a premium placed on memory. Their homes were seldom more than a hundred miles from the college and their fathers followed every calling from bricklayer to merchant prince. But poor or rich, sponsored or select, they were socially ambitious, and a college degree was the badge of their success. It is now important to see how their college experience prepared them for that success.

25. Colleges and Schools, 1st ser., vol. 1, doc. 53a, Conn. Archives; Ebenezer Fitch to Ezra Stiles, 26 July 1780, *Extracts from the Itineraries . . . of Ezra Stiles,* ed. F. B. Dexter (New Haven, 1916), p. 486.

Every social group, however small, possesses an idea, however vague, of the ways in which its members ought to interact and the social goals for which it ought to strive. The social ideal of the colonial college was no different from that of society-at-large. Its recurring motifs, as we have seen, were obedience, respect, humility, and submission, all within the bounds of an established hierarchy. Although the college student was destined to lead society, he was expected to prepare for that role by learning both obedience and acceptance of his assigned place in the microcosm of collegiate society. The last was doubly important, for the place he held in college often predicted with uncanny accuracy his eventual place in civil society.

When Harvard's freshmen matriculated in the autumns of the seventeenth century, the steward provisionally ranked them in his quarter bills according to the "Supposed Dignity of the Families" or a prediction of their future usefulness to the Puritan commonwealth. As he was placed in his class, so a student would recite before the faculty, seat and serve himself at meals, sit in chapel, march in academic processions, appear in the social register of the day, the College Triennial Catalogue, and, as it has been suggested, at the reunions of Harvard men in Heaven. In addition, "the higher part of the class had generally the most influential friends, and they commonly had the best chambers in the College assigned to them. . . . Generally wherever there was occasional precedence allowed, it was very freely yielded to the higher of the class by those who were below." But if anyone, ranked high or low, was found guilty of some breach of acceptable behavior, he could be degraded one or more places until reformation and penitence were manifest.[26]

By 1723, however, class enrollments were bulging into the forties, making the task of placing according to the complicated dual principle of merit and birth nearly impossible. Consequently successive classes were ranked only according to "the Degrees of their ancestors." Each class was divided into

26. *Sibley's Harvard Graduates,* 14 : 533.

three groups, comprising about 10, 20, and 70 percent. The smallest group at the top belonged to the sons of civil magistrates, in Puritan eyes those who had rendered the state the most service in their generations—governors, lieutenant governors, and justices of the peace, in order of the date of their commissions. The second group was reserved for the sons of college graduates, in order of the date of their first degrees. At the bottom, the largest group was made up of the sons of plowmen and publicans, merchants and mariners, and they were assigned places less according to wealth or social status than to a prediction of their future service to society. Religious denomination, length and distinction of genealogy, date of immigration, or political persuasion cut no ice, nor was there any advantage in being the sons of military officers, shipping magnates, or royal councillors.[27]

Within six or nine months after admission, the college faculty officially placed the freshman class by "having their names written in a large German text, in a handsome style, and placed in a conspicuous part of the College Buttery." Understandably, the day was an anxious one for both parents and children.

> The parents were not wholly free from influence; but the scholars were often enraged beyond bounds for their disappointment in their place, and it was some time before a class could be settled down to an acquiescence in their

27. Clifford Shipton, "Ye Mystery of ye Ages Solved, or, How Placing Worked at Colonial Harvard & Yale," *Harvard Alumni Bulletin* 57 (1954): 258–59, 262–63. Israel Williams, the merchant "King of the Connecticut River Valley," discovered that Harvard could be hardnosed about its principles of placing when one of his sons was placed fourth at Yale and another only fourteenth in thirty-six places at Harvard. Only New Haven was impressed that he was a Harvard Overseer (*Sibley's Harvard Graduates,* 8: 314). Peter Harris has established that in the 1720s, when opportunities increased for Harvard and Yale graduates, often in new towns created by a population bulge, offices labelled appointive (justices of the peace and magistrates) became increasingly "hereditary." Placing according to family honor, then, may have had some "psychological compensation" for those families who were being denied political power (*Perspectives in American History* 3 [1969]: 244).

allotment. The highest and the lowest in the class was often ascertained more easily (though not without some difficulty) than the intermediate members of the class, where there was room for uncertainty whose claim was best, and where partiality no doubt was sometimes indulged.

In a day of social sensitivity and fine distinctions, adjustments were frequently required to assuage the sting of wounded pride.

> Samuel Phillips of Andover Esqr. having some time ago entered a Complaint to the President and Tutors that his Son Samuel Phillips . . . had not his proper place in the Class—particularly that he did not rank with the Sons of those Gentlemen who were Justices of the Quorum, when he himself had been in the Commission of the Peace and Quorum a longer Time than any of them—And having, from the late President Holyoke and others in the Government of the College a promise that the records in the Secretary's Office should be consulted, and if it did appear there was a Mistake it should be rectified; Therefore Voted—That Phillips Son . . . do for the future take his place between Vassall and Murray. . . .[28]

Deacon Phillips was a stickler for rights, but he was sensitive enough to see what dangers lay ahead for his son.

> You are now in the most difficult situation, [he wrote] and the eyes of all, above and below you, will be upon you. . . . Every word, action, and even your countenance, will be watched, particularly by those who envy you, and perhaps by those who do not. Therefore keep as much retired as possible, waive all conversation upon it, dont let it appear that you are in the least degree affected with

28. *Sibley's Harvard Graduates*, 14 : 533, 9 : 432–33. On May Day 1746, Robert Treat Paine noted that his class was placed, "to the great uneasiness of a great many" (Diary of RTP, 1745–55, vol. 1, Mass. His. Soc.) For other adjustments, see *Sibley's Harvard Graduates*, 14 : 307, and *PMHS*, 2d ser., vol. 9 (1895), p. 6.

the change. . . . If Murray is uneasy and manifests it to you, say nothing to irritate him. What if you should ask him, whether it would be any ease to his mind if you should continue to stand below him in reciting? But by no means give the most distant hint of yielding your place.

When academic seniority had become so solemn a business, the days of the system were numbered.[29]

The days ran their course in 1767 at Yale and 1772 at Harvard.[30] Each college substituted a simple alphabetical order for the vagaries of social distinction, but for different reasons. Harvard changed because her classes had grown too large to make such fine distinctions; social democracy had little if anything to do with it. Yale, on the other hand, was suffering from a decline in the size of her entering classes and, as one critic of the change insinuated, from "*the Doctrine of Levellism*" as well. Before he was ousted in 1766 by student violence, Yale's President Clap had used placing as a disciplinary club, one of many in his academic arsenal. His successor, Naphtali Daggett, an ancient, unassuming theologian, disliked ceremony and the dignity of office as much as contention and immoderation. His predilections for simplicity and the pervasive reaction from Clap's harshness brought about the change to alphabetical ranking, all within an atmosphere of heightened patriotism and nascent democracy.[31]

The Reverend John Cotton of Plymouth, whose son was attending Yale even though his father was a Harvard man, found the change grossly misguided. In a bitter letter to President Daggett, he tried to turn back the clock.

29. *Sibley's Harvard Graduates,* 9 : 433; Morison, *Three Centuries of Harvard,* p. 105.

30. The change was nearly simultaneous, for although Yale changed its placing system in 1767, it applied only to the incoming freshman class, which did not become the first alphabetized senior class until 1770. All four of Harvard's classes were ranked on the new system in 1772. The manner of change also belies the different reasons each college had for changing.

31. Morison, *Three Centuries of Harvard,* pp. 104–05; Shipton, *Harvard Alumni Bulletin* 57 (1954); Warch, *School of the Prophets,* pp. 255–57.

I'm perswaded it will give great Dissatisfaction if the new
Method takes place; It may perhaps save the Governours
of the College Some Trouble, and prevent some Reflec-
tions from Some few particular Gentlemen, who think
their Sons have not their due Place; But the other way
will disgust Gentlemen in general, whose Sons must perhaps Stand the lowest, and have one brot up by Charity
or of the meanest Parantage often at their Head. . . .

Although his son would be little affected by either system,
Master Cotton made it clear that, if he had known of Yale's intentions when he was considering the choice of a college for
his son, even though he preferred New Haven to Cambridge,
he would have sent him to Harvard.

I believe it will be a general Discouragement to Gentlemen at a Distance and particularly in our Province to
Send their Sons amongst you (whatever Esteem they May
have of your Society upon other accounts) if they must in
this Sort be degraded and no Distinction be made between them & the lowest Sort. Upon the Whole, [he con-
cluded] I would query, whether the new method does not
Savor too much of *the Doctrine of Levellism,* which has
not much Credit in the present Age. . . .[32]

Perhaps in the Puritan fastness of Plymouth in 1768 the
strains of democracy could not be heard. New Haven, however, was different. College towns usually are.

Apparently, few thought so despairingly of Yale's action.
With the resilience of youth, the students seem to have taken
it in stride. David Avery, a junior, gave his impression of the
change to Eleazar Wheelock, the new president of Dartmouth
College. "There appears to be a laudable ambition to excel
in knowledge," he wrote. "It is not he that has got the finest
coat or largest ruffles that is esteemed here at present. And as
the class henceforward are to be placed alphabetically, the
students expect marks of distinction to be put upon the best

32. *Sibley's Harvard Graduates,* 9 June 1768, 8 : 689.

scholars and speakers." If anyone was upset by the loss of social placing, it must have been provincial parents.[33]

The college faculties were equally nonchalant about the loss of ranking because the basic social system of college life remained intact. The students still performed their academic functions according to their places, and they could still be disciplined by degradation. Since everyone knew the normal order, any deviations from it that the faculty enforced still carried the sting of academic justice. But even in its slightly weakened condition, placing did not stand alone in maintaining academic order. Still fully operative were three other modes of social discipline—fagging, customs, and college laws. Together they created a society of imposing vigilance.

A freshman's introduction to college life was an initiation rite of ancient pedigree. Like all primitive rituals, it was designed to promote his acquaintance with the mores and taboos of the society and to cement his allegiance to it. The most zealous agents of initiation, of course, were those who had most recently passed through the fire—the sophomores. But since the college was a microcosm of the larger society, each class held its own prerogatives and responsibilities in a well-defined hierarchy, as the college laws prescribed. "Every Student of this College Shall in Words and Behaviour Shew all Due Honour, Respect and Reverence towards all their Superiours. . . . And Scholars Shall Shew due Respect and Distance to those who are in Senior and Superiour Classes." [34]

The august seniors were entrusted with the oversight of the whole undergraduate society, much like a student government, and especially with preventing the sophomores from lording it over the freshmen in ungentlemanly fashion. The freshmen were naturally grateful, which in turn tightened the seniors' hold upon their deference. One Yale freshman noted with relief that "the sophimores cannot trim us or as it is called

33. E. H. Gillette, "Yale College One Hundred Years Ago," *Hours at Home* 4 (February 1870) : 333.
34. Yale College Laws, 1745, in *Dexter's Yale Graduates*, 2 : 5; *PCSM* 31 (1935) : 330, 350.

discipline us without special leave from the seniors and then they cannot detain us more than 15 minutes at the farthest. And the seniors scarce ever give their leave to discipline us unless in case of a very high insult." Said another, "They use us all like Gentlemen." [35]

Blessed with the grace of age, a senior was fair; a sophomore, predictably, was as "absolute & despotic as the great Mogul." And no wonder he had this reputation: this is how one freshman described his initiation to Yale society.

At the 1st entrance of a Freshman into this College, he is sure to be ordered up & disciplin'd or as the Sophimores term it Trimming.

They endeavour to find some occasion of animadversion against them which they are not long in quest of as he is generally too free with his Superiors—runs in at the Gate before them—sets without leave—or something—

After he has committed the Crime they assemble a dozen good Voices & summon him with a stamp & a step up to my Room—

He entering trembles & is discomposd & 'tis ten to one commits a greater offence than the other—perhaps he forgets to make a bow, then they all fetch a stamp, asking him what he meant to enter so without bowing,—if he bows to one, the rest are affronted & ask him if he like that one better than all the rest—if he bows in an awkward manner they take great pains to shew him keeping him bowing for half an hour almost to the floor.

They ask him what he was ordered up for, "for insulting the Sophs"—"Well what did you insult them for"—

I say you did, don't contradict me, tell me now whether you did or not—I don't think I did—That is not my question you are obliged to answer all questions, answer

35. *The Laws of Yale-College* (New Haven, 1795), pp. 11–12; Edmund Morgan, *The Gentle Puritan: A Life of Ezra Stiles, 1727–1795* (New Haven, 1962), p. 371n.; Jonathan W. Edwards (Yale 1789) to Benjamin Trumbull, Jr., 30 November 1785, Samuel Goodrich (Yale 1783) to Henry P. Dering, 17 November 1779, Yale University Library, New Haven, Conn.

me immediately—I didn't mean to—Did you ever do anything without a meaning—

If he confesses they tell him there is 4 parts to a confession—1st to confess the Crime—2nd to be sorry for it —3rd to ask forgiveness & 4th to promise Reformation—

Sometimes a verbal, sometimes a written confession answers.

If he is obstinate they put the fists in his face, keep him constantly turning around to see those that are behind him—blow tobacco smoke in his face, make him hold a candle, toe a crack, bow to his shadow & when his back is turnd they are continually going in and out to trim him for not bowing—two or three talking to him at once while he all passive obedience & nonresistance is obliged to stand mute & answer only to the questions they ask him—[36]

Being upbraided for peccadilloes was only half the freshman's lot. The other half consisted of running errands. "Every Freshman Shall be Obliged to Go any reasonable and proper Errand when he is Sent by any Student in any Superiour Class; and if he Shall refuse So to Do he may be punished; provided that no Graduate Shall Send a Freshman out of the College Yard, and no Undergraduate Shall Send a Freshman anywhere in Studying Time, without Liberty first had from the President or One of the Tutors." Despite the emphasis on "reasonable and proper," these onerous sorties were subject to abuse, and consequently to resistance by the victims. From as early as 1667 the Harvard authorities tried to legislate against the use of freshmen for "private Errands" or "servile work," especially during study hours. One of their few successes was the prosecution of Joseph Webb in 1682 for "his abusive carriages, in requireing some of the freshmen to goe

36. Journal of William Wheeler (Yale 1785), in Cornelia Lathrop, *Black Rock, Seaport of Old Fairfield* (New Haven, 1930), pp. 39–40; Diary of John Cleaveland (photostat), 12 February 1742, Yale University Library: "This day we were taken up into the Longe garret to be tourmented by the Sophoi moroi and three of my class were fined for unmanners."

upon his private errands, and in strikein[g] the sayd freshmen."
It was against the petty tyrannies of people like Webb that
the freshmen rebelled. So universal was the foot-dragging that
it had to be proscribed by the sacred rule of college custom:
"No freshman shall Loiter by the [way] when he is sent of an
errand, but shall make hast[e] and give a direct answer when
he is asked who he is going [for], no freshman shall use lying
or equivocation to escape going of an errand." [37]

Besides running errands and doing upper-class dirty work,
the lowly freshman could be handed around like a rubber
ball. In his initiation he quickly learned that "a senior sophister can take a freshman from a sophimore, a middle Bache-
lour [B.A.] from a junior sophister, a master [M.A.] from a
senior sophister, & a fellow from a master." If the order was
broken, the full wrath of authority was visited on the offender,
as Samuel Chandler, a junior, discovered in 1734. For his "impudent Carriage" towards Samuel Coolidge, a Master of Arts,
"in taking away a Freshman from him, and falsely assuming
Mr. Flynt [a college tutor]'s name and Authority to do it by,"
Chandler was "debared the Liberty of sending any Freshman
for the space of a month" and degraded eight places in his
class, which put him third from the bottom. Losing the right
to send freshmen probably cost him more face than the degradation. When a noisy Yale upperclassman was convicted
of "Contempt of the Authority" of the college, he forfeited his
own claim to respect by those below him. He was not only
"deprived of the Liberty of sending Freshmen" for several
months, but all freshmen were prohibited from "treating him
with any more than civil Respect." [38]

As in most tribal societies, the mores of the colonial college
were largely customary and transmitted orally from class to
class. At Yale it fell to the senior class to instruct the freshmen
in the college customs, while at Harvard the sophomores were

37. Yale College Laws, 1745, in *Dexter's Yale Graduates*, 2 : 9; *PCSM*
15 (1925) : 58, 70–71, 196; 31 (1935) : 383.
38. *PCSM* 31 (1935) : 383; *Sibley's Harvard Graduates*, 9 : 481; Yale
College Faculty Judgments, 1751–68, 21 January 1752, Yale University
Library, New Haven, Conn.

responsible—and sometimes, as it fell out, irresponsible. In September 1725 three Harvard freshmen complained to the faculty of "being greatly abus'd by the Sophimores, who struck and beat them." When the verdict was in, five sophomores were fined and publicly admonished for being "unreasonable and Imposing, in often taking the Freshmen into the long chamber, so called, there to Indoctrinate them in rules and customs to be observed by them, and admonishing 'em for non-observing the same." But the faculty knew its allies and was quick to add that it did not intend to "prohibit the sophimores in an orderly and suitable way and in a suitable place, to acquaint the Freshmen with such Innocent and usefull customes as they should observe." [39]

The faculty retained the principle of customs with good reason, for the coherence of the collegiate social system depended upon the success of customary law in teaching respect for "Superiours" and impressing the students with the necessity of social gradation. President Clap of Yale believed so firmly in the disciplinary value of the customs that he codified them, certain that, if they were better known by the faculty and students, the government of the college would be "more steady and uniform, and less arbitrary." [40]

Certainly his faith was not misplaced. As a sign of his inferiority, a Harvard freshman could not wear his hat in the college Yard "except it rains, snows, or hails, or he be on horse back or haith both hands full," and outside he had to uncover his head for upperclassmen. He could not laugh or talk saucily or ask impertinent questions before his seniors. At prayers he was forced to stand upright and not lean. He could not call up or down the hallways or across the Yard, toss a ball in the Yard, "mingo" against the college wall, or go into the fellows' "cuzjohn." And if anyone knocked at his door, "he shall not ask who is there, but shall immediately open the door." Yale freshmen chaffed under the same re-

39. *The Laws of Yale-College* (New Haven, 1795), pp. 11–12; Lathrop, *Black Rock*, p. 41; Morison, *Harvard in the Seventeenth Century*, p. 82; *PCSM* 31 (1935): 452–53.

40. Louis Tucker, *Puritan Protagonist: President Thomas Clap of Yale College* (Chapel Hill, 1962), p. 69.

straints as well as others. They were required to "rise when a Superior enters the room" and forbidden to "sit in his presence till permitted." Whistling, eating, kicking, jumping, hopping, dancing, or singing in the streets of New Haven was strictly taboo. And "in passing up or down stairs," they were expected to yield the bannister to their betters. In short, initiative, exuberance and independence were supposed to be checked at the Buttery for the freshman year.[41]

But no social system is perfect, and, to the chagrin of their seniors, many freshmen turned out to be made of spirited stuff. Instead of abject, pliant creatures of their will, the upperclasses often found defiant young bucks on their hands. That too was part of the rite. To earn their own stripes and self-respect, the neophytes had to resist their indoctrination with spirit and ingenuity. Some just brazened it out, but that only brought the faculty down on their heads for contempt of "the Laws of God & this College." Such was the fate of the Yale freshman who, when called before the sophomores in 1752, "went out of the Room in Contempt of them & said these Words, I sware I will not stay here any longer;" he was suspended for four days. The following autumn a new freshman was reported by the sophomores for refusing to cease his nocturnal noise-making, scuffling with one of them in hall before prayers, and replying "Damn'em" to their orders. Since he was so green and operated with such style, he was merely admonished by the faculty. In 1781 William Wheeler exacted his dues from his sophomoric trimmers with diabolical flair. "A few nights since I put round sticks on the stairs which two of them stepping on, they rolld over & tumbled them headlong to the bottom." Probably most encounters were not so decisive. After being "Smartly Reproved" by the sophomores for "Scandleously Reproaching" them, John Cleaveland had to admit that "they got nothing by it—neither did I." The virtue lay in the effort, not the outcome.[42]

---

41. *PCSM* 31 (1935) : 383–84; Lathrop, *Black Rock,* p. 41.
42. Yale College Faculty Judgments, 1751–68, 18 January 1752, 4 September 1753; Lathrop, *Black Rock,* p. 40; Diary of John Cleaveland, 5 February 1742.

The college customs and the fagging system were effective allies of the college authorities in maintaining the discipline that enabled the business of formal education to go on in the classroom undisturbed. Yet customs and fagging were not self-sufficient nor even of primary importance, for, as we have seen, the written college laws were required to bolster the unwritten law of custom. For the creation of an atmosphere of moral guardedness—the heart of the collegiate way of life— the faculty was finally responsible. Acting in the place of parents, they strove to maintain a bastion of moral conduct, religious devotion, and intellectual discipline. If in the process the college served as a relentless instrument of social indoctrination as well, it was no accident. The collegial society simply conformed to the Puritan paradigm.

The best evidence of this is a rubric that appeared in every edition of both Harvard and Yale's statutes in the colonial period. The Yale version of 1745 was the most complete expression of an ideal that permeated old and New English culture.

> Every Student of this College Shall in Words and Behaviour Shew all Due Honour, Respect and Reverence towards all their Superiours, Such as their natural Parents, Magistrates and Ministers, and Especially to the President, Fellows and Tutors of this College; and Shall in no case use any Reproachful, reviling, Disrespectful or contumacious Language: but on the contrary Shall Shew Them all proper Tokens of Reverence, Obedience and Respect: Such as Uncovering their Heads, Rising up, Bowing and Keeping Silence in their Presence.

Although many were legal adults (eighteen years old), college students were always regarded as children—as boys at best, but never as responsible young men.[43]

43. *PCSM,* 1646 and 1734, 15 (1925): 25, 137; 1655, 1692, and 1767, 31 (1935): 329–30, 344–45, 350; Manuscript copy of Henry Allyn, Yale Laws, 1718, Yale University Library, New Haven, Conn.; *Dexter's Yale Graduates,* 1726, 1 : 347; 1745, 2 : 5; *The Laws of Yale-College* (New Haven, 1774), p. 6; ibid., (1787) p. 6; ibid. (1795), p. 11.

Early in his law-making career President Thomas Clap of Yale described his students as "a company of giddy youth" who needed the *"fear of Punishment* or *Shame"* to keep them from "Vice, Vanity and Disorder." The end of punishment for Clap was not the welfare of the individual, a mature young man, but to deter others—children congenitally prone to evil. By the same token, adults were not presumed to be guilty until they could establish their own innocence, but for students the reverse was true. In 1659 the Harvard Corporation put their student charges in just such a corner.

> In case any Student of this Colledge is found absent from his lodging after nine of the Clock at night he shall be responsible for and to all Complaynts of disorder in this kind, that by Testimony of the watch or others shall appeare to be done by any Student of the Colledge as shall be adjudged guilty of the said Crimes unless he can purge himselfe by sufficient witnesse.

Apparently even the faculty, who should have been more understanding, were deficient in justice. In his senior year, at the age of nearly twenty, Samuel Gardner (Harvard 1759) was treated no differently from any Puritan child. "Dr Wigglesworth sent for me," he told his diary, "for not attending his Lecture last Tuesday, when I had my Brother here, and what is worse would not hear my Excuse, hard *Injured innocence*." When a member of the Harvard class of 1710 repented a breach of college order in a letter to President Leverett, he signed it "Your Penitent Child P. Oliver," although he was eighteen. When a student was greeted by the president in his study with "Well, Child, what do you wish?" or heard that the president had resigned his office with the remark, "Should I leave off preaching to 1500 souls . . . only to Expound to 40 or 50 Children, few of them capable of Edification by such Exercises?" the young man quickly got the message and began to satisfy his elders' pessimistic expectations.[44]

44. Tucker, *Puritan Protagonist,* p. 68; *PCSM* 15 (1925) : 205; *EIHC,* 7 June 1759, 49 (1913) : 1–22; *Sibley's Harvard Graduates,* 5 : 538; Morison,

The student's predilection for mischief, of course, necessitated the eternal vigilance of the "collegiate way of living." In the close community of dining hall and dormitory, classroom and library, the inevitable outbreaks of immorality in Adam's heirs could be isolated and doctored by peers and by models of adult rectitude. There were academic and social advantages to such an arrangement, to be sure, but its primary values were moral. In a country where cheap, plentiful land meant that institutions could not be easily endowed as they were in England, the moral emphasis of the college was not unuseful. By providing an education for the sons of New England that was guarded, the colleges prevented an undue alienation of public support. Any college in colonial New England that owed its lifeblood to popular contributions of corn could ill afford to earn the reputation of "a stinking stew of Anti-Christ."

Accordingly the colleges put their most moral foot forward when they appealed to the public for support. In 1671 Harvard replied to an English offer of aid with a darkening picture of its condition. The buildings were "ruinous and allmost irreparable," the students woefully few in number, and "it is wel known to your selves what advantage to Learning accrue's by the multitude of persons cohabiting for Scholasticall communion, whereby to actuate the minds of one another." On another occasion in the eighteenth century, Harvard approached the Massachusetts General Assembly for new residences on solely moral grounds:

> There are Considerable Numbers especially that were admitted this Year, who are oblig'd to take Lodgings in the Town; upon which not only they themselves complain of great Difficulties & Inconveniencies, but the Gentlemen that have the Govermt of that Society do already feel a great Concern in their Minds & have but uncomfortable Views of Mischeifs impending; which they fear they shall not be able to avert, by reason of many being

---

Three Centuries of Harvard, p. 174; Morison, *Harvard in the Seventeenth Century*, p. 522.

necessitated to be so much & so far from their Constant Inspection, & the Slender Authority the College is capable of expecting from the Town.[45]

Even when there were adequate accommodations, the college's moral concern did not diminish. As early as 1660 the Harvard Overseers decreed that "No student shall live or board in the family or privatte house of any inhabitant in Cambridge wthout leave from the President and his Tutors . . . and if any upon such leave obtained shall so live, yet they shall attend all College Exercises both religiouse, and Scholasticall, and *be under College order and discipline, as others ought to doe, and be that are Resident in the College. . . .*" All students and faculty who lived in the college were required to dine in the fellowship of Commons to avoid the "great disorders" of those living out. But Harvard's most characteristic stance as moral guardian was struck in 1738, in response to a proposal to build a bridge over the Charles River, connecting still folksy Cambridge with cosmopolitan Boston. Their first objection, they told the General Court, was financial: Harvard had always received a "very Considerable part of [its] Support" from the revenues of the Charlestown ferry. Their second objection, however, was of greater moment:

> We apprehend, that any nearer and more ready Passage, over the sd River and especially by a Bridge, will cause Such an increase of Company &c at the College, that thereby the Scholars will be in danger of being too much interrupted in their Studies, & hurt in their Morals.

If they could not prevent the devil in their charges from sneaking out, they could at least secure the door against his marauding minions from the outside world.[46]

The colonial college's concern for the morality of its students was second in importance only to the liberal education in the arts and sciences for which it existed. Such moral con-

45. *PCSM*, 21 August 1671, 11 (1910): 338–40; no date, 15 (1925): 310.
46. *PMHS*, 2d ser., vol. 11 (1896–97), p. 202 (my emphasis); *PCSM*, laws of 1734, 15 (1925): 145–46; 13 September 1725, 26 June 1738, 16 (1925): 525, 679.

cern was not an afterthought of anxious ministers. It lay at
the very heart of the social ideal of a collegiate community.
Without it, the thorough education of New England's young
college gentlemen in her social standards would have been
incomplete. The graduates of Harvard and Yale could be considered perfect Englishmen after such an initiation, but without the touch of cold morality, they could not be called Puritans. When they stepped forward on Commencement day, the
college announced to the learned world their proficiency in
"studies of good literature," and to the Puritan community
their "godly life and conversation." Both were essential.[47]

Thus far we have been preoccupied with the social *ideal* of
the colonial colleges, with the characteristics of the "collegiate
way of living" that perpetuated the mores of the larger New
England community. However, a clear and balanced view of
the cultural importance of higher education must pay equal
attention to the students' *actual* social experience. Ideals are
vital to any human enterprise, and above all to education, but
alone they are not sufficient to tell its story.

New England was a society graded by age, which demanded
different behavior of its members at different times of their
lives and expected persons of the same age group to direct all
their activities toward the behavior desired at that age. Young
New Englanders from twelve or fourteen to twenty-one years
were expected to assume in imperceptible, evolutionary stages
the manners, freedoms and responsibilities of adulthood. They
did not constitute a distinct social group, awkwardly trying to
make the transition from childhood to maturity; they had
already in effect made it.[48] But there was one significant

47. Harvard did not grant diplomas to graduates as a matter of course
until 1813; a fee was charged for those who wanted them, and generally
only those going abroad bothered to obtain them (Morison, "Harvard Degree Diplomas," *Harvard Alumni Bulletin* 35 [1933] : 804–13). The phrases
quoted are from George Alcock's B.A. diploma and *New England's First
Fruits* (London, 1643). Morison, *Harvard in the Seventeenth Century*,
p. 281; Morison, *Founding of Harvard College*, p. 436.

48. Ruth Benedict, "Continuities and Discontinuities in Cultural Conditioning," *Psychiatry* 1 (May 1938) : 165; John Demos, *A Little Commonwealth: Family Life in Plymouth Colony* (New York, 1970), chap. 10.

exception—the college student, whose social experience represented a serious disjunction in his cultural conditioning. When the other members of his age group were exercising their maturity in apprenticeship or military service, where the full force of legal and ecclesiastical sanctions operated, the college student was incarcerated in a moral stockade of special privilege and overweening, absolute paternalism. The tensions generated by his anomalous position became so acute in the eighteenth century that only rebellion in the colleges and revolution in the colonies could relieve them.

Every social institution requires some discipline of its members in order to achieve its goals, but the discipline must be appropriate to their particular needs and nature if it is not to defeat its purpose. As the membership of the social institution changes, so must the mode of discipline. Unfortunately, the colonial colleges did not accommodate their exercise of authority to the changing student body. Harvard and Yale, on the eve of revolution, were conducted very much as they had been in the years they were founded, despite student bodies that were about two years older on admission and placed greater value on independence.[49] Maturing young men continued to be treated like sniveling children—sometimes disliked, often disparaged, and always distrusted. Subjected for generations to the indignity of corporal punishment and the impotent annoyance of petty fines and mulcts, the students finally reached the end of their tether in the middle of the eighteenth century and began to offer resistance to their governors.

Whipping was a common punishment at Harvard in the seventeenth century, when boys were small and Satan was strong, but a rising notion of human dignity forced it into disuse by 1718. Yet the colleges knew that "boys will be boys," so a substitute was found in boxing—a sharp smack on the

49. At Harvard the median age of entering freshmen rose from about 15½ years in the seventeenth century to 17 years in 1769. Yale's students in its first forty years (1701–40) were already 16½ (Morison, *Harvard in the Seventeenth Century*, p. 450; Morison, *Three Centuries of Harvard*, p. 102; Warch, *School of the Prophets*, p. 254).

ear of the kneeling culprit. This instrument to compel a student to "any Duty or Obeidience" was jealously guarded by the faculty, and if any undergraduate usurped that right, he could be deprived of sending freshmen, degraded, or expelled, "according to the Aggravation of the Offence." In their zeal to initiate the freshmen, sophomores were frequently caught on faculty territory. When Peter Oliver and several classmates were apprehended for "Boxing the Gentlemen freshmen" in 1708, they escaped the full fury of college justice only because "the Gentlemen Freshmen interceded for us by Drawing up a Petition to the President and Fellows on our Behalf that he would forgive us and pass it by this time." The new spirit had not yet risen.[50]

But by the 1730s a number of students were having no truck with such abuse. One day in 1733 William Vassal, a seventeen-year-old fellow commoner and senior, insolently refused to doff his hat to Tutor Daniel Rogers in the Cambridge marketplace. Following college custom, Rogers proceeded to box his ears for his "Irreverent behaviour." The boy's father, a wealthy Jamaica planter, was livid and hired the best New York lawyer to sue Rogers for £100. In the long judicial imbroglio that ensued, Vassal won his fight but lost on the principle in question. Rogers was found guilty of assault but was only fined £11 (which the college replaced), and the Superior Court reaffirmed the college's right to box, the loss of which the college felt would have been "very hurtfull to the Government of this Society." The following year Elisha Hutchinson appealed to the Harvard Corporation to redress his abuse at the hands of a tutor. Though unsuccessful, his protest did portend the demise of the practice. When Samuel Jordan resisted a tutor who tried to box him for singing in studying time in 1750, boxing was all but dead. It disappeared from use in 1755, and from the college laws in 1767.[51]

---

50. Morison, *Three Centuries of Harvard*, p. 113; *PCSM* 15 (1925): 145, 153; *Sibley's Harvard Graduates*, 5 : 537.

51. *PCSM* 16 (1925) : 630; *Sibley's Harvard Graduates*, 9 : 350–51; Diary of Robert Treat Paine, 27 May 1749. President Clap was still boxing in 1756, but cannot have continued much beyond that date (Yale College

Resistance took other forms as the arbitrary paternalism of the colleges grew more erratic. Before the middle of the century, little if any resistance had been made to the judgments handed down by the authorities. That was only to be expected when students were young, ingenious pranks were a respected ritual of college life, and tutors were reputed to be "Humane and gen'rous, affable and kind, Polite and easy, and of open mind." Those who put cows in the college pulpit, burned the fellows' privy, or cut the rope of the college bell *expected* to be punished for their successes; indeed they would have been disappointed if they had gone unnoticed. But increasingly, pranks gave way to overt acts of violent law-breaking, and the quiet submission of the guilty was no longer forthcoming. Naturally the faculties saw in this a disastrous "Contempt of Authority," which was true, but the students better understood the motives behind it.[52]

Perhaps it started at Harvard in 1747, when three students were degraded for "Laughing while their admonishions were reading . . . for having made a turbulent noise." If so, the virus of rebellion quickly spread to New Haven, where it raged in a particularly virulent form for nearly fifteen years. By the early 1750s, open disrespect for upperclassmen, public admonitions, and the ever onerous tutors was commonplace, but the middle of the decade saw a change. Two students were heavily fined, degraded, and, with fourteen comrades, deprived of sending freshmen for leading a riotous "rake" in the Yard and then having the "bold impudence" to present President Clap with a written protest of his illegal and summary fines. The following month a fearless lad rang the bell even while the president was announcing his rustication for a long record of previous tintinnabulations. On 11 April 1758 David Gardiner was expelled for "Contempt & Disobedience" to a tutor and for fomenting a bad riot—full of gunfire, broken windows, and bell-ringing—which even the tutors

---

Faculty Judgments, 17 January 1756; Diary of Benjamin Trumbull [Yale 1759], 16 January 1746, Yale University Library, New Haven, Conn.).

52. Morison, *Three Centuries of Harvard*, p. 134.

were afraid to try to quell. Even though the riot's seriousness required the town's sheriff, Gardiner was restored after less than two months at home.[53] From 1760 until Clap was forced to resign six years later, Yale looked more like a guerrilla war zone than a seat of the muses. Riots, bell-ringing, town-gown fracases, destruction of property, bonfires, and sporadic gunfire were regular occurrences. And the contempt grew more flagrant. In chapel a student "stood up & prophanely mimicked the President at Prayers," while on another occasion a hunk of cheese was thrown across the dining hall at the departing tutor's head. The culprit pleaded that he was merely a bad shot, having aimed at a fellow student at the opposite end of the hall! Conditions were so terrible that in 1762 one student tried to escape New Haven on a West Indian trader, and another was driven to send a note to the president threatening personally to "skin old Tom Clap's Hide" if any students were expelled.[54]

Undergraduates were not alone in their resistance. Even resident Bachelors, who in previous years could have been expected to support the college authorities and help maintain order, found sources of discontent. In 1761 a number of "Scholars," including two B.A.'s, created a hubbub and then beat a hasty retreat behind a locked door before the pursuit of the president and two tutors. When the authorities demanded entrance—to which they were entitled by college law, and which they were accustomed to make with axes—the reply from within was, "I won't," several times, "You have no Business here; if you come you come at your Perril. The Man that enters Dies." The faculty wisely withdrew, but the four

53. Diary of Robert Treat Paine, 24 April 1747; Yale College Faculty Judgments, 31 January 1755, 7 February 1755, 28 March 1755, 7 April 1758, 11 April 1758.

54. Yale College Faculty Judgments, 16 July 1762, 14 January 1763, 30 January 1764, 25 January 1765. During the disorders at Harvard in April 1768, the focus of the whole affair, a malleable student named Whiting, said at one point, when he was under pressure, that "he tho't of going on board a Man of War" (Testimony of Ward Chipman, 7 April 1768, Harvard Faculty Disorders, vol. 1, Harvard University Archives, Cambridge, Mass.).

scholars were expelled. Some years later, at Harvard, several Bachelors tried to drown their war-weariness in a bottle of rum and ended up with petty fines for riotous behavior. At their interrogation by the faculty, however, "they all behaved with great Insolence, & Persisted in it." One audacious soul boasted: "Pray Gentlemen! What right have you to call me before you? I am surprised you should be ingaged in such Business! What Punishment can you inflict upon me? What do I care for a little paltry Degree which may be bought at any time for twenty shillings. If honor in this Country consists in Degrees, you are very welcome, Gentlemen, to deprive me of yours, for I have two other already." Samuel Langdon, the nerveless president who swallowed this insult, was shortly removed as a result of a student petition that said: "As a man of genius and knowledge we respect you; as a man of piety and virtue we venerate you; as a President we despise you." Even at the height of national need for discipline and order, New England's college students struck out at their governors as if in maddened frenzy.[55] Why? What possessed them to violently depose one president and contemptuously force another's resignation?

The answer surely cannot lie in the boyish exuberance of college pranksters—the situation was much too serious for that. One explanation was offered by the Yale Corporation in 1766, shortly before they reluctantly accepted Clap's resignation. For the official record, they attributed Yale's miseries to the "Spirit of the Times and the Influence of others," meaning the Stamp Act crisis and the Benjamin Gale faction in the Connecticut Assembly, which tried unsuccessfully to obtain the power of visitation over the college and thereby to depose its president. Both charges, however, were somewhat wide of the mark. The Stamp Act was only a year old, while Yale's misfortunes had a long and ignoble history. There was vehement and vocal opposition to Clap's conduct of the college,

55. Yale Corporation Records, 23 July 1761, 1 : 161, Yale University Library, New Haven, Conn.; Harvard Faculty Records, 20 October 1777, vol. 3; Morison, *Three Centuries of Harvard*, p. 162.

but it was the product, not the cause, of Yale's deplorable state. Furthermore, Gale's vitriolic pamphlet war on Clappism began in 1759, but, as we have seen, student rebellion was in full swing by 1755.[56] The memorial sent by three Yale fathers to the General Assembly in 1761 was a more measured expression of the widespread discontent in the colony with student rebellion, and the words point us toward a clearer understanding of the students' behavior.

For the last half Year little or no Study has been done, the Students have had their Minds embroiled with Enmity and a Turbulent Spirit; and have spent much of their Time in caballing against President and Tutors; that their Refractoriness has arisen so high as to Embolden them to contemn the highest Academical Punishments, which have been so often repeated upon them as to Serve only to irritate them into the highest outrage; that Students have by this Means been so enraged for the last half Year as to be guilty of high Violences against the President and Tutors too many and Shameful to be Enumerated.

In the first instance it was Clap's government of the college that generated his opposition. This was the heart of the grievances presented to the Corporation by "all the students except two or three" in March 1766. The most flagrant of Clap's "intolerancies" was "his neglect to publish a law granting appeals to corporation—and in general, that the students don't know by what laws the society is govern'd, as the president (pro arbitrio) makes laws, and alters penalties for past crimes."[57] Colonial college laws bear the unmistakable mark of the president under whom they were drawn, and Yale's laws of

56. Yale Corporation Records, 1 : 173. For the story of Gale's opposition to Clap, see Tucker, *Puritan Protagonist*, chap. 9.
57. Colleges and Schools, 1st ser., 1 : 340, Conn. Archives; *Extracts from the Itineraries . . . of Ezra Stiles*, p. 455.

1745 are a faithful index of Clap's philosophy of government. For most of the twenty-odd penal offences, pecuniary fines, graduated by the nature and repetition of the crime, were deemed sufficient punishment. The rest were thought to be redeemed by public admonition in Hall, degrading, deprivation of sending freshmen, rustication, or expulsion. In practice, however, Clap relied heavily upon fines—"arbitrary and oppressive Exaction" in Gale's view—and expulsion—"unmercifully and without remedy." To the great annoyance of parents and students alike, he frequently exacted more than the sixteen shillings allowed by law, so often that the yearly income from fines alone ranged between £30 and £70 during his zenith of power.[58]

Even more characteristic of Clap's style was the statute that gave the president alone discretionary *"Power"* to make laws by fiat when the existing statutes were inapplicable to the situation. Clap's preferences are thrown into sharp relief by a comparison with the same statute as revised in 1774 by Naphtali Daggett. There both the president *and tutors* were given "a discretionary or *parental Authority* . . . according to the known ancient Customs of the College, and the plain general Rules of the moral Law." And equally important, in the event of heavy punishment, the student had the "Liberty to bring a Petition to the Corporation for Relief therein" if his appeal to the faculty for a rehearing of the case was denied. Due process of law, the right to see copies of judgements, the accountability of the faculty, gentle discretionary authority, the right of appeal—these are conspicuously absent during the reign of "Pope Clap." A student spoke for generations of Yale men when he doodled in the margin of his

58. *Dexter's Yale Graduates,* 2 : 2–18; Tucker, *Puritan Protagonist,* pp. 212–13; Morgan, *Gentle Puritan,* p. 326n. In 1766 the Connecticut Assembly offered Yale an annual grant of £160 if it would reduce its fines. A student doodler testified to Clap's proclivities when he wrote, "If old Tom had all the fines that he has took from the Scholars within this three year, it would build a Chapel as big as Solomons house" (Richard Warch, "Graffiti Olde & Bolde," *Yale Alumni Magazine,* November 1969, p. 39).

textbook, "Old Tom Clap you are quite wrong in your form of government." [59]

But one man, no matter how arbitrary and mean spirited, cannot explain a rebellion of generations. Harvard students, too, took to the streets, and their government was certainly milder in practice, if not in their imaginations. Not by coincidence, the college's explanation of their behavior echoed an earlier Yale theme. In 1769 the Reverend Andrew Eliot of the Harvard Corporation wrote to the great English patron of Whig liberty, Thomas Hollis:

> The young gentlemen are already enough taken up with politics. They have catched the spirit of the times. Their declamations and forensic disputes breathe the spirit of liberty. This has always been encouraged; but they have sometimes wrought themselves up to such a pitch of enthusiasm that it has been difficult to keep them within due bounds. But their tutors are fearful of giving too great a check to a disposition which may hereafter fill the country with patriots, and choose to leave it to age and experience to correct the ardor.

The spirit of liberty was contagious, and no colonial college was able to immunize its students. [60]

In the face of reluctant hometown merchants, they supported the nonimportation and nonconsumption agreements by giving up tea and "foreign spiritous Liquors," wearing homespun, and abolishing lavish public commencements. They took up political topics of current interest in their debating societies and graduation addresses, and transferred the printing of their commencement theses from Tory publishers to Whig. They ranged themselves into military companies and began to drill

59. *Dexter's Yale Graduates,* 2 : 17–18 (my emphasis); *The Laws of Yale-College* (New Haven, 1774), pp. 26–27 (my emphasis); *Yale Alumni Magazine,* November 1969, p. 39.
60. *Colls. MHS,* 25 December 1769, 4th ser., vol. 4, p. 447; Thomas Hutchinson, *History of the Colony and Province of Massachusetts-Bay,* ed. Lawrence Mayo (Cambridge, Mass., 1936), 3 : 135.

for war. In everything, they pulled together for the colonial cause. Tories quietly left, and any person hostile to the Continental Congress was exposed in the public prints as an "Enemy to his Country" and ostracized in the ancient way, a small but characteristic sign of their profound debt to the classical heritage. More than anything else, perhaps, it was this classical education, uniting a knowledge of men, the art of speaking, and the indomitable spirit of the Roman republic, that enabled New England's two thousand college graduates to "influence and direct the great body of the people to a proper line of conduct, for opposing the encroachments of Great Britain on their liberties." [61]

It was in this larger context of the "inalienable rights of Englishmen" that New England's students brought the government of their colleges to its knees and exposed it for the fraudulent anachronism that it was. It was not simply "oppressive" and "arbitrary," though that would have been serious enough; it was also a travesty of true parental government. The faculty did not act *in loco parentis* because, in Puritan casuistry, "the Authority of Parents over their Children is Limited" by God and the civil law, and the college's authority over its students was effectively unlimited. "Every well ordered Government allows unto Children a relief against the Unreasonable Treatments of Unnatural Parents," but the college student enjoyed no such relief. College presidents neither paid "an Honour to their Children" nor avoided extremes of rigor and indulgence

61. Morison, *Three Centuries of Harvard*, chap. 7; *New York Gazette*, 22 November 1764; Edmund Morgan, "The Puritan Ethic and the American Revolution," *WMQ* 24 (January 1967): 8, 12; *Connecticut Journal & New-Haven Post-Boy*, 30 August 1775; Richard Gummere, *The American Colonial Mind and the Classical Tradition* (Cambridge, Mass., 1963), chap. 4; Bernard Bailyn, *The Ideological Origins of the American Revolution* (Cambridge, Mass., 1967), pp. 23–26; David Ramsay, *The History of the American Revolution* (Philadelphia, 1789), 2 : 320. For a convenient summary of revolutionary collegiate activities, see Howard Peckham, "Collegia Ante Bellum: Attitudes of College Professors and Students toward the American Revolution," *Pennsylvania Magazine of History and Biography* 95 (January 1971): 50–72.

in their discipline. And they seldom exercised "a wise mixture of Authority and Love, fatherly Tenderness and Compassion." [62]

It was not the social nature of the college itself that was under attack. Placing, fagging, and college customs were perfectly acceptable to the students both before and after the Revolution. Nor was the moral function of the collegiate way of living assaulted. Students rose up in rage for two reasons, one they could remedy, the other they could not: they were treated like irresponsible children, with suffocating paternalism and erratic arbitrariness at a particularly auspicious moment in American history, and, while their peers were joining the adult world, they were forced to endure a four-year moratorium on maturity. Prisoners of their culture, as well as its beneficiaries, they were unable to alter their anomalous position as the only effective adolescents in a society that did not recognize adolescence. For it was against the very nature of the college experience that they were straining, and no student generation, before or since, has been able completely to break its constraints.

Nevertheless, with the help of the American fight for independence, they were successful in winning the rights and honor that was their due as young adults. In a society where "at the close of boyhood the man appears," the college student fought and won the right to act his age, even if he could not for a time assume his rightful place beside his peers in New England's work. The only pity is that he was forced to obtain by moral violence the liberty which his governors had refused him. [63]

62. Samuel Willard, *A Compleat Body of Divinity* (Boston, 1726), pp. 598–605; Tucker, *Puritan Protagonist,* p. 212.

63. Alexis De Tocqueville, *Democracy in America,* ed. Phillips Bradley (New York, 1966), 2 : 192.

7

The Scholastic Philosophy of the Wilderness

*. . . the scholastic philosophy of the wilderness
to combat which one must stand outside and laugh
since to go in is to be lost.*

Marianne Moore

"In the beginning," John Locke had written, "all the World was *America*." There was no money, no unlimited accumulation of property, and consequently no need for elaborate institutions of government to control human greed. Eminently sociable and peace-loving, men in the state of nature lived "according to reason, without a common Superior on Earth, with Authority to judge between them."

When it appeared in 1690, Locke's picture of the natural condition must have seemed to many Englishmen—to Whigs at least—a superb blend of historical observation and philosophical acuity. But to three generations of New English colonists, it would have appeared overdrawn and dolefully optimistic. For to them, primitive New England had not been a natural paradise of "Peace, Good Will, Mutual Assistance, and Preservation," but rather a "State of Enmity, Malice, Violence, and Mutual Destruction," a living hell ignited by its barbarous inhabitants.[1] The Indians threatened to push them into the sea, and nearly succeeded on several occasions, but the threat of physical annihilation was never so alarming

1. John Locke, *Two Treatises of Government*, ed. Peter Laslett (Cambridge, 1960), bk. 2, sec. 19, p. 298; sec. 49, p. 319.

to English sensibilities—perhaps because they were blinded to the possibility by their supreme righteousness—as the Indian himself. To the English he stood proudly and defiantly against all that they stood for, all that was good, and Christian, and civilized. The Indian, in their lights, was immoral, pagan, and barbarous. So, characteristically, they tried to remake him in their own image through the time-honored but formal institutions of English education—the church, the school, and the college. Needless to say, they failed miserably.[2]

But education, if it is any good, is never a one-way process; sensitive teachers will learn as much from their students as their students will from them. Nor is it always a didactic process; the imitation of intangible qualities and behavior patterns is as powerful an educational force as formal instruction, perhaps more so because of the reinforcement provided by the visible embodiment of those qualities in living models. Accordingly, it would be surprising if the English themselves did not learn a great deal from the original inhabitants in the crucible of the New England wilderness.

The shifting frontier between wilderness and civilization seems an unlikely place for a school, but the cultures that meet there never fail to educate each other. Although one culture may predominate and tend to teach more than it learns, the educational process is always mutual. Because the New English possessed a clear superiority of technology, government, and population, which eventually tipped the cultural scale against the Indians in a saddeningly total way, it is easy for historians to dwell exclusively on the white efforts to civilize and Christianize the Indian. It is easy, but it is also unfortunate, for it neglects the lessons that the English learned from the Indians, lessons which, ironically, helped tip that scale against the Indians' own future.

2. For recent discussions of the English attempts to convert the Indians to "civility," see William Kellaway, *The New England Company, 1649–1776* (London, 1961); Alden Vaughan, *New England Frontier: Puritans and Indians, 1620–1675* (Boston, 1965); Roy Harvey Pearce, *Savagism and Civilization*, rev. ed. (Baltimore, 1965); Ola Winslow, *John Eliot, Apostle to the Indians* (Boston, 1968).

The Indian served as a teacher to the New English in three guises: as neighbor (their hospitable welcomer and uninhibited visitor), as warrior (their mortal enemy or supportive comrade-in-arms), and as example (a tempting model of a different way of life). In each of these roles, significantly, he met his white students on the frontier, where he was culturally secure and they were exposed, often unsure of what they had left behind and not a little tempted by what they found in the woods. In these remote plantations, where it was rightly feared "many were contented to live without, yea, desirous to shake off all Yoake of Government, both sacred and civil, and so transforming themselves as much as well they could into the Manners of the Indians they lived amongst," the Indian found pupils far more receptive to his teaching than he would ever be to theirs. The best of them were young, like the children of Hannah Swarton, who moved from Massachusetts to Maine for "large accommodations in the world, thereby exposing [them] to be bred ignorantly like Indians," but whatever their age, the English soon learned that, when they were in the woods, however uncomfortable they might be in his presence, the Indian was not only the only teacher available but the best as well.[3]

By a stroke of providence that only a Puritan could fully appreciate, the first two Indians who met the New English spoke their language. Samoset was an Algonkian sagamore from Maine "where some English ships came to fish . . . amongst whom he had got his language." Having shipped to Cape Cod with one of them, he was on his way down east when he boldly approached the newly arrived pilgrims at Plymouth and, in broken English, offered to help. According to their governor, William Bradford, "he became profitable to them in acquainting them with many things concerning the state of the country in the east parts where he lived, which was afterwards profitable unto them; as also of the people here,

3. William Hubbard, *The History of the Indian Wars in New England*, ed. Samuel Drake (Roxbury, 1865), 2 : 256–57; Emma Coleman, *New England Captives Carried to Canada* (Portland, Me., 1925), 1 : 204–05.

of their names, number and strength, of their situation and distance from this place, and who was chief amongst them." Even more helpful was Squanto, who had been kidnapped to England in 1614 and accordingly spoke better English than Samoset. This "special instrument sent of God" was their pilot, interpreter, and willing teacher until his death in 1622.[4]

One of the first lessons he taught them, as his brethren would continue to teach each successive wave of settlers, was "how to set their corn, where to take fish, and to procure other commodities." Since the pilgrims had dropped anchor in the "weatherbeaten face" of the New England winter, they had to wait for the spring winds to soften its countenance before they could plant their first crops. But when they did, "either by the badness of the seed or lateness of the season or both, or some other defect," all the English wheat and peas they sowed "came not to good." It was then that Squanto "stood them in great stead" by extending his agricultural knowledge to them. He was only the first of many Indians who were, as the grateful English acknowledged, "our first instructors for the planting of their *Indian* Corne, by teaching us to cull out the finest seede, to observe the fittest season, to keepe distance for holes, and fit measure for hills, to worme it, and weede it; to prune it, and dress it as occasion shall require." In the early years of settlement the Indians' liberal tutelage in the natural life of their woods and fields often provided the English with the slim difference between survival and starvation.[5]

The Indians' generosity is the more remarkable because their only previous knowledge of the English was likely to have been of rapacious seamen and adventurers. As soon as their initial suspicions were laid to rest by the civil conduct of settlers who obviously intended to make permanent residence in their land, they extended the English every courtesy, advice, and endeavour to help them. Roger Williams, who probably

4. William Bradford, *Of Plymouth Plantation, 1620–1647*, ed. Samuel Eliot Morison (New York, 1952), pp. 79–81.
5. Ibid., pp. 81, 85; William Wood, *New Englands Prospect* (London, 1634), p. 70.

knew them better than anyone else, "acknowledged amongst them an heart sensible of kindnesses, and . . . reaped kindnesse again from many, seaven yeares after, when I my selfe had forgotten. . . . If any stranger come in, they presently give him to eate of what they have; many a time, and at all times of the night (as I have fallen in travell upon their houses) when nothing hath been ready, have themselves and their wives, risen to prepare me some refreshing. . . . In Summer-time I have knowne them lye abroad often themselves, to make roome for strangers, *English*, or others." Even in the face of possible affront, they maintained an affable courtesy by sleeping outdoors "by a fire under a tree, when sometimes some *English* have (for want of familiaritie and language with them) been fearefull to entertaine them." It was a "strange *truth*" indeed to those Englishmen who knew them well that "a man shall generally finde more free entertainment and refreshing amongst these *Barbarians,* then amongst thousands that call themselves *Christians*." [6]

The Indians were also generous with their time and patience, for some of them were "very willing to teach their language to any English." When two cultures intersect, as they frequently did in New English houses and Indian wigwams, words are not only the most necessary article of commerce but the easiest medium in which to deal. Most Englishmen were not as fortunate as the pilgrims in having an English-speaking Squanto to help them cope with the American environment and so had to learn something of the Indian's language while teaching him something of theirs. Probably the first words exchanged were the names of natural objects unknown to the other culture. By 1643, for instance, the Indians had incorporated the Englishmen's *chicks, cows,*

6. Roger Williams, *A Key into the Language of America* (London, 1643), in *The Complete Writings of Roger Williams* (New York, 1963), 1 : 36, 46–47. Daniel Gookin, perhaps the second best authority, wrote that "they are much given to hospitality in their way. If any strangers come to their houses, they will give them the best lodging and diet they have" ("Historical Collections of the Indians in New England" [1674], *Colls. MHS,* 1st ser., vol. 1 [1792], p. 153).

goats, hogs, and *pigs* into their vocabulary. But the greatest amount of borrowing was understandably done by the English, who were casting virgin eyes on what to them was a new country. At home they had never seen a *moose, skunk, raccoon, beaver, caribou, opossum, woodchuck,* or *rattlesnake,* so it was necessary for them to learn their names from the Indians, who knew them well. Besides the natural life of New England, the settlers learned to identify many Indian relationships—such as *papoose, squaw, powwow, sagamore,* and *sachem*—and cultural artifacts—such as *moccasin, tomahawk, wigwam, succotash, hominy, toboggan, pemmican,* and *wampum.* Even Indian notions of time were drawn upon. In a decision of the Plymouth colony court in 1641, for example, Englishmen were given one or two "moons" to repair or restore the goods they had stolen from an Indian plaintiff.[7]

The names of a few common plants and animals probably sufficed for most English settlers, but another group of men— admittedly small—needed to go much farther in their comprehension of the Indian langauge. For it was early recognized that "the way to instruct the *Indians,* must be in their owne language, not English." Those learning the Indian language were the Puritan ministers who wanted to bring the Word of the Christian religion to the unconverted heathens around them, in accordance with the stated goals of the colonization of New England. To King Charles I, who issued the charter of the Massachusetts Bay Company in 1629, it was "the principall ende of this plantation" to "wynn and incite the natives of [the] country to the knowledg and obedience of the onlie true God and Savior of mankinde, and the Christian fayth." And so their task was to find or create in the Indian tongue abstractions or analogies for the metaphysical presuppositions of the English religion, a task made doubly

7. Thomas Lechford, *Plain Dealing: or, Newes from New-England* (London, 1642), in *Colls. MHS,* 3d ser., vol. 3 (1833), p. 104; *Complete Writings of Roger Williams,* 1 : 73, 129; H. L. Mencken, *The American Language,* 4th ed. (New York, 1936), pp. 104–07; John Josselyn, *An Account of Two Voyages to New-England* (London, 1675), in *Colls. MHS,* 3d ser., vol. 3 (1833), pp. 251–93; *Plymouth Records,* 17 June 1641, 2 : 20.

difficult by the reticulate complexity of Puritan theology. Although the reception of their message was disappointing for a variety of reasons, some beyond their control, several ministers were at least able to deliver it in the Indians' own language.[8]

When two cultures meet across a common frontier, there exists as much potential for conflict as for cooperation, especially when those cultures are at two very different stages of social development. Even when the chosen leaders of both cultures recognize the futility of war and try to quash the antagonisms and irritations that often feed it, the ardent spirits of the greedy, the proud, and the young can never be thoroughly dampened. In New England the pattern was no different. The initially amicable relations between the English and the Indians soon disintegrated under the pressure of their cultural incompatibility. In 1637, 1675, and almost continually after 1689, Indians made war on the rapidly encroaching Englishmen. And from these opponents the English gradually learned to fight "Indian-style," an ability that once again spelled the difference between their destruction and their survival in the New World.

Not all tribes were hostile, nor at any one time, which meant that some tribes, those who by proximity or treaty had grown closer to the English way of life, were able, if willing, to fight at the side of the English. Fortunately for the English, some tribes always were willing, for the Indians of New England were periodically as divided from each other as their white contemporaries in Europe were.[9] Thus, in the unfamiliar wilderness battlefields of America, it was as much the friendly Indian as his warring brother who taught the New Englishmen how to fight for their very existence.

The first encounter with Indian warfare, during the Pequot war in Connecticut, was too brief for the English to learn very much and too successful for them to need to. In a con-

8. *Colls. MHS,* 3d ser., vol. 3 (1833), p. 106; Edmund Morgan, ed., *The Founding of Massachusetts* (Indianapolis, 1964), p. 320.

9. Vaughan, *New England Frontier,* pp. 37–38, 55.

flict that lasted only a few months, the English troops and
their Mohegan allies obliterated the pugnacious Pequots with
a final surprise attack and superior firepower. Since the Indians had not yet acquired guns from the Dutch and the
French, the English found their fighting methods simply lu-
dicrous. After Mystic Fort, the Pequot stronghold, had been
fired and riddled with English bullets, killing most of its
five hundred inhabitants, the male survivors charged the
English battalia surrounding it with little success; so Captain
John Underhill sent his Mohegans against them "that we
might see the nature of the Indian war." By English standards
this was so ineffective that "they might fight seven years and
not kill seven men. They came not near one another," remarked Underhill, "but shot remote, and not point-blank, as
we often do with our bullets, but at rovers, and then they
gaze up in the sky to see where the arrow falls, and not until
it is fallen do they shoot again. This fight," he concluded, "is
more for pastime, than to conquer and subdue enemies." [10]

Its ineffectiveness, however, was not due to lack of European firearms, as Lieutenant Lion Gardener, the commander
of the English fort at Saybrook, discovered when he went into
the nearby fields to retrieve several victims of an Indian raid.
Not to his surprise, he found "the body of one man shot
through, the arrow going in at the right side, the head sticking
fast, half through a rib on the left side, which I took out and
cleansed it, and presumed to send to the [Massachusetts] Bay,
because they had said that the arrows of the Indians were of
no force." When the Indians wanted to kill their opponents,
especially the English, they had the means and the skill necessary.[11]

Still, the Indians—both friend and foe—were initially impressed with English warfare, which had changed not a whit
from the European style during the seventeen years New

10. *History of the Pequot War*, ed. Charles Orr (Cleveland, 1897), pp.
82, 84. Roger Williams observed the same kind of fighting among the
Narragansetts to the east (*Complete Writings*, 1 : 204).
11. *History of the Pequot Wars*, p. 130.

England had been colonized. When the Connecticut troops emerged from Fort Saybrook to chase their audacious tormentors, they still "beat up the drum," flew their colors, and marched in serried ranks into the nearest champaign field to "bid them battle." The men were "completely armed, with corselets, muskets, bandoleers, rests, and swords," which, as the Indians themselves related afterward, "did much daunt them." The sight of such martial pageantry must have impressed the Indians' sense of ceremony, but it was the ferocity of the English in battle that truly awed them. After the Mystic Fort massacre, Captain Underhill boasted, "our Indians came to us, and much rejoiced at our victories, and greatly admired the manner of English-men's fight, but cried Mach it, mach it; that is, It is naught, it is naught, because it is too furious, and slays too many men." The Indians had little to learn about the art of war, it seems, but the English taught them something about its energetic pursuit.[12]

By the same token, the English learned at least one technique of wilderness warfare from the natives. When Massachusetts sent one hundred soldiers to Connecticut to quell the Pequots, they were placed under the command of four captains and "other inferior officers," a number unusually high by European standards. So Captain Underhill, one of the officers, felt compelled to explain their deviation from the norm to the English readers of his *Newes from America:* "I would not have the world wonder at the great number of commanders to so few men," he wrote, "but know that the Indians' fight far differs from the *Christian* practice; for they most commonly divide themselves into small bodies, so that we are forced to neglect our usual way, and to subdivide our divisions to answer theirs. . . ." Since the Pequot stronghold was ambushed by mass encirclement, a thoroughly European tactic, the American version of "divide and conquer" was not particularly decisive for the English in 1637. However, for more than a century after the outbreak of King Philip's War in 1675, it would prove to be a valuable asset, although on more

12. Ibid., pp. 60–62, 84; Vaughan, *New England Frontier*, p. 40.

than one occasion, ironically, it became a liability. But it was only the first of a whole range of military tactics that the English would learn, however tardily, from the New England natives before the Revolution.[13]

In the initial encounters of Philip's War, which was to be fought largely on terrain very different from Connecticut's rocky forests, the English ensigns still "boldly held up [their] Colours in the Front of [their] Compan[ies]" and the troops still planned to "beat up the Enemies Quarters, or give him Battel, if he durst abide it." But the Indians would have none of this European madness, and continued their own successful methods, "seldom or never daring," as a hostile witness put it, "to meet our Soldiers in the open Field, unless when they have very great Advantage as to their Numbers, or Covert of the Woods and Bushes." Some eight months after the start of hostilities, an American author had to admit to his English readers that "we have as yet had Nothing like to a field Battel with the Indians." Nor would they ever. As one warrior told an English captain, "English Fashion is all one Fool; you kill mee, mee kill you! No, better ly somewhere, and Shoot a man, and hee no see! That the best Soldier!" [14]

The "perfidious Subtlety" of their "timerous and barbarous Enemy" thoroughly frustrated the English. One response, typical of uncomprehending students, was to explain away the obvious effectiveness of Indian tactics as the result of the settlers' own (temporary) inadequacies. The early successes of King Philip's men, wrote the Reverend William Hubbard, the colonies' chief historian of the Indian wars, "must be imputed in a great Measure to our Mens unacquaintedness with the Manner of their fighting, they doing most of their Mischiefs either by Ambushments, sudden Surprizals, or overmatching some of our small Companyes with greater Numbers, having had many Times six or seven to one. [And] possibly also," he

13. *History of the Pequot Wars*, p. 51 (my emphasis); Vaughan, *New England Frontier*, pp. 153–54.
14. Hubbard, *History of the Indian Wars*, 1 : 70–71, 133–34; *Narratives of the Indian Wars, 1675–1699*, ed. Charles Lincoln (New York, 1913), pp. 57, 238.

admitted, more as an aside than a confession, "many of our Overthrows have proceeded from our too much Confidence in our own Weapons, Courage and Martial Discipline. . . ." [15]

Another response, one which would color the whole history of colonial New England, was to adapt as quickly as possible to the uninhibited style of Indian warfare. This had two results, one expected but uncertain and the other unintended but inevitable. As the English had hoped, it ultimately enabled them to defeat their teachers for the hegemony of New England. But their own conduct was lowered to the "barbarous" levels they so self-consciously deplored by two other practices, one an English "improvement" on the Indian style, the other a direct borrowing from the Indians. The English "improvement" was the use of dogs, especially mastiffs. When the Reverend Solomon Stoddard of Northampton recommended to the governor of Massachusetts in 1703 that dogs be used to track Indians and to guard towns, he was well aware that he was departing from "Christian practice." *"If the Indians were as other people are,"* he began, *"&* did manage their warr fairly *after the manner of other nations,* it might be looked upon as inhumane to pursue them in such a manner." And then, like all apologists of war, he proceeded to excuse his own "inhumane" suggestion by dehumanizing the enemy—and in the process a part of himself. "But they are to be looked upon as thieves and murderers, they doe acts of hostility without proclaiming war, *they don't appeare openly in the field to bid us battle,* they use those cruelly that fall into their hands." In short, "they act like wolves & are to be dealt withall as wolves." It was reasoning such as this, tragically flawed by hubris and lack of compassion, that allowed an order to be given in nearby Hatfield in 1675 for a female Indian captive "to be torn in pieces by dogs." [16]

The second practice that diminished the New Englishman's

15. Hubbard, *History of the Indian Wars,* 1 : 132; 2 : 259–60.
16. *NEHGR* 24 (1870) : 269–70 (my emphasis); Increase Mather, *The History of King Philip's War,* ed. Samuel Drake (Boston, 1862), p. 101n.

humanity was scalping, a direct loan from the Indians. On 12 September 1694, the General Court of Massachusetts passed an act confining all friendly Indians within a cordon sanitaire and offering bounties "for every [hostile] Indian, great or small, which they shall kill, or take and bring in prisoner." Volunteer Indian fighters in "greater or lesser parties"—the first American bounty hunters—received £50 per head, volunteers under militia pay, £20, and regular soldiers under pay, £10. Since the provincial treasurer was not about to trust the word of every common soldier, the enemy's scalplock had to be produced to receive the bounty, and, to prevent fraud, a three-month prison sentence and a fine double the amount of the bounty was threatened for trying to pass off a false scalp, especially that of a friendly Indian.[17]

As the situation along the eastern frontier worsened, the government steadily increased the scalp bounties, until by 1722 individual volunteers were receiving £100 per head, a small fortune to poor soldiers, but only a tithe of the actual cost to the country of every Indian taken or killed. But something was obviously gnawing at the New English conscience, for only two months after the act of 1704 was passed, the court amended it in the direction of "Christian practice." Instead of rewarding the killing of "every Indian, great or small," a scale graduated by age and sex was established, so that the scalps of "men or youths [twelve years or older] capable of bearing armes" were worth £100 to any company of volunteers, and women and boys above the age of ten, only £10; no reward was given for killing children under ten years. In a gesture of dubious compassion, such children instead were sold as slaves and transported out of the country.[18]

Aware of the moral dangers inherent in fostering such "barbarous" practices, the General Court was careful to limit each enactment to one year. But necessity was strong throughout

17. *The Acts and Resolves . . . of the Province of the Massachusetts Bay* (Boston, 1869), 1, 175–76, 594. Just how a bona fide scalp was to be distinguished from a false one was not suggested.

18. *Acts and Resolves*, 1 : 530, 558, 594; 2 : 259; Samuel Penhallow, *The History of the Wars of New-England with the Eastern Indians* [1726] (Cincinnati, 1859), pp. 48, 93.

most of the first half of the eighteenth century, and the bounties were renewed year after year in the hope that more volunteers would turn the tide against the eastern Indians. And so they did. Selected techniques of Indian warfare, placed in the hands of a larger English population already possessed of a more advanced technology, eventually sealed the Indians' fate in New England, but not before wreaking upon the English settlers their own subtle form of moral vengeance.

It was regrettable that the English resorted to the Indian practice of scalping, but it was probably necessary if they were to survive in the New World. Furthermore, without trying to explain away their actions, we should place them in historical perspective. Incredible as it may seem, scalping was a humane improvement upon the standard Indian treatment of their enemies, "it being the custome to cut off their heads, hands, and feet, to beare home to their wives and children, as true tokens of their renowned victorie." In his *Key into the Language of America,* Roger Williams translated the ancient Algonquian word for *"to cut off,* or *behead,"* observing that "when ever they wound, and their arrow sticks in the body of their enemie, they (if they be valourous, and possibly may) they follow their arrow, and falling upon the person wounded and tearing his head a little aside by his Locke, they in the twinckling of an eye fetch off his head though but with a sorry [dull] knife." Scalping simply seems to have been reserved for enemies slain a considerable distance from home, "which is their usual Manner, when it is too far to carry the Heads." As soon as the battle was ended, they always made a fire to "carefully preserve the scalps of the head, drying the inside with hot ashes; and so carry them home as trophies of their valour, for which they are rewarded." It was a similar need for proof that prompted the English to encourage the taking of scalps.[19]

But the historical context of scalping included not only the practices of New England but those of old England as well. And even there "barbarism" was not unknown, as Colonel

19. Wood, *New Englands Prospect,* p. 84; *Complete Writings of Roger Williams,* 1 : 78; Hubbard, *History of the Indian Wars,* 2 : 206.

Daniel Axtell discovered in 1660. For his part in the beheading of King Charles I, he was "drawne upon a hardle" to the "Tyborne gallow tree" where he was "hanged, cut downe, his body quickly opened and his intrealls burnt; hee was quartred and brought back to Newgate Prison to be boyled and then, as the [nine] others, [his head] to be sett up as his Majesty pleased." In the seventeenth century, the standards of English justice and Indian revenge were never far apart, and the objects of both had little chance of survival. At least the victims of scalping occasionally lived to a ripe old age.[20]

Fortunately, the great majority of military techniques learned from the Indians carried much less danger of moral contagion than scalping. Their danger was further reduced by the well-known example of Benjamin Church, who was at once perhaps the best student of Indian fighting and one of the most humane military leaders in colonial New England. His personal account of the not insignificant role he played in King Philip's War and in several eastern campaigns into the eighteenth century, published by his son in 1716, might well have served the New English both as a guide to the conduct of Indian warfare and as a casebook of moral restraint in the face of great temptation.

Much of Philip's War was waged in the swampy lowlands of the Plymouth colony and Rhode Island, which gave the Indians an added advantage over their inexperienced rivals. "Every Swamp is a Castle to them," lamented Increase Mather, "knowing where to find us, but we know not where to find them, who nevertheless are always at home, and have in a manner nothing but their lives and souls (which they think not of) to loose . . . and they can live comfortably on that which would starve *English-men*." Each of the local swamps was "so full of Bushes and Trees, that a Parcel of Indians may be within the Length of a Pike of a Man, and he cannot dis-

20. *The Diurnal of Thomas Rugg, 1659–1661*, ed. William Sachse (London, 1961), p. 116. For only a few of the scalping victims who survived, see Penhallow, *History of the Wars of New-England*, p. 76; Hubbard, *History of the Indian Wars*, 1 : 129; *Colls. MHS*, 1st ser., vol. 1 (1792), p. 162.

cover them; and besides, [each] is so soft Ground, that an Englishman can neither go nor stand thereon, and yet these bloody Savages," marvelled a contemporary, "will run along over it, holding their Guns across their Arms (and if Occasion be) discharge in that Posture." The English commanders always ordered their pursuing men out of the swamps at nightfall, "not thinking it Safe to tarry longer in so dangerous a Place, where every one was in as much Danger of his Fellows as of his Foes, being ready to fire upon every Bush they see move (supposing *Indians* were there)." For they had been "taught by late Experience how dangerous it is to fight in such dismal Woods, when their Eyes were muffled with the Leaves, and their Arms pinioned with the thick Boughs of the Trees, as their Feet were continually shackled with the Roots spreading every Way in those boggy Woods." As far as the English were concerned, it was "ill fighting with a wild Beast in his own Den." [21]

But Church, long a resident of the outreaches of the Plymouth colony and Rhode Island, knew the swamps and their red inhabitants well, a knowledge he turned to good advantage when Philip began his assaults on the isolated Plymouth villages in June 1675. Commissioned a captain in the Plymouth militia, he quickly ventured out with raiding parties of colonials and friendly Indians in hopes of catching the "wild Beast in his own Den," having made it clear to the Plymouth Council of War "that if he should take the Command of Men, he should not lye in any Town or Garrison with them, but would lye in the Woods as the Enemy did." In his opinion, forts were "only Nests for Destruction." Once in the woods, he put his knowledge of Indian tactics to work, while continuing to learn from his Indian comrades.

His manner of Marching thro' the Woods was such, as if he were discovered, they appeared to be more than they were. For he always Marched at a wide distance one from

21. Increase Mather, *History of King Philip's War*, pp. 206–07; *Narratives of the Indian Wars*, p. 31; Hubbard, *History of the Indian Wars*, 1 : 85, 87.

another, partly for their safety: and this was an *Indian*
custom, to March thin and scatter. Capt. *Church* inquired
of some of the *Indians* that were become his Souldiers,
*How they got such advantage often of the English in their
Marches thro' the Woods?* They told him, That . . . the
Indians always took care in their Marches and Fights, not
to come too thick together. But the *English* always kept in
a heap together, that it was as easy to hit them as to hit an
House, [and] that if at any time they discovered a company of *English* Souldiers in the Woods, they knew that
there was all, for the *English* never scattered; but the
Indians always divided and scattered.

Another maneuver, which went against European practice,
was to have his men not all fire at once in volleys "lest the
Enemy should take the advantage of such an Opportunity to
run upon them with their Hatche[t]s." He avoided ambushes
by never "return[ing] the same way that he came" and for-
bidding his men telltale fires to satisfy their "Epidemical
plague of lust after Tobacco." And he could "skulk" with the
best of his enemies, always ensuring that he had several Indians in his company because "they exceed most of our
English in hunting & Sculking in the woods, being always
us'd to it; and it must be practised if ever we intend to
destroy those *Indian* Enemies." At the final engagement with
Philip on Mount Hope in August 1676, Church characteristically advised an officer who was given the honor of approaching first that "his custom in the like cases was to creep with his
company on their bellies, until they came as near as they
could; and that as soon as the Enemy discovered them they
would cry out; and that was the word for his Men to fire and
fall on." It was shrewdness like this that leads one to suspect
that, if several crucial pages were missing from the Indian
handbook of war, they were probably taken by Benjamin
Church.[22]

22. Benjamin Church, *The History of King Philip's War*, ed. Henry
Dexter (Boston, 1865), pp. 28, 33, 67, 86, 121–23, 145; Church, *The
History of the Eastern Expeditions . . . against the Indians and French*,
ed. Dexter (Boston, 1867), p. 133.

Church's knowledge of their ways quickly brought him a large measure of success over the hostile Indians. To many an ordinary man this would have presented an overwhelming temptation to visit an understandable rage and thirst for revenge upon his captives. But Church was a man of uncommon mettle. Besides possessing a strong sense of humanity and compassion, he had lived amongst the Indians much of his life and could not erase the instinctive knowledge he had of them as human beings. He was simply incapable of the kind of venomous imprecations Cotton Mather would use in 1689 to arouse battle bound New English soldiers to a fighting pitch. *"Vengeance, Dear Country-men! Vengeance upon our Murderers,"* he cried from Boston's North Church. "Let your *Courage,* in the Name of God be daring enough to Execute that *Vengeance* on them . . . *Beat* them small as the *Dust before the Wind,* and *Cast them out,* as the *Dirt in the Streets* . . . those Ravenous howling *Wolves."* How different was Church's sense of Christian justice when his Indian soldiers presented him with Little Eyes, a Sogkonate who had left his tribe to join Philip upon their making peace with the English and threatened to kill Church at the dance celebrating the treaty. Church's Indians "signified to him that now he had an opportunity to be revenged on him, but the Captain told them, *It was not English-mans fashion to seek revenge; and, that he should have the same quarter the rest had."* [23]

The same scrupulousness on another occasion earned him the "loss of the good Will and Respect of some that before were his good Friends." In July 1675 "a Number of the Enemy . . . had surrendred themselves Prisoners on terms promised" by the captain of the English garrison. "And had their promises to the *Indians* been kept, and the *Indians* farely treated, 'tis probable that most if not all the *Indians* in those Parts, had soon followed the Example of those that had now surrendred themselves; which would have been a good step toward finishing the War," then only one month old. But in spite of all that Church and the captain could

23. Cotton Mather, *Souldiers Counselled and Comforted* (Boston, 1689), p. 28; Church, *History of King Philip's War,* p. 110.

"say, argue, plead, or beg, some body else that had more Power in their hands improv'd it; and without any regard to the promises made them on their surrendring themselves, they were cary'd away to *Plymouth,* there sold, and transported out of the country." It is not difficult to see why this action was "so hateful" to Church.[24]

Equally disturbing to the captain was the barbarous use of prisoners by his Indian soldiers which was countenanced by his superiors. When one of his Mohegans captured a wounded Indian, "some were for torturing of him to bring him to a more ample confession, of what he knew concerning his Country-men. [But] Mr. *Church* verily believing he had been ingenious in his confession, interceded and prevailed for his escaping torture." When the army continued its march, the prisoner's wound "somewhat disinabling him for Travelling, 'twas concluded he should be knock'd on the Head" by his captor before the assembled English troops and their general around a "great fire." "Mr. *Church* taking no delight in the Sport, fram'd an arrant [errand] at some distance among the baggage Horses. . . ."[25]

The following year, as the long war was grinding to a climax, Church decimated most of Philip's forces in a swamp fight, taking or killing 173 men. Although the causes for vengeful action had accumulated beyond number after fourteen months of savage fighting, Church ensured that his prisoners were "well treated with Victuals and drink," so well indeed that "they had a merry Night . . . not being so treated a long time before." And thinking they were giving him cause for joy, "some of the *Indians* now said to Capt. *Church, Sir, You have now made* Philip *ready to dye, for you have made him as poor, and miserable as he us'd to make the* English; *for you have now killed or taken all his Relations.*" They concluded by telling him *"that they believed he would now soon have his head."* But instead of bringing delight to a rancorous spirit, wrote his son, *"this [a]bout had almost*

24. Church, *History of King Philip's War,* pp. 45–47.
25. Ibid., p. 62.

broke his heart." In men like Church, the full meaning of Christian charity becomes palpable.[26]

The success with which Benjamin Church selectively adapted the style of Indian fighting to his own uses stands in doleful contrast to the indiscriminate imitations of other English officers. One of these was Captain Thomas Lothrop, who was sent on 18 September 1675 with a company of eighty men—"the very Flower of the County of Essex"—to escort a wagon train of corn from Deerfield to beleaguered Hatfield. But on that "most fatal Day, the Saddest that ever befel *New-England*," according to William Hubbard, his company was ambushed, and all but seven or eight men killed, "which great Defeat came to pass by the unadvised Procceding of the Captain (who was himself slain in the first Assault) although he wanted neither Courage nor Skill to lead his Souldiers. But having taken up a wrong Motion about the best Way and Manner of fighting with the *Indians* (which he was always wont to argue for) *viz*, that it were best to deal with the *Indians* in their own Way, *sc.* by skulking behind Trees, and taking their Aim at single Persons, which is the usual Manner of the *Indians* fighting one with another; but herein was his great Mistake," Hubbard correctly discerned, "in not considering the great Disadvantage a smaller Company would have in dealing that way with a great Multitude"—the Indians numbered seven to eight hundred that day—"for if five have to deal with one, they may surround him, and every one to take his Aim at him, while he can level at but one of his Enemies at a time. . . . Had he ordered his Men to march in a Body, as some of his Fellow-commanders advised, either backward, or forward, in Reason they had not lost a Quarter of the Number of those that fell that Day by the Edg of the Sword. For the *Indians,* notwithstanding their Subtilty and Cruelty, durst not look an *Englishman* in the Face in the open Field, nor ever yet were known to kill any Man with their Guns, unless when they could lie in wait for him in an Ambush, or behind some Shelter, taking Aim undiscovered." In unseasoned hands,

26. Ibid., pp. 137–38.

the tactics of Indian warfare, like sorcerers' magic, could easily turn upon their apprentices.[27]

Fortunately for the English, not all Indian techniques were double-edged. Two in particular involved only the adoption and use of ordinary native artifacts—the moccasin and the snowshoe. Moccasins, the supreme footwear for fast, quiet forest travel, were made of elk or deerskin, hair side in, "which yet being excellently tann'd by them, is excellent for to travell in wet and snow; for it is so well tempered with oyle," testified Roger Williams, "that the water cleane wrings out; and being hang'd up in their chimney, they presently drie without hurt as my selfe hath often proved." Another advantage was that they were "absolutely necessary for the purpose of adjusting their snowshoes," which were made, said one European, "like a large Racket we play at *Tennis* with, lacing them with *Deers*-guts and the like." "These snowshoes, made in lozenge shape," said another, "are more than two feet long and a foot and a half broad . . . by means of which they easily walk on the snow." In the deep snows of Maine, where the spring sun comes late in the year, both were necessities, as the colonists realized when the theater of war shifted after 1689 to the northern and eastern frontiers.[28]

The need was not unfelt even earlier, for during the first winter of King Philip's War, "the Foot [soldiers] were unable to do any Service in the Depth of the Snow, the Sharpness of the Cold . . . unless they carried Rackets under their Feet, wherewith to walk upon the Top of the Snow." But it was not until 14 June 1704, the same year that the scalp bounty was raised to £100, that the Massachusetts General Court, in an act "for the more ready and better pursuit after the Indian rebels in the winter, upon the snow," ordered that one half of the colonial militia "shall, each of them, at his own charge, be provided with a pair of good serviceable snow-shoes and

27. Hubbard, *History of the Indian Wars*, 1 : 112–13, 212.

28. *Complete Writings of Roger Williams*, 1 : 145; Sébastien Râle, in *The Jesuit Relations and Allied Documents*, ed. Reuben G. Thwaites (Cleveland, 1896–1901), 67 : 135; John Josselyn, in *Colls. MHS*, 3d ser., vol. 3 (1833), p. 297.

mogginsons" before the tenth of November. Officers were to send to Boston lists of their men who had complied with the order so that they might be reimbursed three shillings, and a fine of ten shillings was levied for each neglect. Soon thereafter, to ensure that the militia of each of the four northern counties received sufficient equipment, the court ordered five-hundred pairs of snowshoes to be made. When the time of compliance approached, several companies on the frontiers petitioned the court to raise their reimbursement from three to five shillings since they found that "a pr of good snow shoes, Mogesons & bands will cost 10 *s* money at the least." The military need for this equipment was so pressing that the subsidy was raised without a murmur. And not without reason, for by the following winter, "little or no spoil was done on any of our frontiers; the enemy being so terrified by reason of snow-shoes (which most of our men were skillful in) that they never attempted coming at such a season after." Once again, it was the successful adoption of the Indians' own tactics and technology that gave the English victory and eventually the domination of New England.[29]

People alter their life styles for both negative and positive reasons. They are always to some degree disappointed or unhappy with their present lives, but, perhaps more important, they are also attracted—tempted—by an alternative which seems to answer their dissatisfactions. This alternative life style is generally personified by familiar living models, people whose mode of living conveys an appearance of harmony, integrity, and contentment. When the settlers of New England became disenchanted with their own lives, complicated by the demands of civilization, it was the Indians' more primitive existence that tempted them.

One form of temptation—perhaps among people of different color the most elemental—was sexual. But the attrac-

29. Hubbard, *History of the Indian Wars*, 1 : 158; 2 : 130; *Acts and Resolves*, 1 : 547; 8 : 42, 92, 429; Penhallow, *History of the Wars of New-England*, p. 41.

tion seems to have been all on one side; the Indians never cared to lie with white people, even when they enjoyed sovereign power over their bodies in captivity. Only during wartime, when atrocity stories are normally bruited to condition a people's hatred of the enemy, did the English insinuate that the Indians "Defile any Woman they take alive, afterwards putting her to Death." Such flagrant propaganda could not stand before the impeccable testimony of the many English women who returned from captivity with their chastity and lives intact. As late as 1724 an English woman could say from a year's experience in captivity that "the Indians are very civil towards their captive women, not offering any incivility by any indecent carriage, (unless they be much over-come in liquor,) which is commendable in them, so far." [30]

One explanation for the Indians' lack of interest in English women emerged during the initial stages of the Pequot War, when a sixteen-year-old girl captured from Wethersfield reportedly told her English redeemers that the Indians "did solicit her to uncleanness." This may have been mere wishful thinking, for Edward Johnson told a fuller and much different story. "Having taken these two prisoners," he said, "they did not offer to abuse their persons, *as was verily deemed they would,* questioned them with such broken English, as some of them could speak, to know whether they could make Gunpowder. Which when they understood they could not doe, their prize proved nothing so pretious a Pearle in their eyes as before; for seeing they exceeded not their own Squawes in Art, their owne thoughts informed them they would fall abundantly short in industry, and *as for beauty they esteeme black beyond any colour.*" If Johnson is right, English women were not sexually assaulted because they were not attractive to Indian men, who always preferred their own women. "Wherefore," saw Johnson with his English eyes, "their Squawes use that sinfull art of painting their Faces in the hollow of their

30. *Narratives of the Indian Wars,* p. 30; Samuel Drake, ed., *Tragedies of the Wilderness* (Boston, 1846), p. 125.

Eyes and Nose, with a shining black, out of which their tip of their Nose appears very deformed, and their cheeke bone, being of a lighter swart black, on which they have a blew crosse dyed very deepe. This is the beauty esteemed by them." Perhaps it was no coincidence that to these same Indians the Devil appeared "in a bodily shape, sometimes very ugly and terrible, and sometimes like a *white* boy." [31]

The English, on the other hand, suffered from no such cultural inhibitions. Many of them, men and women, could not resist the physical attraction of these magnificent people of "savage hue." The English found many faults with their initially admired hosts over the course of time, but they could never put aside their unreserved admiration for the Indian physique. The sensuality of William Wood's description is at once a good example and an explanation of the Indians' seductive mien.

> Of their Stature, most of them being betweene five or six foote high, straight bodied, strongly composed, smooth skinned, merry countenanced, of complexion something more swarthy than *Spaniards,* black hair'd, high fore-headed, blacke ey'd, out-nosed, broad shouldred, brawny arm'd, long and slender handed, out brested, small wasted, lanke bellied, well thighed, flat kneed, handsome growne leggs, and small feete: In a word, take them when the blood briskes in their veines, when the flesh is on their backs, and marrow in their bones, when they frolick in their antique deportments and *Indian* postures; and they are more amiable to behold (though onely in *Adams* livery) than many a compounded phantasticke in the newest fashion.

John Josselyn's evocation of Indian women was no less titillating. "The *Indesses* that are young," he wrote, "are some of them very comely, having good features, their faces plump

---

31. *History of the Pequot War,* p. 71; *Johnson's Wonder-Working Providence, 1628–1651,* ed. J. Franklin Jameson (New York, 1910), pp. 149–50, 263 (my emphasis).

and round, and generally plump of their Bodies . . . and as
soft and smooth as a mole-skin, of reasonable good complexions, but that they dye themselves tawnie, many prettie
Brownetto's and spider finger'd Lasses may be seen amongst
them." If the Indians were typically seen as young, wild,
passionate, and alluring, but somehow tainted in the blood—
as dark beauty is often portrayed in literary convention—
the frequency with which the English succumbed to their
aroused passions appears in a clearer light.[32]

For succumb they did. As early as 1631, at the September
session of the Massachusetts General Court, "a young fellow
was whipped for soliciting an Indian squaw to incontinency.
Her husband and she complained of the wrong, and were
present at the execution, and very well satisfied." In the
Plymouth colony, where the English lived more closely with
their Indian neighbors, the opportunity for cross-cultural
unions was greater. During the seventy years of Plymouth's
autonomy, several cases of fornication involving colonists and
Indians appeared on the court docket, only one of which ever
accused an Indian of attempting English virtue. The conduct
of Mary, the wife of Duxbury's Robert Mendame, typified the
direction of New England's sexual solicitations. On 3 September 1639 she was sentenced to be "whipped at cart tayle"
through the town and to wear a badge of sin—the Scarlet
Letter—on her left sleeve forever for "useing dallyance divers
tymes with Tinsin, an Indian, and after committing the act of
uncleanesse with him." Tinsin, who had confessed their crime
through an interpreter, was only whipped at the post with a
halter about his neck "because it arose through the allurement
& inticement of the said Mary, that hee was drawne thereunto."
Singularly exceptional was the case of Sam, an Indian, who
violated Sarah Freeman "by laying her down upon her backe,
and entering her body with his." Ordinarily rape brought the
death penalty, but the court, "considering he was but an

32. Wood, *New Englands Prospect*, p. 54; *Colls. MHS*, 3d ser., vol. 3
(1833), p. 294; Wilcomb Washburn, "A Moral History of Indian-White
Relations," *Ethnohistory* 4 (1957) : 51.

Indian, and therefore in an incapacity to know the horiblenes of the wickedness of his abominable act," commuted his sentence to a whipping and expulsion from the colony. Since this unique violation of the normal pattern of sexual temptation did not occur until 1682, Sam may well have been sufficiently anglicized by his familiarity with the English to exchange, in a moment of weakness or confusion, imported for native standards of beauty and sensuality. If so, it was a costly lapse.[33]

Intercultural dalliance was one thing, and easily handled by English justice and public opinion, but sometimes lust gave way to love, raising the specter of marriage outside the carefully hedged fold. The problem was raised in a formal way in March 1635, when the Massachusetts General Court entertained and then immediately referred to further consideration a question concerning the propriety of Indian-white marriages, but it never regained the court's attention. Instead of civil law, public opinion was left to police untoward affections, with what success we can only guess. Only when a mixed couple was entered in the judicial lists for an offense of a legal nature did the fact of their union come to light.[34]

Probably most couples of necessity lived far from the obdurate center of English society, close to, if not actually in, the tolerant homes of the Indian partners. If the colonial reaction to Joshua Tift, a "Renegadoe English Man of *Providence*," is an accurate measure, mixed marriages were regarded with an unmerciful eye, especially if the Englishman accepted more than a spouse from the Indians. During the first winter of King Philip's War, English scouts wounded and captured Tift, who "upon some Discontent amongst his Neighbours, had turned *Indian*, married one of the *Indian Squawes*, renounced his Religion, Nation and natural Parents all at once, fighting against them. . . . He had in his Habit conformed himself to them amongst whom he lived. After Examination, he was condemned to die the Death of a Traytor" by hanging and

33. *Winthrop's Journal*, 1 : 67; *Plymouth Records*, 1 : 132; 6 : 98.
34. *Mass. Records*, 4 March 1635, 1 : 140.

quartering, "which was accordingly done." "As to his Religion he was found as ignorant as an Heathen"—a clear warning to backsliders—"which no doubt caused the fewer Tears to be shed at his Funeral; Standers by being unwilling to lavish Pity upon him that had divested himself of Nature itself, as well as Religion, in a Time when so much Pity was needed elsewhere. . . ." It was with such transparent disdain for mixed marriages—those divestments of "Nature itself"—that Connecticut outlawed "renegades" in their 1650 code of laws. To discourage "diverse persons [who] departe from amongst us, and take up their aboade with the Indians, in a prophane course of life," the General Court threatened imprisonment for three years "at least" and a fine or corporal punishment. Perhaps legislation could deter mixed marriages to some degree, but it could never throttle the distinctly "heathenish" mode of life that many Englishmen adopted on the remote borders of colonial society. Of all the dangers posed by the "wast howling wilderness" of America, none was more alarming to the New English than that they and their children could be converted from "civility" to "barbarism" by its seductive freedom and its seducing inhabitants.[35]

When the king's commissioners surveyed the state of New England in 1665, bent on pulling the independent Americans firmly under the royal wing, they found that the people of Maine "for the most part are fishermen, and never had any Governement amongst them, and most of them are such as have fled thither from other places to avoyd Justice. Some here are of Opinion," they gloated, "that as many Men may share in a Woman, as they doe in a Boate, and some have done so." If the Maine county court records are any indication, the commissioners had hit upon a hard truth about one notorious New England frontier, but they had only touched the tip of a moral iceberg. Although many men, and women as well, were indicted for adultery and "living apart from one's spouse,"

35. Hubbard, *History of the Indian Wars,* 1 : 162; *Narratives of the Indian Wars,* p. 67; *Conn. Records,* 1 : 530.

they could not compete numerically with those "down easters" presented at the monthly sessions for slander, drunkenness, profanity, assault, trespass, Sabbath-breaking, and, perhaps most telling of all to an orthodox Puritan, neglect of public worship.[36]

The inhabitants of the scattered, lonely farms and fishing villages of Maine represented best those who were, the social critics of the day accused, "contented to live without, yea, desirous to shake off all Yoake of Government, both sacred and civil." And with good reason, for as one plainspoken fisherman informed a Massachusetts minister sent to convert the worshippers of the pine and the cod, "Sir, You are mistaken, you think you are Preaching to the People at the Bay; our main End was to catch Fish." Since their homes had been the brawling seaports of western England, of Cornwall and Devon, not the Puritan villages of East Anglia, no one needed to be told that such men were not highly amenable to the civilized order of the Puritan ideal. In 1639 one struggling official lamented that "every man is a law to him selfe. It is a bad kind of livinge to live in a place where is neather law nor government amonge people." Twenty years later the colony was still so literally lawless that the York County court ordered fifty copies of the latest Massachusetts statutes for the several towns with the pointed observation that "the well regulateing of Civill Societys depends much In haveing good Laws, which must bee first known before they can bee either executed or obeyed, the necessity whereof being of more then ordinary usse to us in these parts." Harvard's president clearly had his northern neighbors in mind when he observed in 1655 that some "account it their happiness to live in the wast howling wilderness, without any ministry, or schools, and means of education for their posterity, they have much liberty (they think) by this want, they are not troubled with strict Sabbaths, but they may follow their worldly bussiness at any

36. *Documentary History of Maine*, 2d ser., vol. 4 (1889), p. 298; *Maine Records*, vols. 1–5.

time, and their children may drudg for them at plough, or hough, or such like servil imployments, that themselves may be eased." [37]

"Down easters" may have been the worst but they were certainly not the only offenders of Puritan sensibilities. The infamous group of Gortonists lived in Rhode Island "without any means for instructing them in the wayes of God, and without any civil Government to keep them in civility or humanity." In her travels through Connecticut in 1704, Sarah Knight of Boston felt that the Indians' polygamous marriages and easy "Stand away" divorces were "too much in Vougue among the English in this Indulgent Colony as their Records plentifully prove, and that on very trivial matters," some "not proper to be Related by a Female pen." But even in the heart of Massachusets, civilized currency had been debased. "There hath been in many professors" of the Puritan faith, scolded the Boston synod in 1679, "an insatiable desire after Land, and worldly Accommodations, yea, so as to forsake Churches and Ordinances, and to live like Heathen, only that so they might have Elbow-room enough in the world." When people moved thus into the shadowed corners of the land, bidding defiance "not only to Religion, but to Civility it self," such places inevitably became "Nurseries of Ignorance, Prophaneness and Atheism," something no good Puritan society could countenance, or did.[38]

At the September session of the Massachusetts General Court in 1642, John Winthrop noted, "we were informed of some English to the eastward, who ordinarily traded powder to the Indians, and lived alone under no government." Whereupon a gentleman was dispatched to confiscate their

37. Hubbard, *History of the Indian Wars*, 2 : 256–57; Cotton Mather, *Magnalia Christi Americana* (London, 1702), bk. 1, p. 15; *Documentary History of Maine*, 10 July 1639, 2d ser., vol. 3 (1884), p. 171; *Maine Records*, 4 July 1659, 2 : 78; Charles Chauncy, *God's Mercy, Shewed to his People* (Cambridge, Mass., 1655), pp. 15–16.

38. *Johnson's Wonder-Working Providence*, p. 223; Sarah Knight, *The Private Journal of a Journey from Boston to New York in the Year 1704* (Albany, 1865), p. 55; *The Necessity of Reformation* (Boston, 1679), p. 7; Joseph Easterbrooks, *Abraham the Passenger* (Boston, 1705), p. 3.

powder and presumably to urge them to more orderly living arrangements. Ten years later, in 1652, the Plymouth court ordered Joseph Ramsden to move "near unto som naighborhood," having "lived with his family remotely in the woods from naighbours." The unsociable Mr. Ramsden evaded the issue until June 1656, when the court insisted that he move by October or have his house pulled down. He moved. In 1675 the same court ordered three men to "frequent the publicke worship of [some town], and live otherwise orderly" or to leave the colony for "liveing lonely and in a heathenish way from good societie." When the civil authority could no longer stem the flow of land-hungry settlers toward the exposed frontier, the church was beckoned to act for it as a last-ditch alternative. If Puritan society could not arrest their movement, Cotton Mather argued, at least the ministry could "Enlighten them; Antidote them; Fortify them with strong *Preservatives*" against the dangers of Indian captivity and popish delusion.[39]

Mather was not exaggerating the dangers of frontier living; they were real and omnipresent and insidious, especially for the children, who were expected to transmit the Puritan ideal across the generations. And they were felt very early. Only a year after he had arrived in Massachusetts, John Winthrop, Jr. was warned by an English correspondent "that ye become not a prey to the spoyler, and your children turne heathen." In 1677 the General Assembly of Connecticut, considering the resettlement of war-torn towns, cited the "woeful experiance in the late warr," which showed that "liveing in a single and scattering way, remoate from townships and neighbourhood" weakened the commonwealth and tempted the "posterity of such, most of them are endangered to degenerate into heathenish ignorance and barbarisme."[40]

The New English conception of white "heathenism" was no idle phantom or religious bugbear; its characteristics were increasingly observable as the two cultures of New England

39. *Winthrop's Journal*, 2 : 80; *Plymouth Records*, 3 : 6–7; 5 : 169; Cotton Mather, *Frontiers Well-Defended* (Boston, 1707), p. 48.
40. *Winthrop Papers*, 9 November 1631, 2 : 55; *Conn. Records*, 2 : 328.

mingled and melded across their common frontier. In addition to teaching them *"Our Vice,"* asked Cotton Mather, "have not we also *Followed* the *Indians?* The Indians are Infamous, especially for Three Scandalous Qualities: They are *Lazy Drones,* and love *Idleness* Exceedingly: They are also most impudent *Lyars,* and will invent Reports and Stories at a strange and monstrous rate; and they are out of measure *Indulgent* unto their Children, there is no Family-Government among them.[41] But, O how much do our people Indianize in every one of those Abominable things!" In a perfect phrase, *"Criolian* Degeneracy" inflicted promising New English youth when they were "permitted to run wild in our Woods." Yet the dangers were not only civil, but eternal as well, for in those notoriously "Ungospellized Plantations," where "no *Minister* of God [is] countenanced," "Satan *terribly* makes a *prey* of you, and *Leads you Captive to do his Will."* And all of New England knew the meaning of captivity. As Hampshire County, in Massachusetts' western extremity, expressed if for King George III, "many of our Children . . . were captivated, bred up in popish and pagan Ignorance, and [educational] inlargement never granted; but have become implacable enemies to your own friends." [42]

The history of colonial New England, like that of most societies, has its share of contradictions and anomalies, but perhaps nothing is more inherently intriguing—or more important to our story—than the diametric difference between the educational power of the Indians and of the English over each other. For beside the doleful failure of English education to civilize and Christianize the Indians stands the impressive success with which the Indians converted the English to their "barbarous" way of living. Benjamin

41. Cotton here followed his father Increase, who contended in 1679 that the chief fault of New England was in family government, in which too many parents and masters were "sinfully indulgent" towards their children. "In this respect, Christians in this Land, have become too like unto the Indians" (*Necessity of Reformation,* p. 5).

42. Cotton Mather, *The Way to Prosperity* (Boston, 1690), pp. 27, 34; Cotton Mather, *A Letter to Ungospellized Plantations* (Boston, 1702), p. 14: Cotton Mather, *The Present State of New-England* (Boston, 1690), p. 32; *PMHS* 66 (1942) : 53–79.

Franklin spoke of a decisive century and a half of American experience when he compared the human results of each process. "When an Indian Child has been brought up among us," he wrote in 1753, "taught our language and habituated to our Customs, yet if he goes to see his relations and make one Indian Ramble with them, there is no perswading him ever to return." But "when white persons of either sex have been taken prisoners young by the Indians, and lived a while among them, tho' ransomed by their Friends, and treated with all imaginable tenderness to prevail with them to stay among the English, yet in a Short time they become disgusted with our manner of life, and the care and pains that are necessary to support it, and take the first good Opportunity of escaping again into the Woods, from whence there is no reclaiming them." [43]

It is too easy, having read only the few novelists who have treated this theme, to underestimate the impact of "Indianization" upon the American character by assuming that it was confined to a mere handful of impressionable children and adult misfits. Nothing could be farther from the truth. In 1782 Hector de Crèvecoeur wondered "by what power does it come to pass, that children who have been adopted when young among these people, can never be prevailed on to re-adopt European manners?" But he was not talking of isolated individuals, "for *thousands* of Europeans are Indians," he wrote, "and we have no examples of even *one* of those Aborigines having from choice become Europeans!" And he does not seem to have been exaggerating for literary effect. Firm figures are impossible to come by, as can be imagined, but judging from New England alone, Crèvecoeur's estimate has the ring of truth. [44]

43. *The Papers of Benjamin Franklin*, ed. Leonard W. Labaree et al. (New Haven, 1959–), 4 : 481–83.
44. J. Hector St. John de Crèvecoeur, *Letters from an American Farmer* (London: Everyman, n.d.), pp. 214–15 (my emphasis). Pierre de Charlevoix tells us that the French "in rather large numbers" were equally captivated by the Indian mode of life and would not return to "civilization" (*Journal d'un Voyage . . . dans L'Amérique Septentrionale* [Paris, 1744], 6 : 32–33).

Between 1689 and 1713, the years of the heaviest Indian depredations along the northern and eastern frontiers of New England, about 600 men, women, and children were taken by the Indians, and less frequently the French, and marched northward into captivity.[45] Of these, 174 (29 percent) definitely returned to New England, having been ransomed or exchanged for French prisoners. An additional 146 captives (25 percent) exchanged their bondage for French naturalization and baptism by the Catholic Church. This means that, if we include those captives who chose to remain with the Indians, anywhere from 25 to 71 percent of English captives may have refused to return to New England. A reasonable estimate, based on the proportion of captives in French and Indian hands in 1705 (5 to 3), would be 40 percent, with 25 percent (146) becoming French Canadians, and 15 percent (90) becoming full-fledged Indians; and some of them became practicing Catholics as well. Indeed this may well be a conservative estimate. For in 1724, during the Three Years' War, the first major outbreak of fighting since the Treaty of Utrecht in 1713, Joseph Stevens wrote the Massachusetts General Court from Canada, where he was trying to redeem two of his sons: "Inasmuch as there are upward of Fifty of our People in the hands of the Indians that have been taken in this War, who unless some speedy care be taken to redeem them will probably turn Roman Catholicks and Embrace their Religion, as *above an hundred others (taken Prisoners Before this Warr)*

45. Coleman, *New England Captives*, lists by name a minimum of 437 captives for this period. From a variety of New English sources to which she refers (chap. 4), we also know that at various times a total of 601 captives remained in Canada, though obviously a certain residual overlap occurred in the figures for years fairly close together. (Two lists exist for 1695 and 1699, however, in which there is no overlap, accounting for 65 persons remaining.) If we add to those persons remaining (assuming for the moment an absence of overlap) the 174 persons who definitely returned to New England, we arrive at an inflated total of 775 persons who may have been captive in this twenty-five-year period. If from that figure we subtract Miss Coleman's definite figure of 437, we get a possible 338 extra captives, which, if we diminish it by 50 percent for inflationary overlap, yields a plausible (and probably conservative) 169 unrecorded captives. These, added to Miss Coleman's 437 recorded captives, yield a total of about 600 captives.

have done, who will by no means be persuaded to Return to their Native Countrey again, but are led on in Superstition and Idolatry." If the Indians were capable of winning the allegiance and affections of 15 percent of all the Americans they captured before 1782, Crèvecoeur's announcement that "thousands of Europeans are Indians" ceases to surprise, but leaves us to search for an explanation.[46]

There were at least three kinds of reasons, each intersecting and reinforcing the others, why so many New Englishmen chose to remain with their Indian captors. Many stayed, in the first place, because they found Indian life morally superior to English civilization and Catholicism more satisfying than Puritanism. According to her Indian husband, Eunice Williams, the celebrated daughter of the Reverend John Williams of Deerfield, "no go" because "her father marry twice times. He no have marry, she go." Sylvanus Johnson, who lived with the Indians from the age of six to ten, "always maintained that the Indians were a far more moral race than the Whites." Another young Deerfield captive, Mary Harris, eventually married an Indian and moved to Ohio, where an English traveller met her in 1751. He wrote in his journal that "she still remembers [after forty-seven years] they used to be very religious in N.E. and wonders how the White men can be so wicked as she has seen them in these woods." About the same time two male captives, recent converts to Catholicism, also condemned New England's fall from religious grace. One said that "he prefers being a slave with the Indians than in his country where there is no religion." (His father was dead, and by New England law, "whoever has been ransomed, if obliged to borrow the money, is bound to service until he have repaid by his labor the sum he cost.") The other sounded a similar note; he refused redemption because "he hated too strongly the English nation where he was almost a slave to give up his religion & liberty." [47]

46. Coleman, *New England Captives*, 2 : 153 (my emphasis).

47. Erwin Ackerknecht, " 'White Indians': Psychological and Physiological Peculiarities of White Children Abducted and Reared by North American Indians," *Bulletin of the History of Medicine* 15 (1944) : 35; Coleman, *New England Captives*, 1 : 120–21; 2 : 88, 312.

Although Puritans resented the Jesuits' perfidious "strata-gem[s] to seduce poor children . . . from the simplicity of the gospel to Romish superstition," they could not gainsay the effectiveness of Jesuit conversion efforts, especially with younger children who in New England had only begun to catechize and to memorize Scripture. The tenacity of belief possessed by two Deerfield girls, captured at the age of seven and eight respectively, testifies to the Jesuits' success in re-ligious education. Several years after her capture, Mary Field and her Indian husband visited her family in their new Connecticut home. She told her brother Pedajah, who had been born after the Deerfield raid, that someday he would be carried off so that he too could enjoy the Indian life and Catholic religion. Indeed, he thought the attempt was once made in Northfield, but he escaped in a canoe. After ten years with the Indians, Hannah Hurst married a thirty-two-year-old Indian widower and received baptism in the Catholic Church. The priest wrote in his register that "she has declared many times she does not wish to leave the Savages, with whom she wished to die a Christian." Among Indian captives from New England her stance was not unusual.[48]

The second explanation for the retentive power of Indian culture is the nature of the adoptive process by which cap-tives were thoroughly integrated into the social life and kin-ship structure of the tribe. After Mrs. James Johnson was adopted by the rich son-in-law of the grand sachem, she later wrote, "I was introduced to the family, and was told [by the interpreter] to call them brothers and sisters, I made a short reply, expressive of gratitude"—a matter of much importance to the Indians[49]—"for being introduced to a house of high

48. John Williams, *The Redeemed Captive Returning to Zion* (Spring-field, 1908), pp. 52–53, 58, 70; Coleman, *New England Captives*, 2 : 78, 96.

49. When Stephen Williams showed some eagerness to be bought by a Frenchman, his Indian captors prevented it and threatened him with death for being ungrateful for his preservation and adoption. "It is no wonder," he wrote, "that children that are small will not speak to their friends when they come to see them, but they will scofe and deride them, because the indians have taught them so, will be angry if they do other-

rank, and requested their patience while I should learn the customs of the nation. . . . I had a numerous retinue of relations, whom I visited daily [and] my new sisters and brothers treated me with the same attention that they did their natural kindred, but it was," she admitted, "an unnatural situation to me." It would not have been to a younger child who had lost one or both of her own parents, as was the situation of many captives. But even Mrs. Johnson, like so many Englishmen who returned from Indian life, had to defend their singular humanity. "Those who have profited by refinement and education, ought to abate part of the prejudice, which prompts them to look with an eye of censure on this untutored race. . . . Do they ever adopt an enemy," she asked, "and salute him by the tender name of brother?" [50]

Adoption was the more serious for the Indians because it was often used to replace fallen sons or daughters. And, as Canada's Governor Duquesne once told Governor Shirley of Massachusetts, "there is nothing so difficult as to get their slaves from them, especially when they have distributed them among their Wigwams to make up for their Dead." Twenty-two-year-old Zadock Steele's description of his adoption brings home the mutual benefits that accrued to both captors and captives.

All the Indians, both male and female, together with the prisoners, assembled, and formed a circle, within which one of their chiefs, standing upon a stage, erected for the purpose, harrangued the audience in the Indian tongue. Although I could not understand his language, yet I could plainly discover a great share of native eloquence. His speech was of considerable length, and its effect obviously manifested weight of argument, solemnity of thought, and at least human sensibility. I was placed near by his side, and had a fair view of the whole circle. After

wise" (*What Befell Stephen Williams in his Captivity* [Deerfield, 1889], p. 9).

50. *A Narrative of the Captivity of Mrs. Johnson* (Springfield, 1907), pp. 67–68, 71, 76–77.

he had ended his speech, an old squaw, came and took
me by the hand, and led me to her wigwam, where she
dressed me in a red coat, with a ruffle in my bosom, and
ordered me to call her *mother*. She could speak English
tollerably well, but was very poor, and therefore unable
to furnish me with very sumptuous fare. My food was
rather beneath a savage mediocrity, though, no doubt
my mother endeavored as far as lay in her power to en-
dear the affections of her newly adopted, yet ill-natured
son. . . . As I was blest with an excellent voice for
singing, I was the more beloved by, and on that account
received much better treatment from my new mother, as
well as from other Indians. I was allowed the privilege of
visiting any part of the village, in the day time, and was
received with marks of fraternal affection, and treated
with all the civility an Indian is capable to bestow.

As Hector de Crèvecoeur realized, there was "in their social
bond something singularly captivating, and far superior to
anything to be boasted of among us." [51]

Finally, many New Englishmen became Indians because, as
two adult converts acknowledged, they enjoyed "the most perfect freedom, the ease of living, [and] the absence of those
cares and corroding solicitudes which so often prevail with
us." When the New English had an explanation for the
startling desertion of their neighbors from the civilized fold,
they refused to impute any major responsibility to the educational inadequacies of their own culture and instead blamed
the natural condition of man as they knew it. "The human
mind is naturally averse to control," said Gen. Benjamin
Lincoln, Revolutionary soldier and Indian expert. "All men
naturally wish for ease, and to avoid the shackles of restraint."
Benjamin Franklin, another Massachusetts man long familiar
with the Indians, singled out the "proneness of human Nature to a life of ease, of freedom from care and labour," but

51. Coleman, *New England Captives*, 2 : 254; *The Indian Captive: or a
Narrative of the Captivity and Sufferings of Zadock Steele* (Springfield,
1908), pp. 70–72; Crèvecoeur, *Letters from an American Farmer*, p. 215.

he argued with unintended irony, "care and pains . . . are necessary to support . . . our manner of life" with its "infinite Artificial wants." The same perspective obviously appealed to the romantic nature of Hector de Crèvecoeur, who planned to move his family to an Indian village to escape the ravages of the Revolutionary war. "There must be something more congenial to our native dispositions," he wrote with undisguised admiration, "than the fictitious society in which we live; or else why should children, and even grown persons, become in a short time so invincibly attached to it? There must be something very bewitching in their manners, something very indelible and marked by the very hands of nature." [52]

What contemporaries saw as the marking hand of nature was in reality the powerful fist of culture, molding in its image its neophytes from another world. When the Reverend John Williams saw "several poor children, who had been taken from the eastward the summer before, . . . in habit very much like Indians, and in manners very much"—the word is crucial—"*symbolizing* with them," he was witnessing the educational impact of a culture marked by an uncommon integrity, by social cohesion, and a unity of thought and action. In short, New English captives stayed with their Indian families because they had become enchanted by

> the scholastic philosophy of the wilderness
> to combat which one must stand outside and laugh
> since to go in is to be lost.

And the arcane complexity of the Puritan philosophy, with its burdens of civility and constraint, could simply not release them from its spell.[53]

---

52. Crèvecoeur, *Letters from an American Farmer*, p. 215; *Colls. MHS*, 1st ser., vol. 5 (1798), p. 10; *Papers of Benjamin Franklin*, 4 : 481–83.

53. John Williams, *Redeemed Captive*, p. 37 (my emphasis); Marianne Moore, "New York," *Observations* (New York, 1924), p. 65.

Afterword

On the eve of revolution New England bore little resemblance to John Winthrop's "Citty upon a Hill." The church was no longer the physical and emotional center of colonial life, having failed at certain points to fulfill its evangelical potential after the Half-Way Covenant and the Great Awakening.[1] The community, while the ideals of harmony and consensus persisted, was fractured by geographical mobility, economic opportunity, and political cacophony.[2] And the family had forfeited much of its moral and educational importance to other institutions, primarily the school.[3]

From this widely shared view of colonial society, two opposite conclusions have been drawn. Lawrence Cremin has argued that, all things considered, colonial education was largely a success. Its characteristic commitment to the "popularization" of the access, substance, and control of education—largely schools and colleges—was an "optimistic and in many ways messianic commitment," befitting America's future role in the world. This "peculiar mixture of religious enthusiasm and secular yearning," he wrote, was "both the boon and the bane of the American commitment to popular education. At

1. By 1760 only 20–25 percent of the New England population enjoyed church membership (William Warren Sweet, *Religion in Colonial America* [New York, 1949], pp. 334–35). ,

2. Michael Zuckerman, *Peaceable Kingdoms: New England Towns in the Eighteenth Century* (New York, 1970); Richard L. Bushman, *From Puritan to Yankee: Character and the Social Order in Connecticut, 1690–1765* (Cambridge, Mass., 1967); Kenneth A. Lockridge, *A New England Town: The First Hundred Years, Dedham, Massachusetts, 1636–1736* (New York, 1970); Timothy Breen, *The Character of the Good Ruler: A Study of Puritan Political Ideas in New England, 1630–1730* (New Haven, 1970); Edward M. Cook, "Social Behavior and Changing Values in Dedham, Massachusetts, 1700 to 1775," *WMQ* 27 (October 1970) : 546–80.

3. Lawrence Cremin, *American Education: The Colonial Experience, 1607–1783* (New York, 1970), pp. 480–86.

its best, it moved men to dream impossible dreams and then set out to realize them; but at its worst, it filled them with unfulfillable hopes that could only be answered in some other, more perfect world." [4]

On the other hand, while recognizing the same basic contours of New England's history, two historians have concluded that, in an important sense, New English education failed. For Ronald Cohen the primary cause of failure was that "there were fewer institutionalized curbs on behavior in New England than in old England," which prevented the "Puritans" from achieving and preserving the "monolithic moral unity" envisioned by Winthrop's "Modell of Christian Charity." [5] In the same vein, Michael Zuckerman has expressed doubts that New England's increasing reliance upon formal education for the socialization of its young represented a real gain, "when men were removed from the supportive web of family and neighborhood, habit and tradition, that had given them security and a sense of easy attunement to the world." While Cremin "remains marvelously assured that [formal] education is the solution," he wrote, establishing his own ideological stance, "many are asking openly if it might not be part of the problem." [6]

Both judgments—negative and positive—appear to capture some of the truth about colonial education. But both suffer from a common fallacy that has long plagued the history of education. In issuing judgments of success or failure, historians fail to treat education as the ongoing *process* of a dynamic culture. Instead, they stand at either end of the chronological spectrum and give marks according to the normative standards of their respective positions, which are compounded of history, ideology, and personal biography.

Those who believe that colonial education failed because

4. Ibid., pp. 561–63.
5. Ronald D. Cohen, "Socialization in Colonial New England," *History of Education Quarterly* 13 (Spring 1973) : 73–82.
6. Michael Zuckerman, review of Cremin, *American Education,* in *Bulletin of the American Association of University Professors,* March 1971, pp. 18–20.

New English culture did not live up to its founders' utopian goals commit what might be called the Tory fallacy. While any culture must be judged by its own goals and values, it is simply unfair and unhistorical to judge the New Englishmen of 1776 by the goals and values of their great- or their great-great-grandfathers. Each generation—which must be defined by behavior rather than prescribed lengths of time—sets its own goals, makes its own choices, and lives by its own values, and it is only by those that its culture and its education should be judged. Consequently, over a period of one hundred and fifty years, there were several distinct yet related New English cultures, each with a configuration of educational processes attempting to shape and preserve its cultural identity.

Furthermore, the values of a culture may be complex, complicated, or merely confused, in which case Edward Cook's distinction between *ideal values* and *operational values* is helpful. Ideal values may be defined as "shared beliefs about how men should behave and how society should function." Operational values, on the other hand, are "the adaption of generalized ideal values to everyday situations and set the limits of accepted behavior. They may or may not correspond precisely with ideal values, though, of course, the divergence between the two cannot be so great as to impair the capacity of the overall value system to explain social arrangements to society." [7] In any given culture, of course, both kinds of values may be in transition or flux, resulting in temporary uncertainty, confusion, or dysfunction for its members as they attempt to pass on their values to their children through education.

On the other hand, those who praise or blame colonial education from hindsight commit the Whig fallacy.[8] By judging a period of history with the knowledge of and an attitude toward all that has happened since, they measure the people

7. *WMQ* 27 (October 1970) : 546.
8. Herbert Butterfield, *The Whig Interpretation of History* (London, 1929); David Hackett Fischer, *Historians' Fallacies* (New York, 1970), pp. 135–40.

of the past by impossible standards, standards which did not exist for them and to which they could not have responded. Hindsight should be used to select topics of study that have meaning and interest for our own times, but not to subject the people of the past to anachronous expectations. We must take their culture on its own terms and treat it as a complex whole in process, not as a static moment in the inevitable progress of the race.

Nevertheless, it is possible to *characterize*—a better word than *judge*—the history of a culture and its educational process without treating them statically or unfairly. For the primary value of the history of education to history in general is to provide seismological readings on the shifting strata of cultural values, both ideal and operational, over time. Since education is designed to preserve and transmit a society's distinctive normative character, that is, its culture, it is the most sensitive instrument for recording the major and minor tremors in the configuration of cultural values. When values become unstable, confused, or contradictory, the agencies of education are the first to sense the change because it is their task to digest and abstract the culture's values into forms intelligible to the young. If the signals they receive from the adult culture are distorted, confused, or weak, the lessons they convey to the young will, accordingly, display the same qualities. This is especially true when the ideal and the operational values of the society seriously diverge.

Such was the case—if I have interpreted the documentary signals correctly—in New England by the middle decades of the eighteenth century. Winthrop's "Citty upon a Hill" was a closed corporate community ordered and bound by love, justice, and mercy. Its chief bulwarks against worldliness and Satan were the family and the church, while the community as a whole was charged with preserving social harmony and moral consensus. It was, of course, a society whose ideal and operational values coincided. When the land was new, the population small and homogeneous, and alternatives few, the founders' vision of a New Zion enjoyed some chance of being realized. But all too soon, immigration, healthy living, and teeming women produced a population so large as to make perfection unattainable, and the social and educational institutions of New England were forced to accommodate themselves as best they could to that reality.

The first and most important institution to change was the family. In England the Puritan family had been a closed, tribal haven for harassed dissenters. To preserve its cultural identity, it had been forced to assume several social functions normally undertaken by traditional agencies, either because Puritan family members were denied access to these agencies, or because their own "puritanism" rejected them. The most important of these functions, of course, was religious education. But once the family felt secure in the congregational orthodoxy of New England, as it began to in the 1660s, it returned its catechetical duties to the church and the school, where they had formerly resided. And not long afterward it sloughed off another set of duties as well. When the racial composition of the labor force began to change, and the field for individual economic opportunity to enlarge, in the early eighteenth century, the family gave over many of its educational responsibilities to the school and the church, or neglected them altogether. This reduced the family's role in apprenticeship to a starkly economic one, especially after the "domesticall government" of society's dependents and deviants was transferred to public institutions.

The school, too, changed in response to New World conditions. On one level, the trend of formal education was toward greater popularization. The elite Latin curriculum for well-to-do boys was gradually replaced in most local schools by a comprehensive English curriculum for children of both sexes drawn from families of a greater range of socioeconomic standings. Whereas Latin had been equated with "Learning" for salvation, the English curriculum was a clear response to the demands of a heterogeneous population for practical knowledge for their earthly business. Yet on another level, the operational values of the school did not change at all. When schools were small, their curriculum uniform, and their students homogeneous, they could work for the individual preparation of Puritan saints. When the size, curriculum, and social composition of the schools changed, however, they were forced back upon the role they had played in England, that of guardian of the social order for an increasing proportion of the youth group. And the continued use of the rod ensured that the lesson of social control would not be lost.

In the religious culture of New England, the institution most subject to change was the church. And yet both the method and credal content of religious education remained strikingly unchanged throughout the colonial period. This meant that the ideal values of New England continued to be those of the founding fathers; the vision of a "Citty upon a Hill" was held before each new generation as the normative standard by which they should measure themselves. Small wonder, then, that successive generations felt themselves to be falling deeper into "declension" as the gap between their fathers' vision and their own operational values widened. For the churches, once described as silent democracies in the face of speaking aristocracies, changed dramatically by the time of the Great Awakening, often reverting to forms and practices of the English Church they had once been forced to spurn. Congregations no longer remained silent, ministers no longer wielded unchallenged authority, membership requirements were loosened, congregational uniformity gave way to begrudging toleration of other sects, and, perhaps most telling of all, economic ambition put intolerable stress upon an ethic that condemned idleness but could not condone worldliness.

The product of all these changes was a culture that, by the middle of the eighteenth century, suffered from a serious disjunction between its ideal values—the values established by the founders of New England—and its operational values—the values formulated in the day-to-day struggle for a distinctive identity. Despite the centripetal force of religious tradition and its founders' vision, New England was sundered by several centrifugal forces at the same time that it was facing powerful challenges—and, as it proved, temptations—from the French and the Indians. The isolated, exposed towns of the frontier, the products of the restless economic ambition of new generations, easily fell victim to the enemy, and in captivity many of their citizens fell from Puritan grace into Catholicism or "savagery." That at least 40 percent of these captives did not return to New England when they had the opportunity is a reliable index of the diluted religious mission of the colonies and of the diminishing hold that the society exercised over its members through education.

Eighteenth century New England was a culture temporarily without a center, a culture that could no longer give all its members a strong sense of being a part of something vital, valuable, durable—something like a religious errand into the wilderness. Not until the thirteen colonies rebelled from the mother country and set off on a new mission of national assertion did education and society in New England recapture the drive and purpose that had founded them.

Index